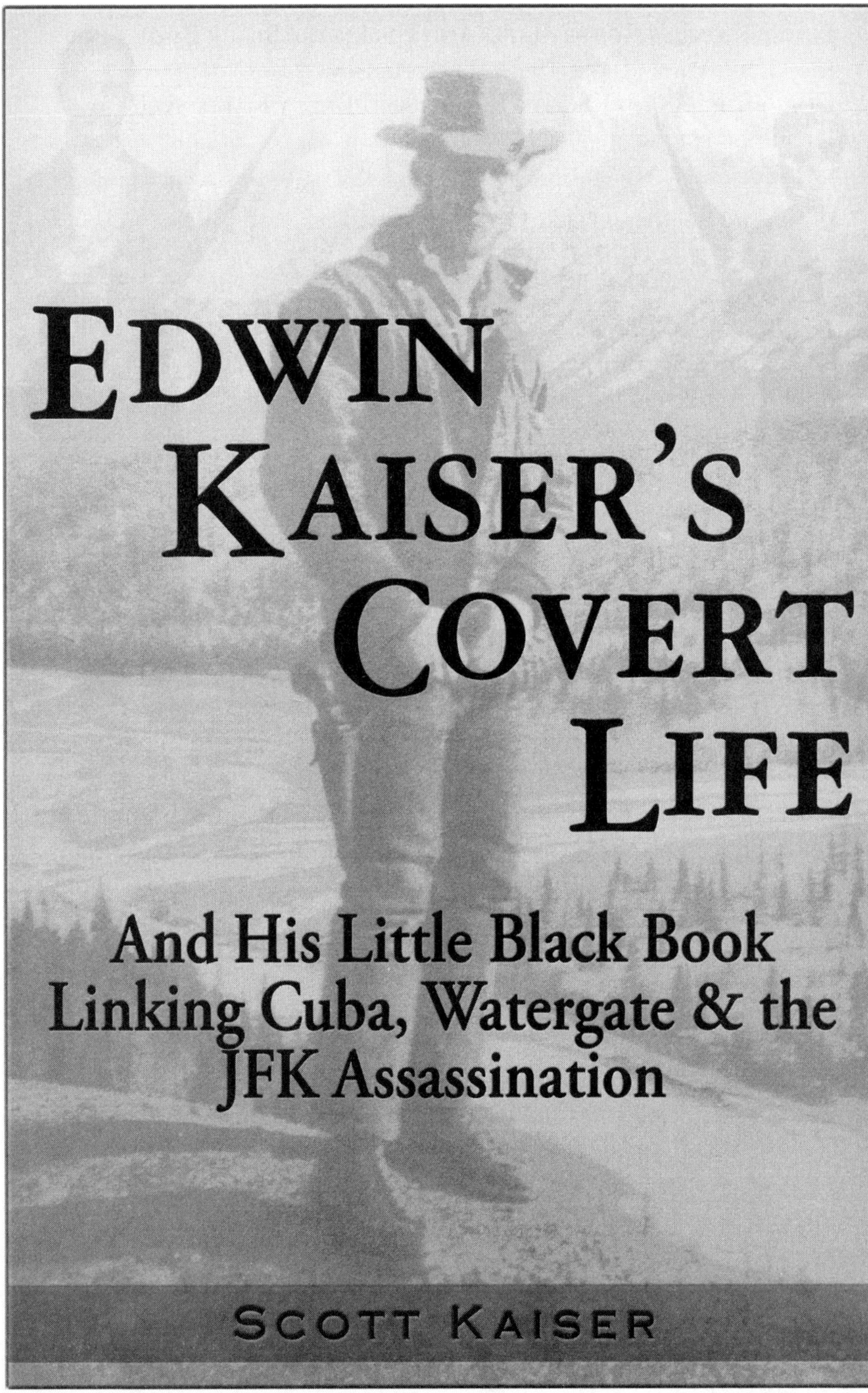

Edwin Kaiser's Covert Life

And His Little Black Book Linking Cuba, Watergate & the JFK Assassination

Scott Kaiser

Published by: Trine Day LLC
PO Box 577
Walterville, OR 97489
1-800-556-2012
www.TrineDay.com
publisher@TrineDay.net

Library of Congress Control Number: 2013937961

Kaiser, Scott.
Edwin Kaiser's Covert Life: And His Little Black Book Linking Cuba, Watergate & the JFK Assassination–1st ed.
p. cm.
Includes index and references.
Epub (ISBN-13) 978-1-937584-46-7
Mobi (ISBN-13) 978-1-937584-47-4
Print (ISBN-13) 978-1-937584-45-0
1. Kaiser, Edwin Benjamin Jr. -- 1933-1977. 2. Kennedy, John F. -- (John Fitzgerald), -- 1917-1963 -- Assassination. 3. Watergate Affair, 1972-1974. 4. Cuba -- History -- 1959-1990. 5. United States -- Biography. I. Kaiser, Scott II. Title

First Edition
10 9 8 7 6 5 4 3 2 1

Printed in the USA

Distribution to the Trade by:
Independent Publishers Group (IPG)
814 North Franklin Street
Chicago, Illinois 60610
312.337.0747
www.ipgbook.com

The year was 1960. My father had just been allowed back into the USA, presumably with his French immigrant visa. He is in Alaska. The gun he carries on his hip is a .44 Magnum Revolver, and he invariably carries it with him wherever he goes.

This book is the first of its kind to provide a full account look into the life of Edwin Benjamin Kaiser, Jr. It also provides a glimpse into the world of those acquainted with him and a quest for the truth regarding the means and motives of certain individuals, which led to his disappearance. He may not have been the perfect husband to his wife, Sonia, but he was a loving father to his two children.

My name is Scott Richard Kaiser. I am his only son and oldest child. I have fathered six of his grandchildren, Jonathan, Amber, Andrew, Ariel, Angelica, and Noah. My sister, Elizabeth Catharine Kaiser-Guanch (married to Daniel Guanch) added three more grandchildren to the lineage, Nathan, Aaron, and Liza. A son, a husband and a father, this book is dedicated to my father, Edwin B. Kaiser Jr.

Prologue

The following is paraphrased from a Freedom of Information Act document that I obtained during the course of my research:

> (Name Unknown) advised that the circumstances surrounding Kaiser's arrest in approximately August of 1960, were as follows:
>
> Kaiser is sitting at the bar at King Mountain Lodge, Anchorage Alaska. He has become involved in an argument. Customers are reporting to the management that Kaiser has a gun and is dry firing it. The gun is obtained from Kaiser and it is discovered that there is a live round in it. He is asked to leave, which he does. Kaiser returns at a later hour carrying a foreign make rifle. He has begun to point it at people and ejects a live round every so often to let them know it is loaded. He is making statements that he doesn't care if he dies tonight. He is also stating that he wants to kill somebody. Kaiser has kept this up for an hour and a half. The manager's wife, unobserved, telephones the Alaska State Police. Kaiser has apparently thought of the telephone and pointing the gun at the manager's wife, makes her carry the phone out from the kitchen and pull it around the corner so that he may observe it.
>
> The Alaska State Police Trooper arrives a short time later and enters the establishment. Kaiser presses the gun against the trooper's body and after a short time, backs him out the door to the outside parking lot and eventually into the car. At this point, the trooper is in the front seat and Kaiser is in the rear seat with the muzzle of the rifle pointed against the trooper's neck. About this time, Kaiser's friend (name unknown) leaves the lodge and walks towards the car. Kaiser moves the rifle to point it at him which gives the Trooper a chance to grab the muzzle. They wrestle in the car and finally Kaiser is disarmed. He is taken to Palmer, Alaska, prosecuted and serves 60 – 90 days in jail. Kaiser states that he does not know the charges.

AN 52-1475

Both John and Robert Kennedy knew of our plots to assassinate Castro, and because of our several failed attempts they decided to pull back, they didn't want information like this to leak out, they broke us up, and had us arrested for operations we were undergoing for them.

P.S. So we took care of them Bastards!

– Osvaldo Coello

Table of Contents

Table of Contents

Introduction

The early sixties to the late seventies was a time of turbulence and social unrest for the United States. Our beloved president John F. Kennedy was assassinated in the streets of Dallas, there was a threat of imminent nuclear war with the Soviet Union, Martin Luther King was slain, followed by the killing of Robert Kennedy as he sought the Democratic nomination for president. Later there would be a botched burglary called "Watergate" that would further shake the American people's belief in the integrity of their government and representatives. Behind these events were men and women carrying out secret orders from seats of power, which origins have been kept from the public. A person who stayed in the shadows, with his secrets hidden among these tragedies and scandals of our era, was my father, Edwin Benjamin Kaiser Jr.

This book seeks to provide the fullest possible account of Edwin Kaiser's dealings with his family and some of the most infamous characters and plots in the last sixty years of American history. I want to help bring to light this member of the "off the books" government assets. What part or parts did Edwin Kaiser play? For whom was he working? What was his influence on our nation's course? I am offering up this account in an effort to rediscover who this man really was. I loved him, he was my hero.

He was my father.

Please allow me to make this explicitly clear; I feel a real need to inform the reader that there is no attempt by myself or anyone involved in this book to solve any of our Nation's dark mysteries. This is an attempt to uncover the workings of a man who graciously taught me what it means to be a man, and, sadly, was taken from me prematurely by forces well beyond his control. If in the pages of this book, I can illuminate some of those areas and workings of our covert establishments, then I will feel truly blessed.

Within this book I will also share with you the tools that I have used to look into the life and dealings of my father. During the long and arduous research of this story, many more questions have been raised than I have been able to answer. As a dedicated family man, attempting to justly tell the story of the man who gave me life and inspired me, I understand that there might be errors and omissions in my research. Please bear with me and please feel free to offer comments, criticisms or corrections to this work.

It is also necessary at certain times to give background information in regards to the people with whom my father was associated and worked. If you are a seasoned Cuba/JFK researcher, a good deal of this may be rudimentary to you. If you are one of those people, I appreciate your patience with me while I help paint a picture for those who are less experienced in these areas. In any case, I do believe, whether a person is experienced or not, this book will help provide some insight as to how, who, what, when, where, and why my father was able to move about and participate in the circles in which he did move. I hope the information to follow, will ignite a spark in any level of researcher to ask more questions and explore new avenues.

Overview

My father, Edwin Kaiser, was a thrill-seeking patriot who became enmeshed with many of our nation's biggest conspiracies. Whether smuggling arms, plotting assassinations or heading underground militia movements, he took part with gusto and without hesitation. In the early seventies, he was the military head of an anti-Castro movement called "Cubanos Unidos." He started to form relationships with other people who were advocates of Cuban liberation. These were men, and a few women, who felt the need to neuter Communism and free Cuba from the grips of Fidel Castro. My father's world of espionage and corruption was spinning out of control, while he tried to balance life at home and the demands of his "job."

What was his job? He had many throughout his years: soldier of fortune, seed peddler, importer, husband, thief, father, assassin, arms smuggler, revolutionary leader, spy, American patriot and the greatest hero a young boy could ever hope for in a father. He was an idealist of his time. A man who loved his country and above that, humanity. He was willing to lay it all on the line to accomplish what he thought was right. My father believed in American freedom above Communism of any flavor. Throughout his short-lived life, he sought out oppressed people and used his brains, brawn and courage to help liberate them. Only the smartest, bravest or most ruthless can participate at this level. At times, he employed any combination of these traits to accomplish his goals and to survive in this secret world.

Through his contacts and dealings in this clandestine world, Edwin Kaiser was able to obtain a confession that by no means solves but adds another perspective from which to view one of our nation's most obsessed-over questions. Who was involved in the conspiracy to kill President John F. Kennedy? That may have been what killed him.

Throughout my research, I have uncovered many government documents which mention my father's name and affairs. Some of them are perplexing in that they have raised more questions than answers.

I invite you, the reader, to conjure your own opinion as to what you think was actually happening over the course of my father's life.

I have also discovered a handful of handwritten documents that my father left behind. These letters and entries paint a picture of an extremely patriotic individual who had offered up his life to the service of the United States military above and beyond all else, except for God. He was a believer – whole-heartedly – in the civil rights of all individuals and dedicated his life to helping those people who needed a hero. My father's stepfather had planned on sending him to Georgetown University, to further his education "and give promise of a good future." My father never got that opportunity. His faculty for spelling and sentence structure is sometimes limited which has led me at times to paraphrase or interpret his writings. As you will see with examination of the original documents, the meaning has not been lost in the translation.

This story is taken in part from my first person perspective as I am his son, Scott Richard Kaiser. I grew up amidst those who were members of my father's organization, an organization comprised of paramilitary mercenaries.

Interspersed with my remembered events is information culled directly from Freedom Of Information Act documents and

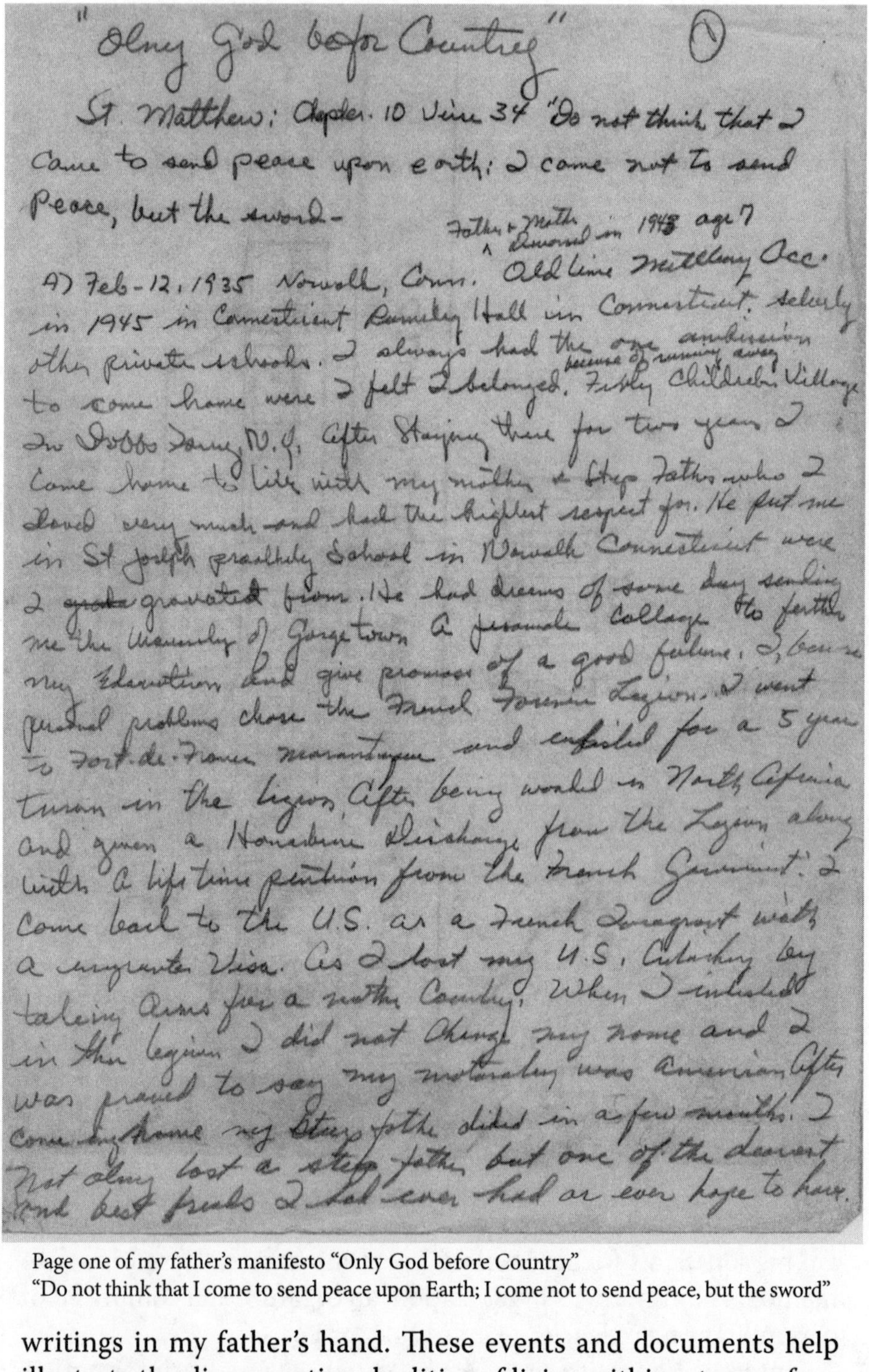
"Olny God befor Country" (1)

St. Matthew: Chapter. 10 Verse 34 "Do not think that I
Came to send peace upon earth: I come not to send
Peace, but the sword-

Father + Mother divorced in 1943 age 7
4) Feb-12, 1935 Norwalk, Conn. Old Line Mutuality Acc.
in 1945 in Connecticut Rumsey Hall in Connecticut. selerly
other private schools. I always had the one ambition
to come home were I felt I belonged. because of running away Fubly Childrens Village
In Dobbs Ferry N.Y. After Staying there for two years I
Came home to Live with my mother & Step Father who I
loved very much and had the highest respect for. He put me
in St Joseph parochial School in Norwalk Connecticut were
I ~~grade~~ gravated from. He had dreams of some day sending
me the University of Georgetown a personal Collage to further
my Education and give promos of a good future. I, because
personal problems chose the French Foreign Legion. I went
to Fort-de-France Martinique and enlisted for a 5 year
turum in the Legion, After being wounded in North Africa
and given a Honorable Discharge from the Legion along
with a life time pention from the French Government. I
Came back to the U.S. as a French Immigrant with
a immigrant Visa. As I lost my U.S. Citizenship by
taking Arms for a another Country. When I enlisted
in the Legion I did not change my name and I
was proud to say my nationality was American. After
Coming home my Step father died in a few months. I
Not only lost a step father but one of the dearest
and best friends I had ever had or ever hope to have.

Page one of my father's manifesto "Only God before Country"
"Do not think that I come to send peace upon Earth; I come not to send peace, but the sword"

writings in my father's hand. These events and documents help illustrate the disconcerting dualities of living within a trove of secrecy. Together, we will examine the evidence of the man behind the mission, the truth behind the secrecy, and finally, the cost of knowing too much.

During my adolescence, my father's affiliation with certain, clandestine affairs was rapidly increasing. Shadowy men would sweep through the house. I watched, meeting these enigmatic figures only to truly know them later in life. The hushed conversations in the family room were the norm for me and my mother. Among the many men who held court with my father were E. Howard Hunt (Watergate, CIA), the Navarro brothers (Fervent anti-Castro activists), David Sanchez Morales (JM/WAVE operations chief and suspect JFK assassination), and his closest co-worker, Frank Sturgis (July 26th Movement, Bay of Pigs, JFK, Watergate).

My dad gave no reason or explanation to his involvements. He was a man of secrecy, as were the other individuals working by his side. Although he gained respect by doing what he did, he was also greatly influenced by this powerful crew. He was an opportunist and if a situation called for a big adventure – he wanted to be part of it. However, it was a precarious time for him as he wrestled with the safety of his family and the sensitive information he possessed. He was quiet but never nervous; his unshakable disposition prevented him from showing fear. He carried his secrets in an attaché case, the one thing that would never leave his side.

My father disappeared shortly after my 13th birthday. I say disappeared because my mother never viewed the body. Unfortunately, due to our financial constraints at the time, it was suggested by the mortician to cremate my father, according to my mother there were two other men in suits in his office.

"I don't remember who they were, they could've been from the FBI or the CIA," she said, "they would not allow me to view your fathers body.... It was the pressure from those men that had me thinking about the cost of burying your father that led me to cremating him."

It should also be noted that my mother was not allowed to identify the body.

My father's body was identified by Rudy Junco of Rudy's Meat Market in Hialeah, Florida. It was in the basement of Rudy's Meat Market where I had attended secret Cubanos Unidos meetings with my father.

On the morning of the day of his disappearance, my father sat me down to give me an important message. In a gravely serious tone, he said, "If anything were to happen to me, I want you to know that your Uncle Frank is not as nice as you think he is."

He then played a recorded conversation in which "Uncle" Frank Sturgis (a.k.a. Frank Fiorini) confessed to being a key participant in the assassination of President John F. Kennedy. That same afternoon, my mother answered a phone call at work, only to learn that her husband had died on the local docks down at the marina. The reports show the cause of death to be multiple injuries; blunt force trauma caused by falling from some wooden planking into the Bilge of the ship. The attaché case that he always carried around with him was never to be seen again.

I began to develop a deep desire to connect the dots in my father's life. I made a decision to request and then analyze the FBI & CIA files obtained through the Freedom of Information Act (FOIA). And I began to unravel part of the mystery of who my father was, his involvement in the covert world, and clues regarding my father's disappearance/murder and who may have been his murderer.

This is a story about life choices and the ideals that led my father to fight in the same arena as some of the most dangerous and infamous men in our nation's history.

I received a letter dated June 13, 2011 from the FBI, which basically states that our government still deems it necessary to keep some of information concerning my father *classified*.

> "FOIPA Request No: 1128166-000 Subject: Kaiser, Edwin B. JR.
>
> Dear Mr. Kaiser,
> This disclosure is in further response to your Freedom of Information Privacy Act (FOIPA) request to FBI Headquarters (FBIHQ) for records concerning the above-mentioned subject and administrative appeal number 2010-0644 to the Department of Justice/Office of Information (DOJ/OIP).
>
> By letter dated January 29, 2010, the DOJ/OIP advised that some of the information responsive to your request is classified and that material would be referred to the Department of Justice Review Committee (DRC) for further review and determination on whether the information warrants continued classification under Exec-

> utive Order No. 12958. <--- (Meaning, a National Threat to Security).
>
> For your information, the DRC has completed their review of the requested material and it was determined that the information warrants continued classification pursuant to Title 5, United States Code, Section 552 (b)(1). However, minor changes have been made to pages two through four of file 139-HQ. 4089 serial 2413. This serial consisting of four pages has been reprinted and forwarded to you.
>
> Should you choose to contest the results of the DRC, you may file a Civil Complaint in the United States District Court for the judicial district in which you reside or have your principal place of business, or in the District of Columbia, which is also where the records you seek are located."

I am fairly convinced that there is a lot more to the story than what you're about to read. Although this story is quite detailed in its time line, it seems to me that someone does not want me to have what could possibly be some very incriminating evidence.

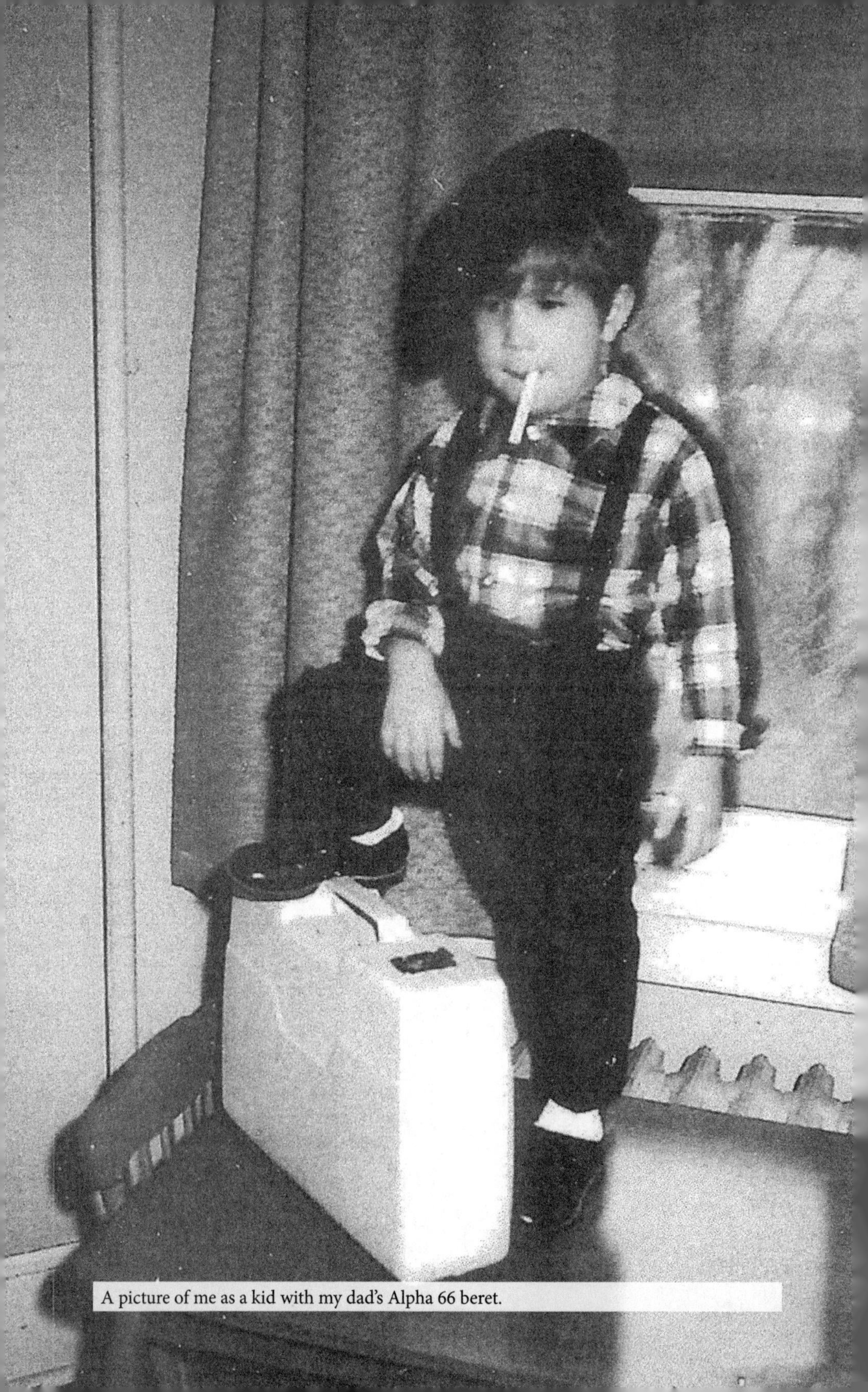

A picture of me as a kid with my dad's Alpha 66 beret.

Chapter One

My Thirteenth Birthday

On January 18, 1977 my father came home early, and Wilfredo Navarro was with him. My sister and I were home alone, and our mother was at work. It was my 13th birthday and my dad said, "I've got something for you." He handed me a $100.00 bill and said, "I have another surprise for you. Follow me to the bedroom."

I followed him with anticipation. He pulled a rifle out of a big plastic bag and said, "I want you to have it." Boy! I was excited! My eyes just lit up, and I had a huge smile on my face. I felt like my father was treating me like a man, and I didn't need my BB gun anymore. My dad said, "This is an M-1 Carbine. Your Uncle Frank gave this to me, and now I want you to have it." We put the gun in the closet in my parent's bedroom, and as we were walking out of the bedroom he said, "Don't mention it to anyone."

Wilfredo Navarro was sitting at the dining room table with a birthday cake that he had just set there. Minutes later, there was a knock at the back door. It was my "Uncle" Frank Sturgis. My father wanted a picture taken, so we all gathered around the table, and I sat next to Navarro while my father stood up behind him with my sister, Elizabeth, in his arms. Dad asked Frank if he would take the picture, and he did. After the picture was taken they all started to sing Happy Birthday to me.

Chapter Two

Home Sweet Home

The Kaiser family in Miami November 1968

Our first rental house after moving from Alaska was located near the Hialeah Race Track off of Palm Avenue in East Hialeah. My father spent his time getting reacquainted with old friends, while my mother had her hands full with two children. This photograph was taken by my grandmother. I assume that this is where my father's involvement in the Cuban affairs began or re-started.

Soon after this photograph was taken, we moved to our final destination, a house my grandmother helped my parents purchase in West Hialeah. The house I grew up in was located at 6585 West 8th Lane, Hialeah, Florida. And that's where many of my new found "uncles" would come to visit.

In order to get a good look at who my father was and what it was that motivated him to sacrifice friends, family, financial gain and ultimately his life, I ask you to indulge me as I start at the beginning.

Edwin Kaiser's Childhood:

Edwin Benjamin Kaiser, Jr., was born on February 12, 1935, in Norwalk, Connecticut. He was born to Edwin Benjamin Kaiser, Sr. and Elizabeth Catharine Gage Kaiser. They would divorce when he was only seven years old. He was sent by his father to stay in a military school. At home, his mother was a heavy drinker. He felt abandoned and unwanted, and unable to understand the complexities of his family life.

This is a photo of my father, Edwin Kaiser, at the age of seven standing outside his parent's home in Norwalk, Connecticut. My grandfather took this picture before Edwin was shipped off to military school. I guess the salute was his way of saying goodbye to my grandparents.

My father had a hard time trying to adjust to his new surroundings while having to live in military school. He was seven when he was enrolled and remained there for two years until he started getting into fights and tried repeatedly to escape.

He would often scale the fence at night to escape the world in which he was now living. Many times, he was caught just outside the common yard by the guards patrolling the fence lines. He would be escorted back to his bunk by the capturing officers. The military school finally had to expel him for fighting. This wasn't the first of his fights as reported by the school. The school's dean requested that both of his parents be called in for a conference but only his mother showed, she said, "This is the very reason his father had him boarded in military school. Ever since our divorce," she said, "Edwin has been so hard to manage and it's taken a toll on all of us." Little Edwin, soon after, found himself living back at home with his mother.

One afternoon when my dad was about eleven years old, my grandfather called my grandmother asking her if he could have Edwin for the weekends. She was happy to hear that his father would be soon on his way to pick up their child. My grandfather said, "I'll be there Friday night, just make sure he's ready to go by the time I get there." Edwin packed his suitcase and sat outside the front porch anxiously waiting for his father to arrive, but his father never showed up. He was heartbroken, wondering if it was his fault that his father never showed.

He asked his mother "Did I do something wrong? Why didn't dad come?" She didn't know how to answer him, other than, "I'm sorry your father didn't come." He was a little boy having to deal with the pain of loosing his parents to a divorce. Feeling abandoned, his belief system and character now began to reflect the remembrances of officers whom he had respected during his time in military school. There is not much documented or known about my father's early teen years. I am sure, without a doubt, there were some fights and run-ins with the law.

At seventeen, he was picked up in a stolen car, for speeding, by the Norwalk police. When the police officer asked for his identification, he lied and replied with a fictitious name. Along with theft of an automobile, the charge was increased to include providing false information. He spent the night in jail before seeing the magistrate. My grandmother posted bond, and later when he went to court, the judge ordered him to pay his court costs, a fine and placed him on parole.

Then later in 1952 after a dishonorable discharge from the U.S. Marines, he went to Rushville, Illinois where he broke into a restaurant, stole a loaf of bread, milk and cracked open the register and took money. He was quickly picked up by the police. After his day in court my father made a plea deal with the District Attorney, they would release my father back into the custody of his parents in Norwalk, but Edwin had to write his parole office once a month to let them know where he was and what he was doing.

Rather then going back home my father took off in the opposite direction and headed for Los Angeles California where in 1953 he soon committed another burglary, but this time it would include assaulting a police officer. A nearby pedestrian witness the brutal beating the police officer received and called for additional back up. Soon a flurry of police officers arrived and wrestled my father to the ground. He spent time in the Los Angels Detention Center.

Edwin was suppose to appear weekly for meetings with his probation officer, but decided to abandon California and headed back to Norwalk, Connecticut.

Back in Connecticut, Edwin's habit of wrecking havoc didn't seem to fade. Holding down a job was not his forte, as his appetite for adventure started to grow.

In the *Meriden Record*, Friday, January 20, 1956, the headline on page four of the paper read: Knife-Attacker Is Committed To State Hospital.

> Norwalk, Jan 20, 1956: A twenty year old boy who attempted to attack a detective with a knife here yesterday was ordered and committed to the Fairfield State Hospital today. Edwin Kaiser, was injured when the detective subdued him, was committed under orders from the psychiatric staff at Norwalk Hospital where he was taken for treatment. A police department spokesman told this story.
>
> Kaiser had come to the detective bureau and asked the officer to whom he talked to call in another detective so he could kill him, "for personal reasons." The other detective, William Smith, had investigated a break in at a store run by Kaiser's stepfather about a year ago, and Kaiser had been arrested and convicted of the burglary.
>
> When the detective wouldn't call Smith, he said, Kaiser first pulled a knife on him and then attempted to snatch his gun.
>
> In being subdued, Kaiser suffered head injuries for which he was admitted to the hospital where psychiatrists later decided upon his commitment to the Sate Hospital.

Is it any wonder that my father would then run off to Haiti and join the French Foreign Legion only a year later?

The story is one morning my father said to his mother, "I'm going out". He didn't say another word, he just left. For all she knew, he was picked up by the cops for a crime he may have committed, or took off to one of his buddies house.

Edwin Kaiser, the U.S. Marines and the French Foreign Legion:

In 1952, Edwin Kaiser joined the United States Marine Corps. He was only seventeen years old, and would receive a dishonorable dis-

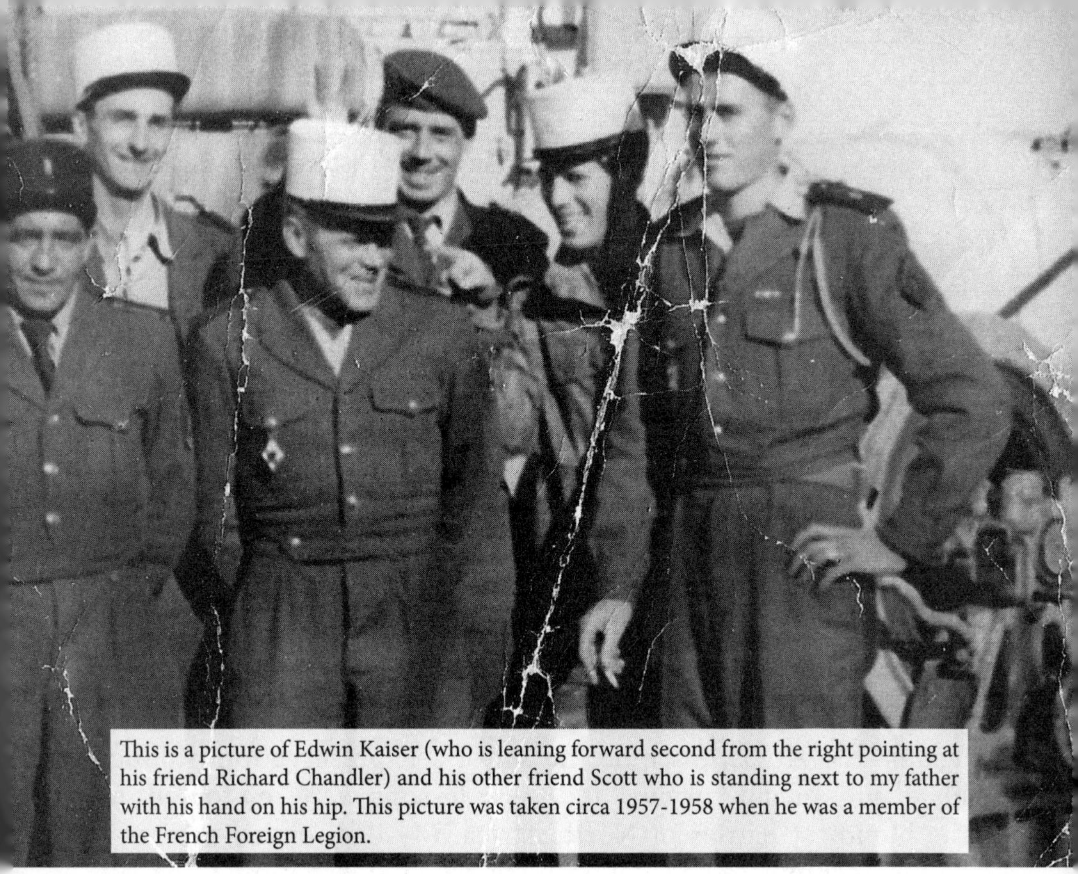

This is a picture of Edwin Kaiser (who is leaning forward second from the right pointing at his friend Richard Chandler) and his other friend Scott who is standing next to my father with his hand on his hip. This picture was taken circa 1957-1958 when he was a member of the French Foreign Legion.

charge. Apparently, five months after joining the U.S. Marine Corps, he was released for assaulting his superior officer. He moved back to Connecticut, and into my grandmother's home, with no money or prospect of a job. He then began an unsuccessful pattern of seeking employment. My grandmother would often remind me of how much a pain in the ass my dad was growing up. She always called me the top man of her totem pole, and said dad was often very difficult. That difficulty in managing my father as a child was a harbinger of things to come. He had been nurturing an appetite for adventure since childhood, and decided to take a bold step. My father left his family and his fiancé and enlisted for a five-year tour in the French Foreign Legion. In 1957 at the age of twenty-two he graduated from boot camp in Sidi Bel Abbès, Algeria.

The Legion was comprised mostly of men of action, thieves and prisoners. I don't know how else to put it, but my father was always kicking someone's ass, and from all accounts seemed to fit in pretty well with his other Legionnaires. He saw some of the fiercest battles in North Africa as the Legion was attempting to subdue rebel uprisings in Algeria and surrounding area.

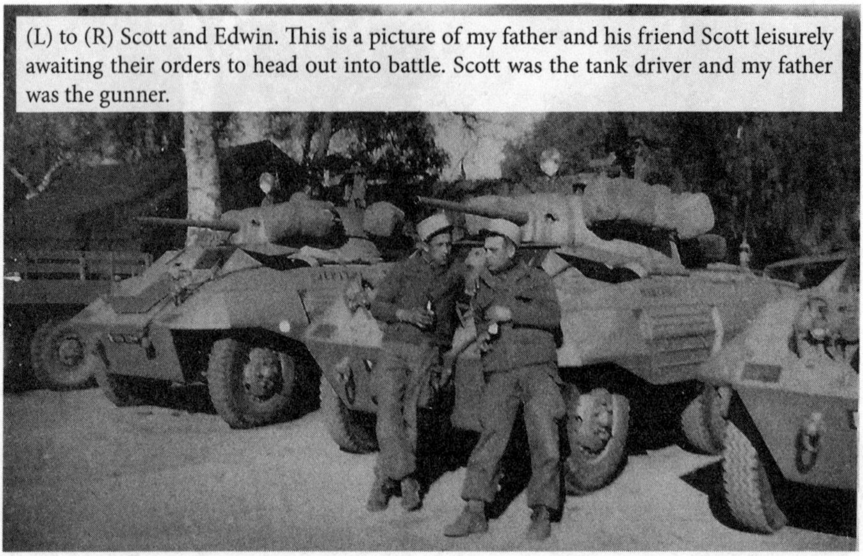

(L) to (R) Scott and Edwin. This is a picture of my father and his friend Scott leisurely awaiting their orders to head out into battle. Scott was the tank driver and my father was the gunner.

My father was wounded three times in hand-to-hand combat against the Arabs, learning the art of self-preservation. Killing his enemy meant survival and these lessons were reinforced in the bloodiest battles of North Africa. My dad, by his own account, accumulated a total of thirty-seven kills, winning several medals for conduct and valor. There were two other Americans that fought alongside him, and they became his closest friends: "Scott," and "Richard." My father honored his "brothers in arms" by naming me Scott Richard Kaiser.

During a much deserved rest and relaxation in the city of Sidi Bel Abbès (home of the French Foreign Legion until 1962), he was seriously injured in a bar fight, alongside Scott and Richard. Help from fellow Legionnaires arrived, but a bit too late. His head had been split open by a barstool, and he was thrown through the bar's plate glass window. Injuries to his head and leg led to a stay at the local hospital. To his dismay, while lying on his hospital bed, he was handed his honorable discharge papers by his superior officer. He had given one year of service to the French Foreign Legion, and was now mustered out with a pension from France, and the respect of his colleagues.

Edwin Kaiser Attempts a Return to the United States

My father had been honorably discharged from the Legion, but then found himself a man without a country, living in

North Africa. The big question for him was: "Where to go next?" It was not in his plan to be done with the Legion so soon. But my father had not realized that when he signed up for the Legion, he would lose what he cherished most: his United States citizenship. He had signed up to fight under his legal name, and proudly stated that he was an American citizen. Apparently, when a U.S. citizen takes up arms under another nation's flag, even if it is a friendly nation, that person has their U.S. citizenship stripped. He began to write his mother often, longing for home. He sought the return of his citizenship through the U.S. Embassy in Paris.

During his time waiting to hear from the government, my father felt abandoned by his parents, school and now his country. His mother petitioned her senator and congressman, but received no reply. His stepfather also wrote to his congressman pleading for my father's return so that my grandmother would stop crying herself to sleep every night.

My grandparents

My grandmother then went a step further and wrote a letter to President Dwight Eisenhower on her son's behalf. Her inquiry was finally answered by First Lady Mamie Eisenhower, on April 10, 1959. Mamie's reply was: "Of course, I understand perfectly your desire to have your son return to this country. Whether or not anything can be done I do not know, but I am referring your letter to the proper officials in government. I am sure that someone will be in touch with you further about this matter."

Weeks turned into months with no word from the U. S. Government about my father's whereabouts, nor anything about any efforts to return to him the United States. It would take a few years from the time of his discharge before he could finally return to the U.S. (I have no idea what he was doing during this time), under less-than-defined circumstances. He was assigned Alien Registration Number 11832410 by the U.S. Embassy in Paris in 1960. He finally flew home in 1961, landing with an immigrant status at the Idlewild Airport in New York City. He then hitchhiked from New York to a reunion with his elated mother and stepfather back home in Norwalk, Connecticut.

Without work and low on finances, life after returning from overseas wasn't easy for my father. Although back on American soil, he had not regained his U.S. citizenship. This caused understand-

MURVON SEED COMPANY

VOLUNTEER 6-2143 BOX 389 NORWALK, CONNECTICUT

April 28. 1959

Los Angeles Police Department
Los Angeles California.

Gentlemen—

On September 8. 1953 my son Edwin Kaiser, Norwalk, Conn. was arrested by your Police Department.

During 1957 my son joined the French Legion and in 1958 was seriously wounded in the leg and consequently was medically discharged from the legion. Now he is unable to obtain a passport until I am able to obtain a written statement from your Police Department stating that he served his time as a youth for his foolish act and was released to his

A letter written by my grandfather requesting a sworn statement by Los Angles California Police Department for time served for burglary and assaulting a police officer. The letter of "time severed" from the LAPD was apparently to be instrumental in assisting and helping my dad receive his passport. My grandparents had no idea how severe or serious Edwin's leg wound was.

MURVON SEED COMPANY

VOlunteer 6-2143 BOX 389 NORWALK, CONNECTICUT

Mother—

I have been trying for five months attempting to gain this Visa or passport for my son and now I find that Statements mentioned above from your Department is necessary before I can secure a passport.

Will you please send me a letter and statement that my son served his time in full for his foolish act so that I can forward to French Paris Embassy

Surely you can appreciate how I feel as I want my son home with me— He is 23 years of age now and fully realizes how wrong he was in his youth— An anxious Mother

MRS HAYWARD H SMITH
BOX 389 NORWALK CONN

The continuation and page 2 of the letter.

ADDRESS OFFICIAL COMMUNICATIONS TO
THE SECRETARY OF STATE
WASHINGTON 25, D. C.

DEPARTMENT OF STATE
WASHINGTON

In reply refer to
VO 150 Kaiser, Edwin B.

APRIL 23 1959

Dear Mrs. Smith:

Your letter of April 7 addressed to Mrs. Eisenhower concerning your desire to have your son, Edwin B. Kaiser, return to the United States has been referred to this Department for reply.

The records of the Department show that Mr. Kaiser has made application at the American Embassy at Paris for documentation to enable him to return to the United States. The Embassy recently communicated with the Department requesting a clarification of certain aspects of your son's case. An appropriate reply was forwarded to the Embassy on April 1 furnishing the requested information. It is believed that the Embassy is now in a position to give further consideration to your son's application.

You are assured that the Embassy will be of all possible assistance to your son and will handle his case as expeditiously as circumstances permit.

Sincerely yours,

Joseph S. Henderson
Joseph S. Henderson
Director, Visa Office

Mrs. Hayward H. Smith,
Murvon Seed Company,
Box 389,
Norwalk, Connecticut.

Mr. Irwin,

This is a letter from the Department of State in response to my grandmother's letter she wrote to Mrs. Eisenhower.

REPUBLIC OF FRANCE, CITY OF PARIS
EMBASSY OF THE UNITED STATES OF AMERICA } SS :

I, Edwin B. Kaiser, Jr. hereby volunteer to make this statement. Iam writing this being in my sane mind. I was born in NORWALK, CONNECTICUT, U.S.A., on the 12 th. day of Feb. 1935.

Having diffaculties with my family, fiance and friends over very personel matters, I left the U.S.A. with allintentions of joining the FRENCH FOREIGN LEGION.I had then and now the intentions of returning to my home, family, and country.

In the FOREIGN LEGION, I engaged u under my own name my own country that I love, and would never go against politically or in war. When asked on entering the LEGION my nationality I proudly said AMERICAN. My date of liberation was 12-12-1958.

Now my only problem to get back home to family and country, is by means obtaining a visa. I never knew I would forfiet my citizenship enterring the LEGION. Irealize I have made a grave mistake. I now appreciate the UNITED STATES, much more then the average man. I would like to devote my life to the Armed Services of the UNITED STATES, if Iam accepted by the country and service. I left the U.S.A. Aug. of 1957

Iam dear country very
truthfully yours..........

Edwin B. Kaiser Jr.

Subscribed and sworn to before me this 22nd day of January 1959

John R. Burke
Vice Consul of the United States of America at Paris, France, duly commissioned and qualified

566

duplicate.

Copy of a letter that my father wrote from the U.S. Embassy in Paris and could have been the genesis of his lifelong involvement with service to the country he loved so dearly. Pay close attention to the last paragraph. He is offering to devote his life to the Armed Services of the United States if he is accepted by the country and service.

THE WHITE HOUSE
WASHINGTON

Augusta, Georgia,
April 10, 1959.

Dear Mrs. Smith:

Of course I understand perfectly your desire to have your son return to this country. Whether or not anything can be done I do not know, but I am referring your letter to the proper officials in government. I am sure that someone will be in touch with you further about the matter.

Sincerely,

Mamie Doud Eisenhower

Mrs. Hayward H. Smith,
Murvon Seed Company,
Box 389,
Norwalk, Connecticut.

Left: Letter from Mamie Eisenhower to my grandmother regarding the reinstatement of my father's U.S. citizenship

able friction

MURVON SEED COMPANY

VOLUNTEER 6-2143 BOX 389 NORWALK, CONNECTICUT

May 25, 1959

Mr. Donald J. Irwin,
Congress of the United States,
House of Representatives,
Washington, D.C.

Dear Mr. Irwin:-

Acknowledging with thanks your letter of May 21st.

I am enclosing a copy of a letter that Lieutenant Edward F. Rooney who is in charge of the local Norwalk Police Youth Bureau kindly gave to me. You will note that Mr. Rooney wrote this letter to the American Embassy in Paris May 13th.

Regarding the pertinent records of the Rushville, Illinois Police Department covering my Step Son Edwin Kaiser, This was an incident when he was a teen ager "Wanting to see the World" was arrested for stealing a loaf of bread and some milk along with some other boys, because they were broke and hungry.

This boy is now 23 years of age and these foolish teen age incidents are behind him.

It would seem to me that our American Embassy is in a position to tell this boy he can come home-just on the strength of Mr. Rooney's letter, or will they prefer to continue the hardship for this boys Mother as well as the boy himself.

This matter has been going on for approximatly six months now at a cost of $200.00 per month to me. After all the boy has to eat and sleep.

You can feel free to forward any of this correspondence to the American Embassy and rest assured anything that you can do to convince the Paris Embassy to send this boy home will be greatly appreciated. All they have to do is wire me for Air Transporation and same will be forwarded at once.

Sincerely,

Right: What was my father doing in Illinois? And so far from home at such a young age. Was he drawn into some type of Mafioso?

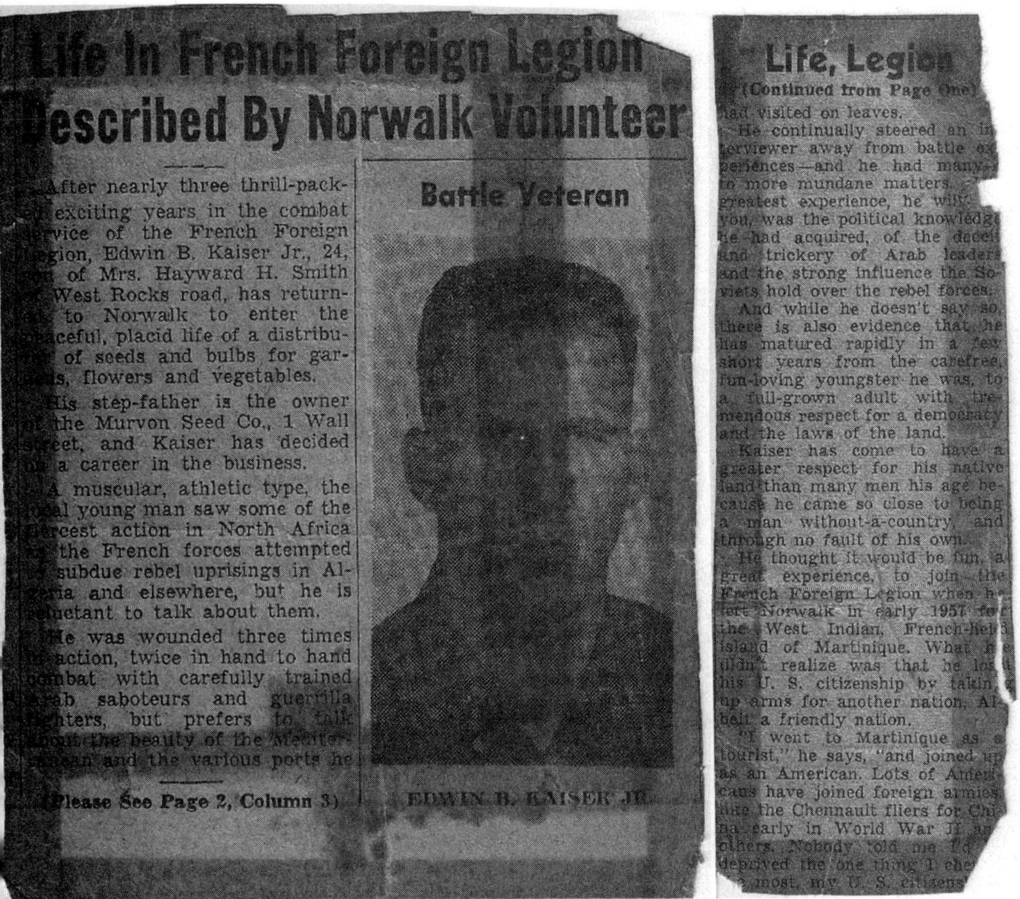

Life In French Foreign Legion Described By Norwalk Volunteer

After nearly three thrill-pack- exciting years in the combat vice of the French Foreign gion, Edwin B. Kaiser Jr., 24, of Mrs. Hayward H. Smith West Rocks road, has return- to Norwalk to enter the aceful, placid life of a distribu- of seeds and bulbs for gar- s, flowers and vegetables.

His step-father is the owner the Murvon Seed Co., 1 Wall eet, and Kaiser has decided a career in the business.

A muscular, athletic type, the al young man saw some of the rcest action in North Africa the French forces attempted subdue rebel uprisings in Al- ria and elsewhere, but he is luctant to talk about them.

He was wounded three times action, twice in hand to hand mbat with carefully trained ab saboteurs and guerrilla hters, but prefers to talk out the beauty of the Mediter- anean and the various ports he

(Please See Page 2, Column 3)

Battle Veteran

EDWIN B. KAISER JR.

Life, Legion

(Continued from Page One)

had visited on leaves.

He continually steered an in terviewer away from battle ex periences—and he had many— to more mundane matters. greatest experience, he will you, was the political knowledge he had acquired, of the deceit and trickery of Arab leaders and the strong influence the So- viets hold over the rebel forces.

And while he doesn't say so, there is also evidence that he has matured rapidly in a few short years from the carefree, fun-loving youngster he was, to a full-grown adult with tre- mendous respect for a democracy and the laws of the land.

Kaiser has come to have a greater respect for his native land than many men his age be- cause he came so close to being a man without-a-country, and through no fault of his own.

He thought it would be fun, a great experience, to join the French Foreign Legion when he left Norwalk in early 1957 for the West Indian, French-held island of Martinique. What he didn't realize was that he lost his U. S. citizenship by taking up arms for another nation, Al- beit a friendly nation.

"I went to Martinique as a tourist," he says, "and joined up as an American. Lots of Ameri- cans have joined foreign armies like the Chennault fliers for Chi- na early in World War II and others. Nobody told me I'd deprived the one thing I che most, my U. S. citizens

A local newspaper article about my father after his arrival from France and also after his honorable discharge from the French Foreign Legion. It speaks of his experience in hand-to-hand combat, his dearly and deeply held Patriotism and touches on his education in the dealings of our enemy's governments.

with his mother, as she would provide for his needs while he was jobless. The pressures of this living situation led him to leave home in late 1961 and move to Alaska. He began working as a lumberjack. His new home was a log cabin.

My father shared a cabin off of Mile 78 and Glenn Highway in a field bordering Chickaloon Road about two-and-a-half miles past the bridge on King Mountain Lodge with a man whose name remains a mystery (redacted in the FBI/CIA files). This cabin was close to the military testing grounds outside of Fort Richardson, Alaska. He had befriended soldiers in the area, who were working on a training mission of large proportion. His associations led him to question a U.S. Army sergeant about the nature of their training exercises. He learned that their co-op training was called "Operation Willow Freeze." This Cold-War training would consist of U.S. soldiers conducting military exercises in the Alaskan wilderness. It was being done in order for the soldiers to become acclimated to the harsh environment similar to that of the Soviet Union, directly west of them in eastern Siberia.

My father in his cabin, which he shared with a friend who was then spending time in a California prison. This is where he would survive by living off moose and caribou that he hunted.

My father became friends with many of the servicemen while in Alaska. During a conversation with some pals, he was given information by an Army sergeant. The sergeant told him that after Operation Willow Freeze began, gas was going to be transported to Gulkana, Alaska, in 5,000-gallon tankers. The sergeant went on to state that 1,250 tankers would drive to a halfway point near my father's residence at King Mountain Lodge. There, he could await the convoy of vehicles. When the convoy arrived he could empty the gas out of the tankers, which would then return to Ft. Richardson for another supply of gas. He could store the fuel on his land and then resell the gas to the locals in order to make money on which to live.

According to reports from the base commander, there were several hundred vehicles set aside for Operation Willow Freeze. And one evening, my father ran into an enlisted man who notified him of an overturned military vehicle that was abandoned in the Willow Freeze testing zone. He was told that the vehicle had some supplies and that he could probably help himself to inconsequential items like rations without calling attention to himself. He was given the approximate location and headed out on the icy, snow-covered roads. With the help of two friends, they spotted the overturned vehicle, and found the vehicle abandoned. The truck contained a gas generator, some food, blankets and according to the FBI documents two M-2 carbine rifles. My father and his friends quickly and thoroughly stripped the vehicle of its contents, including the generator, blankets and even the rear axle, which had been torn off the truck during the accident. The FBI became involved and everybody cracked under questioning, except my father. His cohorts had implicated him to authorities only a few days after the incident.

Under the tarpaulin near the tree is were my father kept his 55-gallon drums of gas taken from the U.S. Government. A spare gas can would be attached to his truck while he would travel long distances on hunting expeditions.

He was convicted for theft of government property and was sentenced to eighteen months in an Alaskan prison. It should be noted that my father was already in prison, when questioned about this incident. His prior arrest and conviction was the result of an assault with a deadly weapon from the opening story of this book. This sentence of 18 months in jail for theft of government property was subsequently reduced to probation.

I find it odd that my father would only serve 60-90 days in jail for threatening an entire bar with deadly force and then taking an Alaskan State Trooper hostage at gunpoint. It is also strange to me that he was charged with theft of government property and his sentence was reduced to probation. The fact that the word "reduced" was used in the memo makes me think my father was already receiving a helping hand from someone unseen, who held a great deal of power.

Two out-going cables were generated by the CIA, one completely redacted. It was believed that around this time the "three-letter agencies" took a serious interest in my father. This was most likely due to his experience in the French Foreign Legion, his proclivity for theft and his utter disregard for authority. The two cables are now officially redacted by the CIA and the FBI in its entirety.

The following are excerpts from much later FBI reports where they are detailing my father's first run-ins with the law before and immediately after his return from the French Foreign Legion.

AN 52-1475

Operation Willow Freeze, in February, 1961, the United States Army maintained a gasoline supply station on the property of KING MOUNTAIN LODGE. He advised that KAISER used to associate with the military personnel daily and apparently became quite friendly with them during the time they were stationed there. He stated he personally never visited this group of men, but that KAISER ate with them and on one or more occasions supplied them with caribou and moose meat. He recalls that one morning, at approximately 6:00 AM, KAISER came and woke him and said he had some gas coming. Subsequently, a military tanker pulled into the yard by the cabin and thereafter filled several empty barrels with gasoline from the tanker.

He stated he feels that at least eight barrels of gas were obtained. He stated he does not know how KAISER arranged this deal and he does not know the name of the military man who brought the gas, and he could not identify him or the truck at this time. He stated KAISER sold some of the gas and that the rest was used in his truck. He stated there is no gas left.

He cannot recall the names of any people who purchased gas from KAISER.

52-765

~~PAGE TWO (MM 105-NEW)~~

HE IS A WHITE MALE, BLONDE HAIR, 68 INCHES IN HEIGHT, WITH A "PANTHER" TATTOO ON HIS UPPER RIGHT ARM. HAS EXTENSIVE ARREST RECORD UNDER FBI NUMBER 243.334B WHICH INCLUDES ARRESTS SINCE 1952 ON NUMEROUS CRIMINAL CHARGES INCLUDING BURGLARY AND LARCENY, AGGRAVATED ASSAULT, ASSAULT WITH A DEADLY WEAPON, AND THEFT OF GOVERNMENT PROPERTY. IN 1961 WHILE IN ALASKA, HE WAS SENTENCED TO SERVE 18 MONTHS ON A CHARGE OF ASSAULT WITH A DEADLY WEAPON. IN NOVEMBER 1961, KAISER ENTERED A PLEA OF GUILTY TO A CRIMINAL INFORMATION CHARGING VIOLATION OF TITLE 18, UNITED STATES CODE, SECTION 641 FOR THEFT OF GOVERNMENT PROPERTY OF A VALUE EXCEEDING $100 AND IN DECEMBER 1961 HE WAS SENTENCED TO A TERM OF 18 MONTHS. THE LATTER SENTENCE WAS SUBSEQUENTLY REDUCED TO PROBATION.

[redacted] B7C B7D

~~ADMINISTRATIVE~~

~~RE BUREAU AIRTEL TO MIAMI CAPTIONED, ED KAISER; NEUTRALITY~~

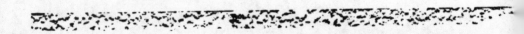

~~END PAGE TWO~~

Chapter Three

Sonia Kaiser

When released from jail, my father embarked on a road trip from Alaska that eventually led him to gainful employment at a local hospital and a meal at a White Castle restaurant in Saint Paul, Minnesota. While there, he spotted a beautiful twenty-two-year-old eating her meal alone in her car in the parking lot. He noticed her but was too hesitant to make an approach, and she drove off.

My mother, Sonia Kaiser in 1962.

My father convinced his friends that they needed to follow her, so they drove off in pursuit. As they caught up to her, he was holding his arm out the passenger window trying to hand her something. She grabbed it through the window as the cars sped down the road, but she was perplexed. She stopped her car at the next red light, and asked him if he realized what he just handed her? He replied, "Yes, my Alaskan driving license. I didn't know how else to stop you." He introduced himself. She replied, "My name is Sonia Cartier." He asked her if she would be nice enough to give him a ride back to his friend's house. She felt no fear after having a brief conversation with Edwin and gladly accepted to give him a ride.

He began to relate to her his adventures in the French Foreign Legion and his current road trip from Alaska. Sonia was amused and found him to be an interesting young man. The adventurous Edwin had succeeded in catching the attention of this young girl's eye.

He asked Sonia for a date. He wanted to take her out the next day, but he was about to be admitted back into the hospital ... and she already had a boyfriend! His leg had not healed well, from the wound he received when he was in the French Foreign Legion. The doctors in Algeria did not do a good job at re-attaching a severed tendon in his leg and had not close the wound properly. The surgeons in Saint Paul decided that they had to re-operate on his leg in order to try and fix it.

It was decided that the wound would require immediate surgery. This left my father crestfallen, as he was unable to go on the date. My mother went to visit him even though she was dating another man. When Sonia arrived at the hospital, the staff already knew about her, and how popular she was with my father.

He convinced Sonia to get a wheelchair and wheel him out of the hospital before he was discharged. She put him in her car and drove him to his friend's house where he had been staying. When they arrived, he said, "I just wanted to introduce you to my friends." She was a bit upset that my father had left without being properly discharged ... just to introduce her to his friends, but I am sure she was a bit charmed as well. Sonia convinced Edwin that he should return to the hospital, and stay until the doctors would properly release him. The hospital staff was relieved to see him back on the premises, and his treatment was completed.

After being released, he visited Sonia at work and asked her to lunch. She was shocked when he took this opportunity to propose to her. His powers of persuasion led the startled Sonia to say "yes" to his proposal even though they had only known each other a few weeks. The young lovers took a trip to South Dakota, and on September 1, 1962 they were married. From there, they headed to Alaska, where they set up a home as a newly married couple.

My father's employment history remained a problem. He was back in the country, he loved so dearly, but was still not a citizen. He was hired for various odd jobs but nothing had the longevity or excitement he was seeking. My father secured employment at a nearby corner store, but soon left for lack of excitement. Fortunately, around the same time, he met a manufacturer of silk garments who needed help importing his textiles from Hong Kong.

My father began working with this man and on many occasions would also take the measurements of clients. These fittings often were held at my parent's apartment. Sonia wanted her husband to have a better job, and was quite shocked to learn that most of the garments were being outfitted for pimps and prostitutes. According to my mother, my dad was not thrilled about his work either, but it was the only immediate work that he could find.

In October of 1962, my mother was able to convince my father to move to Norwalk, Connecticut, where they could stay with his mother. They lived at my paternal grandmother's house until my father helped her move to Miami Beach in November 1962. My parents then moved out of my grandmother's house and moved in with my father's Aunt Dorothy (Dot) in Norwalk.

My father would travel to Miami to visit his mother, and on a trip back from Miami in late January 1963, he expressed to my mother how beautiful Miami was. He seemed full of excitement, especially about meeting several Cubans there. My mother was already preparing for the worst hoping they weren't going to pack their bags and move again, after all she already had a job. As my mother was listening to my father's adventures while visiting Miami he said, "And, I also met two Americans by the names of Frank Fiorini and Lee Oswald." My mother said, "he seemed impressed with the amount of people protesting against Fidel Castro."

It was in Miami where my father would meet Wilfredo Navarro, a Cuban exile, whose parents were imprisoned by Fidel Castro in Cuba. Wilfredo had a brother, Roerme, who was constantly at his brother's side. My dad sympathized with the Navarro's plight, and heard many adventurous stories from Bay of Pigs veterans in Miami. Through Wilfredo, my father met, and soon became best friends and a co-worker, with Frank Sturgis, a veteran of the Bay of Pigs, as well as other missions of intrigue.

Paraphrased from Page Three of My Father's Letter:

"Silent Majority" I still believe action speaks louder then words. I met more and more Cubans and got involved in their problems more and more and as I did I understand that to help them in their fight in Cuba would help cut off the head of the snake who is biting us. Who is poisoning our sanity with drugs and drugs lead to pimps and prostitution. The streets in the United States today are a good example, our public parks our young generation. Thank God not all of it, but it is a start that has to be stopped in my mind. So I worked with different Cubans and different groups training them with what knowledge I had in automatic weapons, explosives and guerrilla warfare.

I have been on call at any time 24 hours a day, sometimes sleeping only when I could not go any further because of exhaustion. There was no pay for this in the terms of money. My pay was the possible hope of making this country a better place for my children to grow up in. In this fight for the Cuban cause, I had the honor to meet several men who I have the deepest respect for; among them, Frank Fiorini. We have spent many hours, days, weeks and months together for the same cause. I first met him at the home of a Cuban by the name of Wilfredo Navarro who was with an agency by the name of Cubanos Unidos, "United Cubans" We worked hard to get that agency going to better our chances to do something in the fight. We brought different groups together and trained them in the everglades, but the...

Please pay particular attention in the part of this letter when my father writes, "I had the honor to meet several men who I have the deepest respect for; among them, Frank Fiorini. We have spent many hours, days, weeks and months together for the same cause. I first met him at the home of a Cuban by the name of Wilfredo Navarro who was with an agency by the name of Cubanos Unidos, "United Cubans."

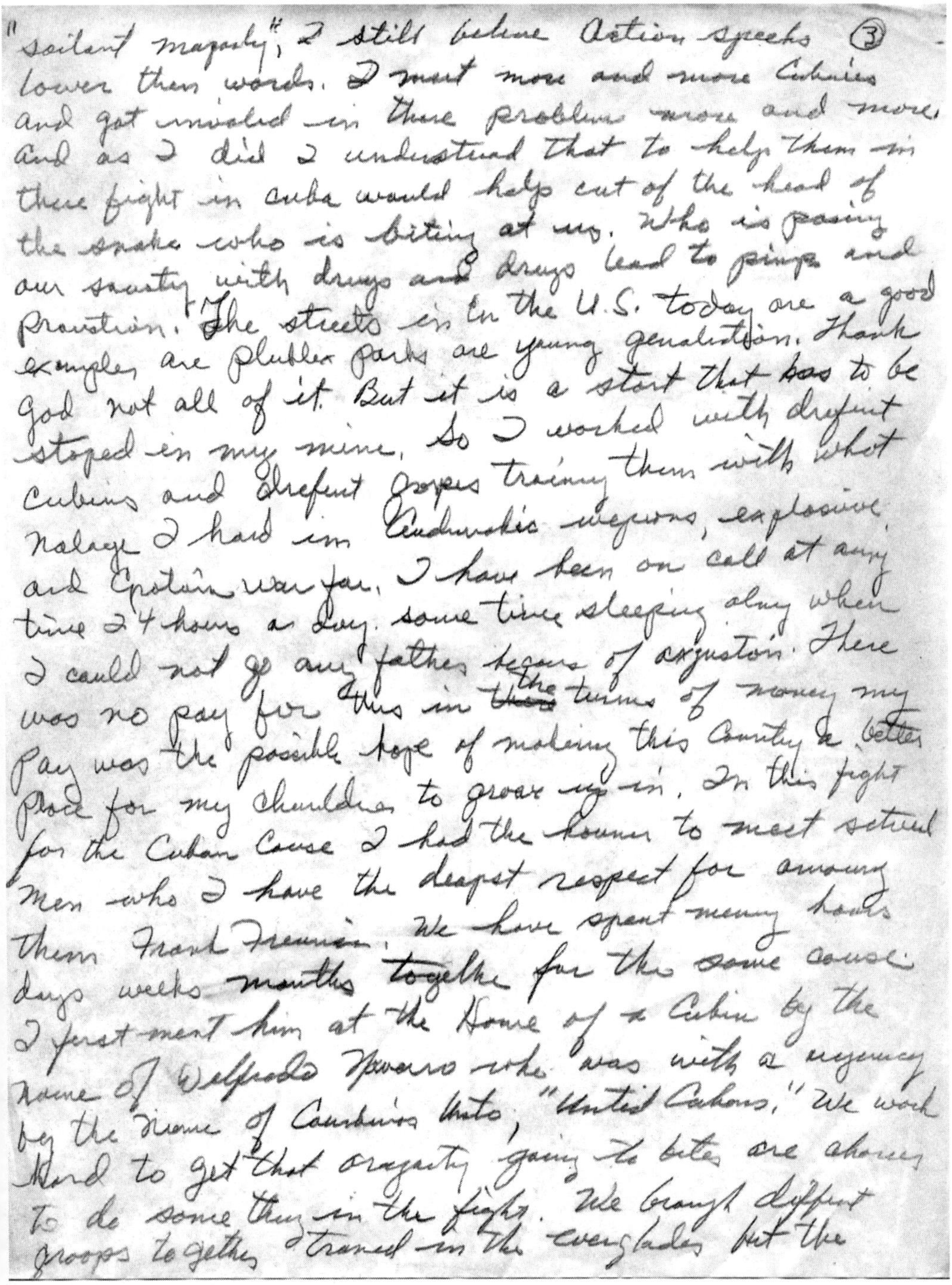
"sailent majesty", I still belive Action speeks ③ -
lower then words. I meet more and more Cubaies
and got invaled in there problems more and more.
And as I did I understand that to help them in
there fight in cuba would help cut of the head of
the snake who is biting at us. Who is posing
our sausty with drugs and drugs lead to pimps and
prostiton. The streets in the U.S. today are a good
examples are plubblic parks are young genaration. Thank
God not all of it. But it is a start that has to be
stoped in my mine. So I worked with drefent
Cubins and drefent groups training them with what
nalage I had in Autumatic wepons, explosive,
and Gurilla war far. I have been on call at any
time 24 hours a day. some time sleeping alny when
I could not go any father because of exzustoin. There
was no pay for this in ~~thes~~ the terms of money my
Pay was the possible hope of making this Country a better
place for my chuldren to groow up in. In this fight
for the Cuban Cause I had the houner to meet actual
men who I have the deapst respect for among
them Frank Freminin. We have spent meny hours
days weeks ~~months~~ togethe for the same cause.
I first meat him at the Home of a Cuban by the
name of Welfredo Navarro who was with a orgency
by the name of Commbrios Unto, "United Cubans." We work
Hard to get that oragaty going to bitter are chances
To do some thing in the fight. We brough diffent
groops together trained in the everglades but the

Page three of my father's manifesto. He talked about working with Cubans and different groups, training them with his knowledge of automatic weapons, explosives and guerrilla warfare.

Frank Fiorini (a.k.a. Sturgis) was a man described by my father, as a man with a volatile temper of Italian descent.

Frank Sturgis in the late 1950's while working with Fidel Castro to overthrow the Batista regime. After Communist influence reared its head in Cuba, Frank would help the head of the Cuban Air Force, Pedro Diaz Lanz and his brother defect to the United States. During this time Sturgis worked as a soldier of fortune and a contract agent for the CIA. Although the 1975 Rockefeller Commission report found that Frank Sturgis was not an employee or agent of the CIA either in 1963 or at any other time. However, Frank Sturgis was involved in helping the CIA organize the Bay of Pigs invasion.

Chapter Four

"Uncle" Frank Sturgis

Frank Fiorini (Sturgis) was born in Norfolk, Virginia, on December 9, 1924. In 1942 Sturgis joined the United States Marines and during the Second World War served in the Pacific. He also served in the United States Army from (1950-52).

In 1956 he moved to Cuba and in 1958 made contact with the CIA at the U.S. Consulate in Santiago de Cuba. Over the next few years he worked as an undercover agent for the agency. His control officer was Sam Jenis.

The CIA formally denies that Frank Sturgis ever worked for them. They deny Sturgis ever being on their payroll or an active employee of their agency. They deny that Sturgis was ever a contract agent for them. Isn't that what the agency is supposed to do, deny?

Frank Sturgis was involved in Cuban anti-Castro activities, and Watergate. Speculation exists that Sturgis was one of the "tramps" arrested immediately after the John F. Kennedy assassination. This speculation has no solid base, but in 1963, Sturgis did report to the FBI that he had a "fistfight" with Lee Harvey Oswald. Investigator Bob Smith of the private group "Committee to Investigate Assassinations" uncovered this report in Fall 1972. The report may be the first link discovered between the JFK assassination and Watergate. To put it into context, Oswald was shown to be involved in Cuban related activities, and the burglars were Cuban, many Bay of Pig's veterans. If these things are true, a connection could exist.

Sturgis Time Line

December 9, 1924 – Frank Angelo Fiorini born, Norfolk VA.

1942 – Joins U.S. Marine Corps Reserve.

1945 – Honorable discharge.

1948 – Joins U.S. Naval Reserve.

1950 – U.S. Army, stationed in Germany.

September 23, 1952 Fiorini petitions a Norfolk court to have his name changed from Frank Angelo Fiorini to Frank Anthony Sturgis.

1958 – Serves in the Cuban Army, in an intelligence capacity.

1959 – Drops anti-Castro leaflets over Cuba.

1961 – Bay of Pigs (Sam Jenis, CIA contact.)

22 Dec 1961 – A CIA memorandum documents Sturgis' involvement in the CIA's leafleting over Cuba.

1963 – FBI report (submitted by Sturgis) that Frank Sturgis engaged in a "fistfight" with Lee Harvey Oswald in Miami. Investigator Bob Smith of the private group "Committee to Investigate Assassinations" uncovers this report in Fall 1972.

1972 – Bernard Barker introduces Sturgis to fellow Watergate plumber E. Howard Hunt, although according to some, the two knew each other much earlier in time.

June 17, 1972 – At 2:30 am, five burglars arrested at the Watergate complex: Bernard Barker, Virgilio Gonzalez, Eugenio Martinez, James W. McCord (CREEP security director), and Frank Sturgis.

September 15, 1972 – Five Watergate burglars plus E. Howard Hunt and G. Gordon Liddy indicted.

January 1973 – Sturgis told Andrew St. George that while in prison, "I will never leave this jail alive if what we discussed about does not remain a secret between us. If you attempt to publish what I've told you, I am a dead man."

February 7, 1977 – Sturgis is a suspect in the killing of my father.

May 7, 1977 – In an interview with the *San Francisco Chronicle*, Frank Sturgis claims "that the objective of the Watergate break-ins was to locate and destroy the photographs of our role in the assassination of President Kennedy.

It doesn't take a genius to figure out that Watergate was a CIA setup. We were just pawns." Frank Sturgis as quoted by Jim Hougan in *Secret Agenda*.

The July 26th Movement

Its name originated from the failed attack on the Moncada Barracks, an army facility in the city of Santiago de Cuba, on July 26, 1953. The July 26th Movement was re-organized in Mexico in 1955 by a group of eighty-two exiled revolutionaries including Fidel Castro, his brother Raul, Camilo Cienfuegos, Huber Matos, Argentinean Ernesto 'Che' Guevara and Frank Sturgis.

Their task was to form a disciplined guerrilla force to overthrow President Fulgencia Batista. A report on Sturgis dated October 8, 1958, by the CIA, stated "Subject is in custody of Cuban Army Military Intelligence Service on suspicion he acted as a 26th of July Movement courier between Miami and Santiago de Cuba. Details of activities in Cuba contained in DBF 8393, July 30, 1958." [CIA FOIA F810351D01854] On October 10, 1958, the CIA generated an index card (deleted)-02765) that Sturgis did indeed infiltrate the 26th of July Revolutionary Movement as a courier for Fidel Castro in Cuba. According to Sturgis, CIA Agents in the American Embassy in Havana, gained his release.

Felix Rodriguez, Evan Rosales, Pepin Pujol, Jan. 3, 1959, Santiago.

Additional Info in Regards to "Uncle" Frank Sturgis

According to declassified FBI documents, Sturgis participated in an anti-Castro leaflet dropping raid over Cuba with Pedro Diaz Lanz, who was at one time the former Chief of Staff of the Cuban Air Force.

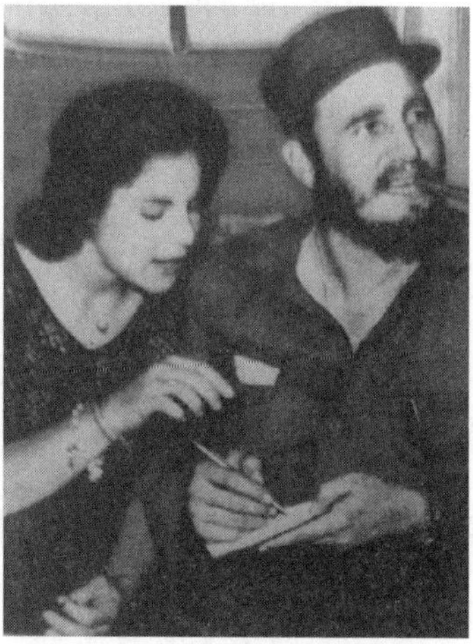

Sturgis became involved with Marita Lorenz who at the time was also having an affair with Fidel Castro. In January 1960, Sturgis and Lorenz took part in a failed attempt to poison Castro. He was also involved in helping the CIA organize the failed Bay of Pigs invasion.

Sturgis was also a member of "Operation 40." He later explained about his role in this assassination squad saying that Operation 40 would, upon orders, assassinate members of the military or the political parties of the foreign country they were going to infiltrate, and if necessary, some of their own members who were suspected of being foreign or double agents.

Marita Lorenz testified before the House Select Committee on Assassinations and during her testimony, she claimed that Sturgis had been one of the gunmen who fired on President John F. Kennedy.

In an article published in the *Florida Sun Sentinel* on 4th December 1963 journalist James Buchanan claimed that Sturgis had met Lee Harvey Oswald in Miami shortly before the assassination of John F. Kennedy.

Buchanan claimed Oswald had tried to infiltrate the anti-Communist Brigade founded by Sturgis. When he was questioned by the FBI about this story, Sturgis claimed that Buchanan had misquoted him regarding his comments about Oswald.

My father left behind two little black books. In these books are names, phone numbers and addresses of many important, famous and infamous men. One page in particular stands out with regards to Frank Sturgis and Lee Harvey Oswald.

The name "Lee" appears near an early entry for Frank Fiorini, "Ferennie" with what I believe to be Frank Fiorini's address. There is a crossed out phone number 866-9085. During that time, area codes were being used, but you could still dial local numbers using just seven digits. This has led me to believe that this number could probably be a 305 area code, which was then the area code for Miami and its surrounding suburbs.

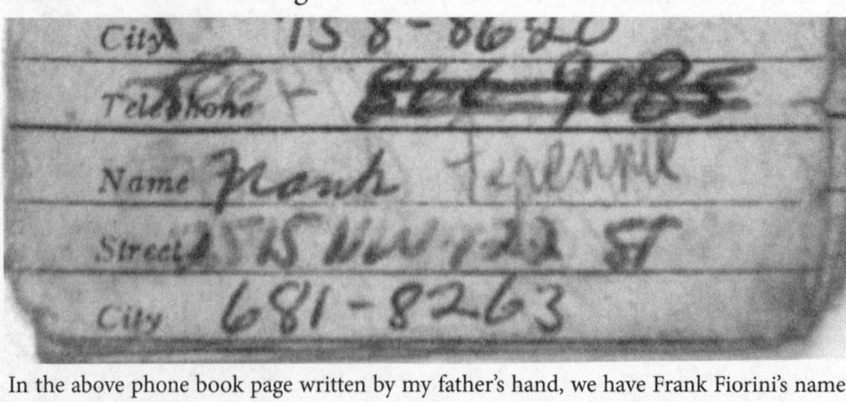

In the above phone book page written by my father's hand, we have Frank Fiorini's name (mis-spelled as Ferennie) with the name "Lee,"and phone number directly above it. This is one of two entries with the name Lee in my father's phone book. Considering the placement of the name, is it possible that this entry may be referencing Lee Oswald?
Lee Oswald's phone book had Frank Fiorini aka Sturgis found in it. The real name of FRANK STURGIS, FRANK FIORINI, appeared twice in OSWALD'S address book.

On June 17, 1972 Sturgis, Virgilio Gonzalez, Eugenio Martinez, Barnard Barker and James McCord were arrested while removing electronic devices from the Democratic Party offices at the Watergate Apartment and Office Complex in Washington, D.C.

While in prison Sturgis gave an interview to Andrew St. George, and said, "I will never leave this prison alive if what we discussed about Watergate does not remain a secret between us. If you attempt to publish what I've told you, I am a dead man."

In November, 1977, Marita Lorenz gave an interview to the *New York Daily News* in which she claimed that a group called Operation 40 which included Sturgis and Oswald were involved in a conspiracy to kill both Kennedy and Castro.

Frank Sturgis died on 4th December, 1993.

A CIA report published information acquired in Miami in mid-July 1965, concerning the continuing involvement of Isadore Irving Davidson in the recruitment of Cuba exiles to go to the Dominican Republic as part of the Organization of American States (OAS) Force, and the plans of Cuban exiles hoping to recover Cuba after the Dominican situation was settled. According to Cuban exile Julio Aton Constanzo Palau, Davidson was acting on "orders from President Lyndon Johnson" and Johnson had asked Constanzo to increase the number of Cubans to as many as possible.

Constanzo claimed he was working with President Johnson, and that he had appointed Frank Fiorini in charge of about 3,000 men, and their goal was to set up a "Government in Exile".

Several U.S. Senators were in support; however, Senator Robert Kennedy was very much against this. 109-12-210-5290.

From a post to me by David Lifton on the Education Forum:

"I think everyone studying this matter should also be aware of another piece of critical evidence – an undated postcard received by Robert Oswald (from Dallas) that is postmarked January 10, 1963. This is WC Exhibit 324 (16 WCH 916), and reads (typed out line by line) as follows:

> Dear Robert,
>
> Sorry I took so long in saying "Thank you" for the nice Xmas
> present you sent June. I was out of town for a few days so I

didn't hear about it until after Xmas. Please send pic. My regards when you write him, I seem to have mislaid his address.

Your Brother,
Lee

P.S. Marina says "Hello""

"If true, this text suggests that Lee Harvey Oswald made a brief 'out of town' trip for a few days or longer just following Christmas, 1962. (Remember: he was at a Christmas party, brought there by George DeMohrenshieldt). Marina Oswald was questioned about this postcard by the HSCA and denied he was gone for the length of time necessary to make a bus trip to Florida. (I do not have the page reference immediately at hand). 'FWIW,' I think the whole 'bus trip' idea provides a possibly incorrect context.

"Robert Oswald's testimony about the postcard is at Volume 1, p. 390. He simply acknowledges it exists, and at that point it is mentioned as being Warren Commission Exhibit 324.

"If Lee Oswald in fact left town for a few days or longer, I don't think he went by bus (which was the way the HSCA questioned him). I would assume he was flown somewhere, maybe somewhere and then back again."

Furthermore, I have researched the phone number crossed out by simply submitting my question to the Miami Dade Public Library.

QUESTION:

Please be advised that I am in search of a number listed in my father's phone book as 866-9085 this number would have been a Miami or Miami Beach number, my father's name was Edwin Kaiser, the name of "Lee" and the number itself was placed above my father's associate Frank Forini aka Sturgis, it may have some significant historical meaning. I would appreciate any help and am thanking you in advance.

Scott Kaiser

RESPONSE:

Dear Mr. Kaiser;

Thank you for your question. We looked in the 1961-62 R.L. Polk Miami Beach City Directory and found the following name: 'A R Schaye.' It is possible that someone lived with him but there was no "Lee" listed.

Helen Muir Florida Collection
Miami-Dade Public Library System
101 W. Flagler Street
Miami, FL 33130
Tel.: 305.375.5023 Fax.: 305.375.3048

Here are some answers to questions I asked my mother:

Q: Can you tell me about the time that dad helped Grandma move to Florida and when this happen?

A: Well your father and I had just gotten married on September 1, 1962 and I wanted to go to Alaska with your father since I've never been there before, we stayed there for a little over a month before we decided to move to Norwalk. Your father couldn't hold down a job so moving to where your grandmother lived at seemed like a good idea so we could have some help, but when we got there your father was in for a big surprise because your grandmother already decided that she was going to move to Florida. Your father helped her move sometime in mid November 1962. I'll never forget it because we had a terrible snow storm that year and your grandmother said to me that she would rather take her chances with a hurricane then have to live in this crap.

Q: So where did you and dad move to if you where no longer living with Grandma?

A: We moved in with your father's Aunt Dorothy, she was your great Aunt Dot.

Q: I see, how long was dad down in Florida for?

A: He was there for quite some time, I was already working at my job for a few months before he returned home, so it had to be sometime in January.

Q: When he came back from his Florida trip did he say anything to you about it? As far as why it took him so long in returning back home.

A: Your father just loved his adventures, he loved hanging around other people more then he did his own family at times. He said he met lots of Cubans while he was down there and he started talking about Fidel Castro that was the first time I ever heard of him.

Q: Who Fidel?

A: Yes, Castro.

Q: I see, you said, dad had met lots of Cubans down there, can you recall or tell me who those Cubans might have been? Do you remember any of their names?

A: Oh it's been such a long time ago, what was his name? Navarro, Wilfredo Navarro that was his name, that's when your father also met Frank Sturgis too.

Q: Did you ever meet Frank?

A: Yeah, but much later.

Q: When you say much later, can you tell me when you first met him?

A: Just as soon as we arrived in Florida your father introduced me to him.

Q: What did you think of Frank?

A: I didn't like him, I didn't like him at all, he just looked like someone you couldn't trust.

Q: Is there anyone one else dad may have met while he was in Florida that you can think of? And, who is this Lee in dad's phone book?

A: Oh my God! Yes, I forgot about your father telling me he had met Lee Oswald too.

Q: How do you know it's Oswald?

A: Your father loved to talk and brag about how he joined the Marines at the age of seventeen then later joined the French Foreign Legion, we were only married for a few months and that's all he practically talked about, he said he had met some guys while in Florida, two Americans in Miami or Miami Beach who were also in the Marines and they were protesting against Castro. Your father told me that when he had met Frank Sturgis he also met Lee Oswald in Florida.

Q: Do you suppose that's how Lee's name got in Dad's phone book?

A: I would say so, your father met a lot of people and anytime he met someone he would write their name and phone number in his address book.

Q: Hmmm? Interesting, when you heard about Kennedy getting shot and the government blamed Oswald for it what did you think?

A: Well you have to remember that it was nearly a year later. I didn't think much of Oswald because I couldn't believe that Kennedy got shot, it was all over the news and radio, the TV news showed him getting shot, I mean he was slumped forward and all I could see was the cameras just panning back, someone else got shot too, and all you could see was the car just taking off, it was complete chaos and pandemonium, people were just running everywhere.

Q: After the government arrested Oswald and then two days later he gets shot what did you think?

A: I couldn't believe it, I mean how stupid is that? They just shot the man who shot Kennedy, or may have shot Kennedy, but now we'll never know.

Q: So you mean to tell me that it never crossed your mind that the Lee Oswald dad met in Miami could have been the same Oswald that may have killed the president?

A: No, I didn't give it any thought, wished I had, I would've asked your father if it was the same guy, but I didn't.

Q: Okay, fair enough, did dad say anything after he found out that Oswald got shot?

A: No, your father had no expression what so ever, after watching it on TV your father went right to the kitchen and made himself and me a sandwich, and that's because I was already seven months pregnant with you.

Q: Speaking about that and being pregnant with me, can you tell me again about your trip to the doctor's office?

A: Your father was suppose to give me a ride to my gynecologist, but like always he was nowhere to be found so I ended up driving myself, it was there at the doctor's office that I heard about Kennedy getting shot. A nurse came running in and made the announcement, I was listing to it on the radio in my car until I got home then I watched it on TV.

Q: Where was dad the day you went to your doctors? That had to be on November 22, 1963 right?

A: Right, I don't know where your father was, I didn't see him until late that evening.

Q: Hmmm? Didn't you ask dad where he was?

A: Yes I did, all he said was he was out with his friends drinking, so I left it alone because I didn't want to get upset while I was pregnant with you.

Q: Okay, well, I have one more question I'd like to ask you.

A: What?

Q: When Brett was down here asking you questions why didn't we talk about any of this stuff?

A: Because Brett didn't ask me any of these questions and we didn't show him your father's phone book or the letter's your father wrote, all he got to see was the CIA documents and the book that Weberman sent me.

My father and Frank spent a good amount of time together, and I know they exchanged many war stories. Early on in their friendship, still sometime in the 1960s, Uncle Frank mentioned to my dad how he had lost hundreds of men at the Bay of Pigs invasion, and how hundreds more were currently jailed in Cuba.

Sturgis described how he planned to start another anti-Castro group and attempt to free Cuba from the grips of Castro. My father was intrigued by these stories, but he needed to return home to his family in Norwalk.

MM 105-8342
RJD:jll
1.

On November 27, 1963, ALAN COURTNEY, Radio Interviewer, Miami Radio Station WQAM, Mc Allister Hotel, Biscayne Boulevard, Miami, Florida, furnished the following information:

About one year ago COURTNEY had GERALD PATRICK HEMMING and three other individuals on his radio program. He interviewed them concerning their training anti-CASTRO troops in the Florida Keys. At the conclusion of the program, a telephone call was received at the radio station from a young man who said he was from New Orleans, was formerly in the U. S. Marine Corps, and wanted to volunteer his services.

COURTNEY recalled that this young man gave a name such as HARVEY LEE, OSWALD HARVEY, or OSWALD LEE. COURTNEY turned this telephone call over to DAVEY (LNU), one of the participants of the radio show. DAVEY and OSWALD talked on the telephone a short period of time and may have made an appointment to meet at a later date.

COURTNEY advised that JOHN MARTINO, 2326 Alton Road, Miami Beach, Florida, claimed he received a report that LEE OSWALD was in Cuba between September and October, 1963, and went there by way of Mexico. MARTINO further claimed that during the past year OSWALD distributed pro-CASTRO literature in Miami, had the literature printed by a Miami printer, and paid for the printing by a check signed by the Fair Play For Cuba Committee.

COURTNEY advised that he could not verify the above information and was reporting it for any possible value it might have.

Chapter Five

Back to Norwalk

Sonia was employed at the Red Roof Inn restaurant in Norwalk, where her salary paid the family bills. Meanwhile, my father would frequent bars, and spend most of his time within his circle of friends.

One day, my father received a letter from his old French Foreign Legion friend, Richard, who was still living in Paris. Richard inquired whether my father might be able to help him move back into the United States. My father contacted immigration offices and spoke to an immigration officer on Richard's behalf. The immigration offices response was: "in order to sponsor Richard, he must have a solid job offer, a place to live, and an American citizen as a sponsor." My mother (and father) then became Richard's sponsor.

Father believed that this process would be simple and that Richard would be able to move back with his family. Both parties filled out the proper paperwork, but my father was crushed to find out Richard's application had been denied. He nonetheless told Richard to fly over with his family.

Whether it was dumb luck, an incredibly fortuitous oversight, or some intelligence apparatus at work, my father was able meet Richard and his family in New York, and then off to Connecticut. Richard was able to buy a home for his family.

My mother and father also moved into the house with Richard and his family. My dad soon found employment as a tree surgeon, but was then injured. He had been struck by a falling tree. Mom was called at work by the hospital notifying her that her husband was ready to be picked up. She wondered what had happened to him this time?

The nurse said, "He broke his leg." When my mother arrived, he was already hopping around on his crutches. A little boy walked up to him and said, "Mister what happened?"

My dad replied, "A pigeon kicked me." The youngster was amazed at the strength possessed by what must have been an immense bird. Mom and Dad shared a laugh, and left the hospital. It wasn't so amusing to my father in later years, as he would find out his leg never healed correctly, and he would walk with a limp for the rest of his life.

My father and Richard would constantly exchange war stories from their days in the Legion. Sonia found the testosterone level in the house sometimes a bit unbearable. In one alcohol-fueled instance, my father placed his hand on the counter and stabbed himself in the hand with a knife, in a show of poorly-thought-out bravado.

Once again, he found himself having to go back to the hospital. At the emergency room, the doctors informed Edwin that he had severed a tendon. He would never again be able to straighten out his pinkie finger. That evening when he returned home, Sonia broke the news to him that she was pregnant with their child. My father borrowed some money from Richard to celebrate with cigars.

On November 22, 1963 my mother was seven months pregnant with me and found herself alone and on the way to her gynecologist. While in the waiting room with the doctor, a nurse came running in and said, "An announcement has been made that President Kennedy has just been shot in Dallas, Texas." Sonia wept as she drove home alone listening to the radio reports.

My father wasn't at home, he had been gone all day. He arrived at the house much later that evening. My mother met him as he entered the front door and asked my father if he had heard the news. He said, "Yeah! And I hope they get that son of a bitch who ever did it! That person does not deserve to live."

After hearing about Lee Oswald's arrest my mother said it was all over the news, the TV and radio, everyone was just talking about it, she said, "and I really never given it any thought. A few days after his arrest, I watched the news and saw Oswald get shot." My mother said, my father showed no expression whatsoever, he went right to the kitchen and made himself a sandwich. She said to me later in life: "If only I could've remembered your dad telling me he had met a man in Miami named Lee Oswald, I would've certainly asked him if he thought it was the same guy?" My mom continued, "I guess, I was in shock just watching the man who shot the president get shot himself on TV and it had me in awe. I mean, how stupid is that? She said, and now we'll never know.

My father's 8mm movie of JFK's funeral.

My father drove to Washington, D.C. to film the funeral proceedings of the 35th President of the United States with his 8mm movie camera. He phoned my mother to say that he would be home the following day and that he would stay the night in Washington with some friends who he met there. My mother has no idea who he met, and what happened on this trip to our nation's Capital.

Nothing seemed the same after my father's return home. My mom felt that the world was "going to hell in a hand basket." The new year did not seem festive, with the exception of the arrival of their son, me, Scott Richard Kaiser. I was born on January 18, 1964.

Our family life stabilized through 1967, as we continued living with Richard and his family in Norwalk. This all changed when Richard went missing one morning.

He was found by my father in the garage. Richard was supposedly working on his car while it was running. The garage door was down, and the carbon monoxide had quickly killed him. My mother didn't think it was suicide, but no one could prove he was murdered. According to my mother Richard was happy living back in the United States, he had bought a house for his family, found work and settled down, but my father thought that it was the pressures of not knowing anything else other then war. I mean after all, Richard was an American, who fought for the French Foreign Legion and had been a Legionnaire for quite sometime.

In late 1967, my father packed the family up, and we moved back to Anchorage, Alaska. My mother was pregnant and in September of 1968, my little sister, Elizabeth Catharine was born. She was named after my paternal grandmother, Elizabeth Catharine.

The winter weather in Alaska was more than Mom could bear. My sister and I were always getting sick, and Mom didn't have much help financially. My father didn't exactly help in taking care of us. I needed an ear operation and the doctor suggested that it should be done in warmer climate. Dad called his mother who was living in Florida at the time and told her that the family was moving down there.

My father, me and my mother in Alaska, 1967.

Paraphrase from Page Two of My Father's Letter:

After his death I moved to Alaska, then on one of my trips back to Connecticut I met and married my wife, this was in 1962, I have been married now eleven years. I have a son nine and a daughter four. Because of a operation on my sons ear we were advised to have it done in a warmer climate not in Alaska. My mother lived in Florida at that time so we moved from Alaska to Florida. The operation was performed in a hospital in Miami Beach and we have lived in that area for over four years now. It was then that I started getting wrapped up in the Cuban problems. Abraham Lincoln once said that "progress" true progress starts in your heart. The Cuban people not only had in their heart the cry for freedom, justice, a new democratic government in Cuba but also the cry for "progress" they knew that the Monroe Doctrine made by President Monroe, which was made to protect the Americans, North, South and central from infiltration from other government foreign and abroad was not Kennedy. I asked myself? Do I have to see New York, Chicago or Dallas Texas? Budapest, Algeria, Vet Nam or even like that

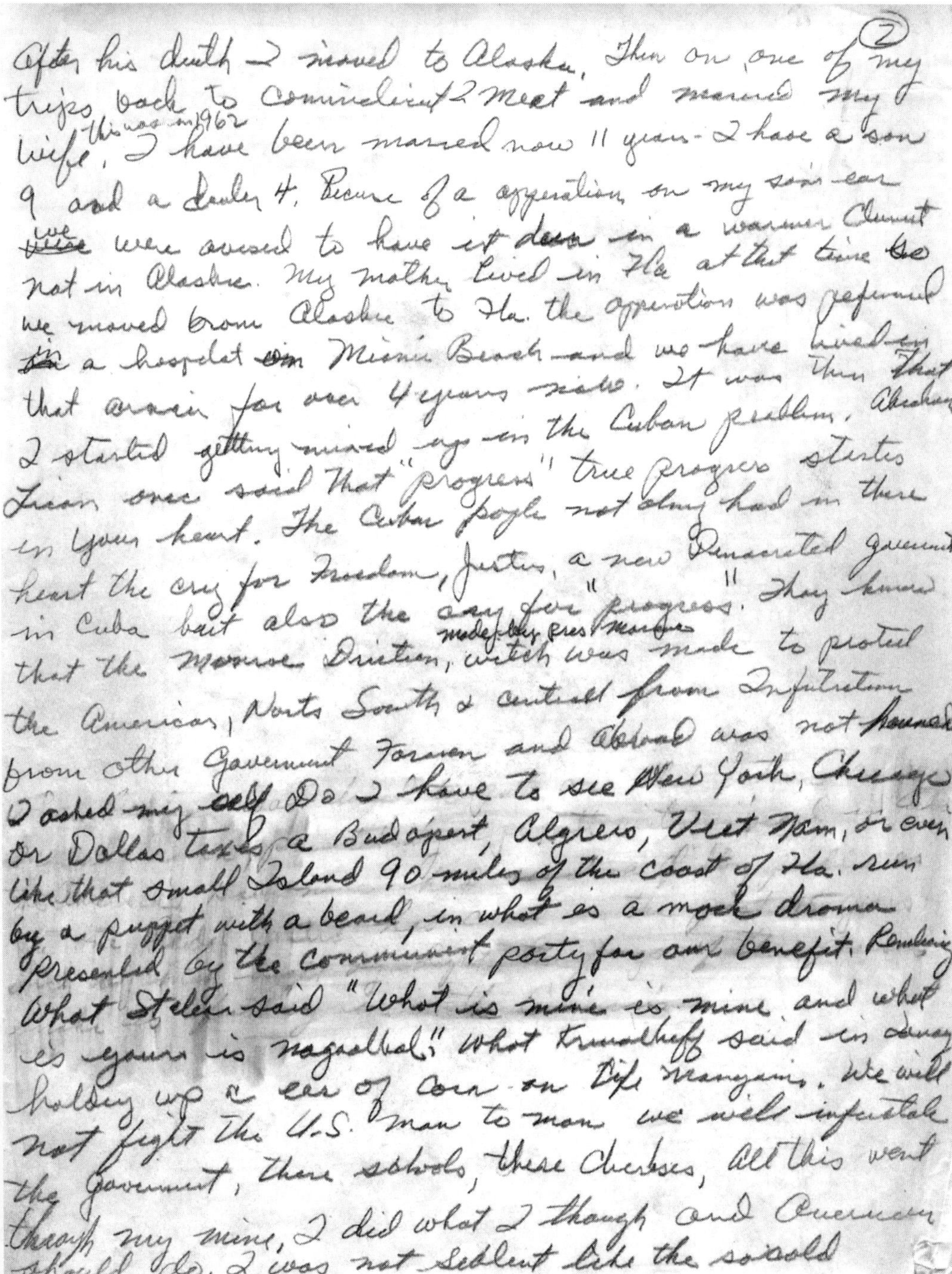
2

After his death I moved to Alaska. Then on one of my
trips back to Connecticut I meet and married my
wife. (this was in 1962) I have been married now 11 years - I have a son
9 and a daughter 4. Because of a operation on my son's ear
we were advised to have it done in a warmer climate
not in Alaska. My mother lived in Fla at that time so
we moved from Alaska to Fla. the operation was performed
in a hospital in Miami Beach and we have lived in
that area for over 4 years now. It was then that
I started getting mixed up in the Cuban problem. Abraham
Lincoln once said that "progress" true progress starts
in your heart. The Cuban people not only had in there
heart the cry for freedom, justice, a new Democratic government
in Cuba but also the cry for "progress". They knew
that the Monroe Doctrine, (modified by pres. Monroe) witch was made to protect
the Americas, North South & central from Infiltration
from other Government Forces and Abroad was not honored.
I asked my self Do I have to see New York, Chicago
or Dallas Texas a Budapest, Algiers, Viet Nam, or even
like that small Island 90 miles of the coast of Fla. run
by a puppet with a beard, in what is a mock drama
presented by the communist party for our benefit. Remembering
What Stalin said "What is mine is mine and what
is yours is negotiable." What Krushchev said in during
holding up a ear of corn on Life Magazine. We will
not fight the U.S. man to man we will infiltrate
the Government, there schools, these Churches, All this went
through my mind, I did what I though and American
should do. I was not silent like the silent

Page two of a handwritten letter by my father where he is explaining our move to Miami and his life's adventures.

small island 90 miles off the coast of Florida run by a puppet with a beard in what is a mock drama presumably by the communist party for our benefit. Remembering what Joseph Stalin said, "what is mine is mine and what is yours is negotiable" what Nikita Khrushchev said in February holding up an ear of corn on *Life* magazine. We will not fight the United States man to man we will infiltrate the government, their schools, their churches, all this went through my mind, I did what I thought any American should do. I was not silent like the so called...

Chapter Six

The Kaisers Move to Miami

The family arrived in Miami in November 1968 and it wasn't long before my father would meet up again with Wilfredo Navarro. At this time in Miami, JM/WAVE, the second largest CIA base of operations outside of Langley, Virginia was winding down from its previous glory. However, operations like JM/WAVE do not completely disappear overnight.

From Wikipedia:

> JMWAVE or JM/WAVE or JM WAVE was the codename for a major secret United States covert operations and in-

telligence gathering station operated by the CIA from 1961 until 1968. It was headquartered in Building 25 on the South Campus (formerly the site of Richmond Naval Air Station, an airship base about 12 miles south of the main campus) of the University of Miami in Miami, Florida. It was also referred to as the CIA's "Miami Station" or "Wave Station".

JMWAVE underwent its first major development when it was established as the operations center for Task Force W, the CIA's unit dedicated to "Operation Mongoose" – a U.S. effort to overthrow President Fidel Castro's Communist government in Cuba. JMWAVE was also active in some form during the failed U.S.-sponsored "Bay of Pigs" invasion of Cuba in April 1961. The JMWAVE operation grew out of an earlier fledgling CIA office in Coral Gables.

The station's activities reached their peak in late 1962 and early 1963 – the period of the Cuban Missile Crisis. Under Ted Shackley's leadership from 1962 to 1965, JMWAVE grew to be the largest CIA station in the world outside of the organization's headquarters in Langley, Virginia, with 300 to 400 professional operatives (possibly including about 100 based in Cuba) as well as an estimated 15,000 anti-Castro Cuban exiles on its payroll. The CIA was one of Miami's largest employers during this period. Exiles were trained in commando tactics, espionage and seamanship and the station supported numerous exile raids on Cuba.

The main front company for JMWAVE was "Zenith Technical Enterprises, Inc." In addition, about 300 to 400 other front companies were created throughout South Florida with a large range of "safe houses", cover businesses and other properties. With an annual budget of approx. U.S. $50 million (in 1960s dollars; U.S. $50 million in 1962 dollars are worth U.S. $333 million in 2006 dollars (PPP)[10]), the station had a major impact on the economy of South Florida, creating a local economic boom – particularly in the real estate, banking and certain manufacturing sectors. It also operated a fleet of aircraft and boats – this has been described as the third largest navy in the Caribbean at the time after the main U.S. and Cuban navies. JMWAVE's activities were so widespread that they became an open secret amongst local Florida government and law enforcement agencies.

> On June 26, 1964, *Look* magazine published an exposé by David Wise and Thomas B. Ross which revealed that Zenith was a CIA front. The University of Miami authorities denied knowledge of the CIA operation (though Shackley would claim privately that University President Henry King Stanford was fully aware) and JMWAVE changed its main front company name from Zenith to "Melmar Corporation."
>
> By 1968, JMWAVE was increasingly regarded as obsolete. There was also concern that the station would become a public embarrassment to the University of Miami. Consequently, it was deactivated and replaced with a substantially smaller station at Miami Beach.

Although the CIA's operations seemed to be scaled down, The Cuban people were still screaming out for a free Cuban government and for the assassination of Fidel Castro on what seemed like every street corner. My father had found something that he felt he could put his whole heart behind and knew exactly what he wanted to do. He made friends with – or was assigned to – several Cubans in Miami and quickly picked up their language.

Inconspicuously nestled in a wooded area next to what is now the Metro Zoo, the CIA's JM/WAVE headquarters had a sign on its door that read: Zenith Technical Enterprises. Organizing and supplying the CIA's secret war against Castro, it became the largest employer in South Florida. Run by veteran clandestine boss Theodore Shackley, his chief of operations was David Morales. As head of propaganda and psych warfare activities, David Phillips was a frequent visitor who had all 300 Agency officers handling the anti-Castro Cuban groups reporting to him. PHOTO COURTESY OF BRAD AYERS

Chapter Seven

Edwin, Wilfredo and Frank

My father and Frank Sturgis had first met each other in the early 60s in the Miami area through Wilfredo Navarro. After our move to Hialeah, the two became reacquainted and were good friends. Sturgis had mentioned to my father that he was a leader in an anti-Castro organization called the International Anti-Communist Brigade, and that he also led the charge of the 2506 Brigade in the Bay of Pigs invasion. The 2506 was designed to overthrow Fidel Castro's Communist regime. Frank said that everything that could possibly go wrong went wrong. The planes that were supposed to arrive didn't. Our men got captured by Castro's government, and our president deserted us. Sturgis said, "I hated Kennedy and he deserved to bite the bullet."

Manuel Artime (saluting) at the Orange Bowl Stadium with President and Mrs. Kennedy. Many researchers claim that after this ceremony, President Kennedy met with Mike McLaney (Mafia liaison) in Miami to discuss plans for the overthrow of Fidel Castro.

After the Republican Party victory with Richard Nixon in the election of 1968, the Cuban exiles believed there would be a political change concerning Cuba. Several political exile leaders held meetings to make future plans but according to Sturgis his former revolutionary friend, Manuel Artime Buesa, would report that there would be no change. Nixon would not attempt to send troops back into Cuba, or contribute to the anti-Castro committee in seeing the overthrow of Castro's regime. Sturgis said that Artime had served with him in Fidel Castro's revolutionary army to overthrow President Batista and also with the 2506 Brigade.

During the night of April 14/15, 1961, a diversionary landing was planned near Baracoa, in Oriente province, which is at the far eastern end of the island. There were 164 Cuban exiles commanded by Higino "Nino" Diaz. Their mothership, named La Playa or Santa Ana, had sailed from Key West under a Costa Rican flag. Several U.S. Navy destroyers were stationed off shore near Guantanamo Bay to give the appearance of an impending invasion fleet.

The reconnaissance boats turned back after detecting activities by Cuban forces along the coastline. In the 1970s Artime organized the Miami Watergate Defense Relief Fund, collecting $21,000 for the convicted Watergate burglars, a number of whom were veterans of the Bay of Pigs operation.

In 1969, my father started talking about a free democracy for Cuba. He started with a basic propaganda agenda against Cuba's government. He would draw cartoons of Fidel Castro, and have them published in the *Miami Herald* showing Castro holding a gun to his head blowing his brains out. He would also make pamphlets that opposed Castro's regime, and passed them out in Miami's Cuban community. Long before he moved to Miami, there were other anti-Castro groups such as Interpen, International Anti-Communist Brigade and Alpha 66 just to name a few. All of which, had previous ties to the JM/WAVE activities.

Frank Sturgis mentioned to my father that a friend of his, Orlando Bosch Avila in U.S. District Court had been sentenced to ten years for ship bombings in the United States. In 1969, Manuel Artime contacted a U.S. Congressman seeking his support to have Bosch acquitted of his crimes. Bosch was later released on good behavior.

Orlando Bosch and friend.

Sturgis said that Jorge Canosa was head of another anti-Castro group called "The Cuban Representation in Exile" (RECE), and that RECE had sent an infiltration team into Cuba. There were plans to send other groups that were called the "Second National Front of Escambray" (SNFE) and "Alpha 66." Those two groups would later split into two. The Cuban Nationalist Movement under Felipe Rivero Diaz also planned terrorist activities in Canada, hoping to get the British involved in going to war with the Americans against Cuba.

Sturgis said that he and twelve other Americans, committed to military activities against Cuba, went into Mexico and then to British Honduras where they were arrested, and deported back to the United States. Sturgis had one plan to infiltrate those countries using terrorist activities, and then blame Fidel Castro for the destruction of their power plants and other buildings.

My father was excited to be a part of what was going on in Miami. He couldn't believe how much action he had been missing, but he was a father and a husband. Once, he had been in Miami, a short time, he knew what interested him, and he was ready. My father would never miss out on an opportunity for adventure again.

Cubanos Unidos

My father saw an opportunity to be at the birth a new anti-Castro organization. He, with the help of Frank Sturgis, Wilfredo Navarro and most likely with some sort of support from JM/WAVE, resurrected (in name at least) an organization called the "*Cubanos Unidos*" which means, "United Cubans." The three of them started to recruit Cuban males with an anti-Castro ideology.

My father and Wilfredo Navarro in Hialeah, Florida 1970's.

Dad suggested to Navarro that meetings could also be held at our house on West 8th Lane in Hialeah. There they could sit in the back yard, drink their Cuban coffee, smoke their Cuban cigars and discuss the birth of their new organization, the Cubanos Unidos.

Sturgis said that if they would be able to unite all of the anti-Castro groups into one, creating a large entity, it might grab the attention of the U.S. Government. Sturgis believed that the U.S. Government could assist them in the funding of their operation to overthrow and assassinate Fidel Castro.

Late one evening in our backyard, my father, Navarro and Sturgis were enjoying drinks and discussing their plans for this new organization. Eventually, Navarro got into his car and went home. Soon after, Sturgis and my father got into in argument over who would hold which position in the organization. The argument rapidly devolved into the throwing of blows.

I ran out of the house to see what was going on. I started to scream at the two of them to stop, but my cries fell on deaf ears. Neither man would listen. There were bloody mouths and bloody noses! I ran back into the house, yelling to my mother that, "Dad and Uncle Frank are outside fighting."

Mother called the police, saying, "There are two idiots fighting in my back yard and one of them is my husband." By the time the police arrived, Sturgis was gone. The police officers questioned my father.. Dad told them that he had hurt himself shadow boxing! The next morning Sturgis and my dad chose to forget about their disagreement and were again, thick as thieves.

My father began to gather information and again started to spread anti-Castro propaganda with cartoons in the *Miami Herald*. He soon realized that propaganda alone wasn't working, aside from raising a few eyebrows. They needed a different approach if they wanted Castro out of office. The political atmosphere of that time bred a new crop of underground organizations.

My father deferred leadership of the Cubanos Unidos organization to Wilfredo Navarro, and from that point forward, my father would be recognized as the military head of the group. Supposedly, my dad couldn't risk an investigation by the U.S. Government for immigration or neutrality matters. He was, after all, no longer a citizen of the United States. This posed a good question: How was my father able to get so deep into the anti-Castro movement, in a hot bed of CIA activity, if he was a white Caucasian and didn't have his U.S. citizenship?

According to my father, Wilfredo Navarro had been involved in revolutionary matters going back as far as 1960. The two were hard at work recruiting people for their organization, and the only thing that could possibly have gotten in their way was lack of funds. Navarro told my dad he wasn't worried.

Navarro was in contact with Gordon DiBattisto who had banking connections in America and Europe. DiBattisto said that he would be willing to invest $50,000 if the Department of State would condone their plans. Navarro was to either confirm these plans or resign.

The Department of State replied that it could not make any suggestion as to what action DiBattisto or the Cubanos Unidos organization should take. The United States Government did not want them to violate the United States neutrality laws or involve the U.S. in any political situations. But what the U.S. Government wasn't aware of at the time was that my father, Sturgis, Navarro and DiBattisto were already communicating with representatives from the CIA. FBI 105-18743.

Gordon DiBattisto was an Italian-American who claimed to be a millionaire. Wilfredo Navarro stated to the FBI that at the time he was a secretary to Maurice Ferre, who was a former six-term Mayor of Miami (1973-1985). Ferre had been the first United States mayor born in Puerto Rico (Ponce) and the first Hispanic Mayor of Miami. He was also an unsuccessful candidate in the 2010 elections for the U.S. Senate seat. http://en.wikipedia.org/wiki/Maurice_Ferre.

Maurice Ferre

During the early 1970s, Ferre was a Miami City Commissioner and already very wealthy. It was around this time that Gordon DiBattisto planned to leave for New York in order to conduct a large press conference, rally and fund-raising drive. He said he planned to hand out a considerable amount of my father's propaganda material to stimulate exiles in the New York area to prepare a mass propaganda effort against Castro and the government of Cuba.

At that time, the Cubanos Unidos were planning for infiltration and sabotage missions against Cuba, which would involve sending their members into Cuba to work among members of the Cuban Armed Forces. There they would try to sabotage gasoline storage facilities and electrical plants in Cuba.

Selling Bonds to Raise Money For CU

On February 25, 1970, José Elias de la Torriente appeared at the Miami office of the FBI accompanied by his assistant, José Velez. Torriente resides in Coral Gables, Florida, and is a retired Vice President of Collins Radio International. In the October, 1998 issue of John F. Kennedy, Jr.'s *George* magazine, David Wise reported on how the NRO had "lost" $6 billion in U.S. taxpayer's money, and specifically mentioned the fiasco surrounding the construction of the HQ building, for which Collins/Rockwell served as a cover company for the CIA.

During the past six months Torriente had been engaged in an effort to unite the Cuban exile community in an effort to liberate Cuba. Torriente made available some papers relating to an organization known as Cubanos Unidos. He said he was not aware of the identities of who was responsible for the distribution of the papers of Cubanos Unidos, but that he believed it was as attempt by these people to sell bonds to Cubans in Miami under the impression that they were bonds of the Torriente group. FBI 105-18943.

José E. Torriente at far right, photo taken just days before his assassination.

Sinking Ships and Supplying Guns

My father called Sturgis and told him that the night before, the chief of the paratrooper section for the Cubanos Unidos, Frank Castro, has been ambushed while in his car in Miami. The paratroop section of the Cubanos Unidos was known as 'Alcones Dorados' and were located at the Commercial Airport in Homestead. Florida. SJ 105-12631.

This paratroop section was mainly a private Cuban social club and only representatives of the CIA knew that the club was an "arm" of the Cubanos Unidos. FBI Special Agent Robert Dwyer indicated that Alpha 66, a militant anti-Castro group, was continuing plans to carry out infiltrations with other group into Cuba.

Juan Marquez Hernandez, who had been active in Alpha 66 operations, was planning to join the Cubanos Unidos. The group was talking about sinking a Russian ship while en route to Cuba. This information was forwarded to Henry Kissinger at the White House, , and to the State Department, CIA, Secret Service and Defense Intelligence Agency. Copies were also sent to the Attorney General, the U.S. Customs Service, the Coast Guard and the Alcohol and Tobacco Tax Division.

At that time discussions were being held concerning an attack on a Soviet ship, Wilfredo Navarro asked Tomas Arencibia to quit his job, his position with Alpha 66, and work for the Cubanos Unidos full time. The group Alpha 66 was a Miami-based anti-Castro organization, which had landed a thirteen-man infiltration team into Cuba, during April 1970, and subsequently claimed responsibility for sinking two Cuban Government boats.

Besides my father, Sturgis and Navarro, the people with the Cubanos Unidos included Gordon DiBattisto, Roerme Navarro (Wilfredo's brother), Jose "Pepin" Fortuno, Navarro's uncle, Tomas Arencibia and Rafael Orosman.

One day, Sturgis said that my father got very drunk and when they left Navarro's office, and they got to the lobby downstairs my father began ranting and raving about a Russian ship, which was en route to Cuba. He said he wanted them to help him sink it, but when everyone decided not to go along with my father's plan, he became more belligerent, and said he was going to sink it himself.

Gordon DiBattisto had to catch a plane back to Newark, and he saw my father and a Cuban male enter an alley near the office building as he and the Navarro brothers drove by. He could see that my dad had a gun out, and was threatening the Cuban with it. He and the others got out of the car and walked into the alley. There Sturgis took the .45-caliber pistol away from my dad, took out the bullets and then handed the gun back.

Sturgis said that my father carried this gun with him all the time. DiBattisto said he told my dad he would think about his offer only because he was too scared to turn him down, at the time, considering the state my father was in.

Jose De La Torriente, who was a Cuban leader in Miami, had been negotiating to obtain two islands in the Caribbean which could be used as a training and operational bases for the Cuban exiles. One of the islands is Isla Beata just South of the Dominican

Republic. Torriente also went to Puerto Rico with Edwin Kaiser during June 1970. The other island is Île à Vache, just South of Haiti. The ex-president of Cuba, Carlos Prio Socarrás, was negotiating for this island.

The Cubanos Unidos held a meeting to introduce the Americans who were backing their organization. The Americans were Frank Fiorini and my father. Fiorini called himself "Chief of the Intelligence Section of the Cubanos Unidos." (Headquarters comment: Fiorini, an American pilot, has cooperated with Cuban exiles in the past. He has participated in air strikes over Cuba.) [SK] Cite TDCS DB-315/03129-70.

A source who was acquainted with the leaders of Alpha 66 advised that despite the arrest of Andrés Nazario Sargén who was the Secretary General of Alpha 66, the organization was proceeding with its plans to carry out the infiltration of another group into Cuba.

On June 11, 1970 Nazario claimed that these men were again at a training camp, and were eager to leave for Cuba as soon as possible. Nazario didn't furnish details of the location of the camp, but said there were two separate groups of five or six men, and these men would be landing at four different sites in Cuba. Each group would have at least two fully-automatic weapons that were supplied by my father and Sturgis.

Nazario said that the new military leader of Alpha 66 was José Rodriguez Perez, who Nazario said, was the former military leader of the MIRR (Movimiento Insurreccional de Recuperacion Revolucionaria) group of Orlando Bosch Avila. Another Alpha 66 military leader who returned to the training camps was Euclides Mendez, who was also known as "El Indio" or David Sanchez Morales, former chief of operations of JM/WAVE out of Miami.

As I was going through the CIA files I noticed a name Arencibia. I tracked him down, still living in Miami. I called a Tomas Arencibia to ask him some questions about my father, he told me he knew my father, and said "he thought my father was a brave man." After talking to him for awhile on the phone, I was hesitant to ask him about Euclides Mendez, who was also found in the same set of CIA documents as Arencibia was found.

I asked a question about Euclides Mendez, who's nickname was "El Indio," and Arencibia said that Euclides Mendez was in fact David Sanchez Morales. I wanted to catch all this on tape, so I would have a good transcript of our conversation, but I hadn't purchased my dictaphone yet. I was excited to talk to him about my father, now that I was able to locate him. After purchasing a dictaphone, I called Arencibia back, several times, but he would no longer answer my phone calls.

There is no hard evidence that Morales joined the Cubanos Unidos, my father's anti-Castro group, although Arencibia said that Morales would take part in some of the Cubanos Unidos training camps, Morales would often come over our house in Hialeah with Frank Sturgis. I didn't know who this Morales was until late in life, when I seen a picture of him, then I remembered this guy coming over to our house.

Alpha 66 had also acquired two stolen rubber rafts with silent motors for use in their next operation. Orozco Loreto Santiago, Reinol Rodriguez and possibly one other left South Florida on some type of boat trip, but the exact nature was not disclosed. In all probability it was a trial run.

Men representing the Cubanos Unidos including both Navarros, Arencibia, Sturgis and my father conducted this phase of the impending infiltrations along with Orozco and Juan Marquez.

"El Indio" and Arencibia, are military leaders with Alpha 66 and "El Flaco" Valdes, also from Alpha 66 who had joined the Cubanos Unidos were at the home of Marquez who was accompanied by Alberto Ruiz.

Navarro, Sturgis and my father had suggested that Marquez leave Alpha 66 and join the Cubanos Unidos. My father claimed that CU had unlimited resources and a considerable amount of arms and supplies. Sturgis said that the objective of CU was to attack a ship going to Cuba, rather than infiltration. Marquez agreed to consider the proposal.

Marquez said that he had decided to give Andres Nazario "a real surprise" by refusing to participate in the next Alpha 66 operation and join the Cubanos Unidos. Marquez said he had met with members of the CU and told them that he was going to join. Marquez also told the CU that he had a fast "Formula," a twenty-three-foot boat that was purchased by him with Alpha 66 funds, and he planned on keeping it hidden for his own use and the use of CU.

Marquez also said that he had a 57mm recoilless rifle and an adequate supply of ammunition. He had located a man experienced in the use of these weapons. He said the man's name was "Hemmings." This was in reality Gerald Patrick "Gerry" Hemming, who was the founder of Interpen, which was the Intercontinental Penetration Force, a group of anti-Castro guerrillas who trained at No Name Key in the early 1960s. Marquez planned to arrange practice sessions with the 57mm rifle prior to carrying out any operation.

Marquez made mention to the Navarro brothers that Sturgis and my father were talking about sinking a Russian ship on its way to Cuba, but Marquez considered a foray into the center of the Cuban Government fleet as a more feasible possibility. He told the Navarros that with this 57mm rifle it would be possible to easily sink ten or twelve Cuban boats in a matter of minutes and then escape. The Cubanos Unidos were indeed making plans to sink a Soviet vessel.

They were getting the cooperation of Hernandez and Orlando Bosch Avila, all members of MIRR. This organization had helped transport exiles on expeditions to Cuba. The group had two V-20 fiberglass boats in the Miami River to be used in the operation. Roerme Navarro, a graduate of the Cuban Naval Academy and his brother Wilfredo were backed by DiBattisto, the Italian-American who claimed to have unlimited financial support from business firms that lost heavily when Castro seized power in Cuba.

The CU had no hard information to indicate the specific location of any Soviet vessels during their runs to Cuba, but they closely monitored the U.S. Coast Guard and Marine communication frequencies hoping it would provide the target's location.

Establishing Bases on Surrounding Islands:

On July 30, 1970 my father said he was leaving for the island of Martinique in the Caribbean where he would try to make arrangements to set up a military base for operations against Cuba. By August 3, he had returned from Martinique after he was arrested and questioned for twenty-eight hours by the French Intelligence officials before he was released.

The initial purpose of this visit was to obtain permission to set up a base for operations against Cuba. The French authorities told my father they would cooperate if and when he obtained a formal request from the United States Government. My father said that his military plans were to involve an operation which would leave the Florida Keys by boat and attack the Cuban Naval Academy near Havana.

About twelve men would participate in the raid and after the mission, would return to Florida. After about two days, they would return to sea to meet the mother ship, and then go on to Haiti. My father said the military mission would then leave from Haiti for a second attack.

Training activities and recruiting for maritime and infiltration courses were held in the Miami area out in the Everglades. Previous training has been conducted in private homes throughout the Miami area. My father would notify all the members of the CU in the *Sunday Miami Herald* where the next meeting would be held the following Saturday. The announcements would be printed around my father's propaganda cartoons, and in a code that only the group would know.

During one such meeting at our house, I watched my father display some of his judo techniques in our living room. Morales, both Navarro brothers, Sturgis and Rudy Junco all moved the furniture that was in the living room out of the way. I was instructed for the hundredth time that children were to be seen and not heard.

Sitting at the dining room I noticed that the popcorn my father placed on the stove was going up in flames. I was trying desperately to get my father's attention but all he kept saying was to be quiet, so I quietly whispered under my breath, "OK Dad, I won't mention that the kitchen is on fire."

My father then ran into the kitchen grabbing a glass of water putting out the fire. He said, "Why didn't you say something?"

I replied, "But Dad, I tried telling you, and you kept telling me to be quiet."

Uncle Frank and the others found it funny, and started to laugh. Frank said, "Go easy on the kid Ed, its not his fault."

CIA to Assassinate Nixon?

I also wanted to tell you what Eugenio Martinez and Jose Pujol told me. I was told that in 1968, when Nixon was running for president, all the Cuban people rallied around and fought to get him elected. They believed that Nixon would change our policy to Cuba. Once he learned, Manuel Airtime told everyone that there would be no change. This was around the time Nixon was butting heads with Richard Helms over the Bay of Pigs documents, and Helms refused to give them to his Commander in Chief. Nixon then shut down CIA operations into Cuba, among the thirty remaining "frogmen" stationed in Moa Bay Cuba was Eugenio Martinez.

After two assassination attempts failed, the CIA plotted Watergate to have Nixon removed from office. The reason the plot to assassinate Nixon failed is because my father backed out, therefore, there was no patsy to blame.

Chapter Eight

Ed Kaiser in Haiti

My father visited the island of Haiti on September 10, 1970. Like his trip to Martinique, he was apprehended by government officials who questioned him as to his intentions while on the island. My father told them about the possibility of recruiting men to help infiltrate Cuba, but the President of Haiti, "Papa Doc" Duvalier would have nothing to do with either my father or his military plans. My father said that Duvalier showed signs of fearing Castro. Duvalier told my father he was to leave his country immediately or face death.

François "Papa Doc" Duvalier. He was elected President of Haiti in 1957. As he moved toward an absolutist regime, he declared himself President for life in 1964. This and other corrupt and despotic measures helped precipitate the end of U.S. aid to Haiti. Papa Doc died in 1971.

Duvalier had developed a 'cult of personality' in Haiti and even claimed to be the physical embodiment of that island nation and began to revive some of the traditions of voodoo.

By the time my father returned to the shores of his beloved United States, he was already devising a plan to assassinate "Papa Doc" Duvalier.

My father who has been interviewed in the past concerning other matters on Haiti said, on February 27, 1970 that he had furnished the following information to the FBI:

My father said that in December, 1969, he met Robert (Last name unknown) in Coral Gables, Florida, who was a Haitian exile. My father proposed to Robert that he could help free Haiti of the present government, if in return the new Government of Haiti would promise to make their land bases against Cuba. In a December, 1969, meeting held in New York City between my father and

UNITED STATES DEPARTMENT OF JUSTICE

FEDERAL BUREAU OF INVESTIGATION

File No. 97-615

Miami, Florida

MAR 2 5 1970

RE: UNKNOWN SUBJECT;
HAITIAN REVOLUTIONARY GROUP,
NEW YORK, NEW YORK,
[redacted] B7D
REGISTRATION ACT - HAITI

EDWIN BENJAMIN KAISER, JR., 805 West 30th Street, Apartment 16, Hialeah, Florida, is a 35 year old mercenary and soldier of fortune whose past activities have resulted in numerous arrests and convictions.

KAISER, who has been interviewed in the past concerning other matters, on February 27, 1970, furnished the following information:

In December, 1969, he met ROBERT (Last Name Unknown), Coral Gables, Florida, who is a Haitian exile. KAISER proposed to ROBERT that KAISER could help free Haiti of the present government if in return the new Government of Haiti would promise to make land bases available to Cuban exiles for military operations against Cuba. ROBERT referred KAISER to [redacted] a Haitian exile in New York City, having telephone number [redacted] ROBERT also contacted a [redacted] in Canada concerning this proposal. B7C

In December, 1969, a meeting was held in New York City between KAISER and [redacted] concerning KAISER's plan. [redacted] did not attend but reportedly said that anything [redacted] decided would be agreeable with him. [redacted] listened to KAISER's plan but did not seem impressed with it and no further action was taken on this matter.

KAISER said he has not initiated any further

ENCLOSURE

ENCLOSURE

(Name unknown) this person did not attend the meeting, but reportedly said that he would be agreeable with my father.

My father said, "it was necessary to form a Cuban Government in exile" and since the United States Government will not recognize such a government in the United States, my father would like to establish one in some Caribbean or Central American Republic. My father said he contacted a Haitian exile in New York, and proposed such a government in exile be established in Haiti.

The Haitian exile in New York sent this proposition to some Haitians exiles in Montreal, Canada. My father was later notified that the Haitian exiles were working on a plan to kill President François Duvalier of Haiti, but they did not carry it out because Fidel Castro in Cuba had over 15,000 Haitian guerrillas trained to take over Haiti in the event Duvalier was assassinated. The Haitian exile committee would be afraid of a revolt, and what would be come of the Haitian exiles in Cuba, thinking that a mass genocide would erupt in Cuba. 2-2005-7 Referred to CIA/B1.

Chapter Nine

Training in Everglades

On September 15, 1970, my father said that, "on the previous Saturday, he had participated in a military training exercise with about 32 other men in the Florida Everglades. The instruction was given by a former U.S. Army lieutenant and the training was under control of a Captain (first name unknown) Hickey, who was the commanding officer of a Fort Lauderdale or Hollywood, Florida, National Guard unit."

Two weeks later, on September 29, 1970, he approached Wilfredo Calvino and Adolfo Rodriguez who were standing on a street corner in Miami. Calvino was not certain how my father happened to know them or if he previously knew Rodriguez. My dad did know that Rodriguez had gone AWOL and Rodriguez admitted to Calvino that about six months previously, he had been approached by my father.

He asked Rodriguez if he would be willing to smuggle arms out of the armory at Fort Jackson. Rodriguez thought that was a good idea and he knew of a pasture near Fort Jackson which could be used as a landing strip to pick up the arms. Calvino mentioned to my father that during the past couple of weeks he had seen Wilfredo Navarro and him together. My father made no further proposal.

During the next several weeks Rodriguez and Calvino represented an Anti-Communist Cuban Commandos Organization who had signed a unity agreement with Cubanos Unidos wherein the two organizations agreed to cooperate. No money or property was transferred from either organization and they both continue to cooperate, but they operated independently.

My father made mention that he could supply an airplane and knew of a "Frank Sturgis," a pilot who could fly the arms out of the U.S., where someone could file down the serial numbers on all the weapons making it difficult for the U.S. Government to track them.

Two days later, on October 1, 1970 an inquiry was made at Rodriguez' home in Miami by U.S. Army Intelligence. They were told that Rodriguez had returned to his Army unit at Fort Jackson. Specialist Kenneth Barrick who was a part of the United States Army AWOL Apprehension Team removed Adolfo Rodriguez from the office of the FBI and lodged him in the South Miami jail.

Chapter Ten

Sneaking onto U.S. Military Bases, Impersonating a Military Officer and Leaving with Supplies

In early 1971, my father and Frank Sturgis entered an army surplus store and purchased some army fatigues. Dad then wore these army fatigues to Homestead Air Force Base in Florida, and when he arrived at the entrance to the base, he flashed his ID quickly, and distracted the guards by saluting them. My father was then allowed to drive onto the base. After driving around for awhile he spotted the Officer's Club and quarters buildings. He stopped, entered the officer's quarters building and moments later walked out with a lieutenant's uniform and an ID badge.

When my father arrived back at our house in Hialeah, he began to duplicate the ID badge to make him appear as a solider in the U.S. Army. He carefully removed the photo of the person and replaced it with his own. Only a couple of people knew about this improbable mission. Probably only Sturgis and Wilfredo Navarro.

The next time my father visited Homestead Air Force Base everyone there knew him as *Lieutenant* Kaiser. During this visit he went to the Supply Building and ordered a small quantity of supplies, those items included pencils, paper-clips, stamp pads, binders loose leaf, index cards, card files and several more items he needed in order to draw up a plan of action for the Cubanos Unidos.

My father needed Sturgis to help him out if they were going to get their hands on guns and ammunition. Sturgis had long ago mentioned to my father that he used to do some gun-running in the early 1960s, and was up for whatever my father had in mind. So they headed out to Homestead again, only this time, to pull off a much more difficult ruse.

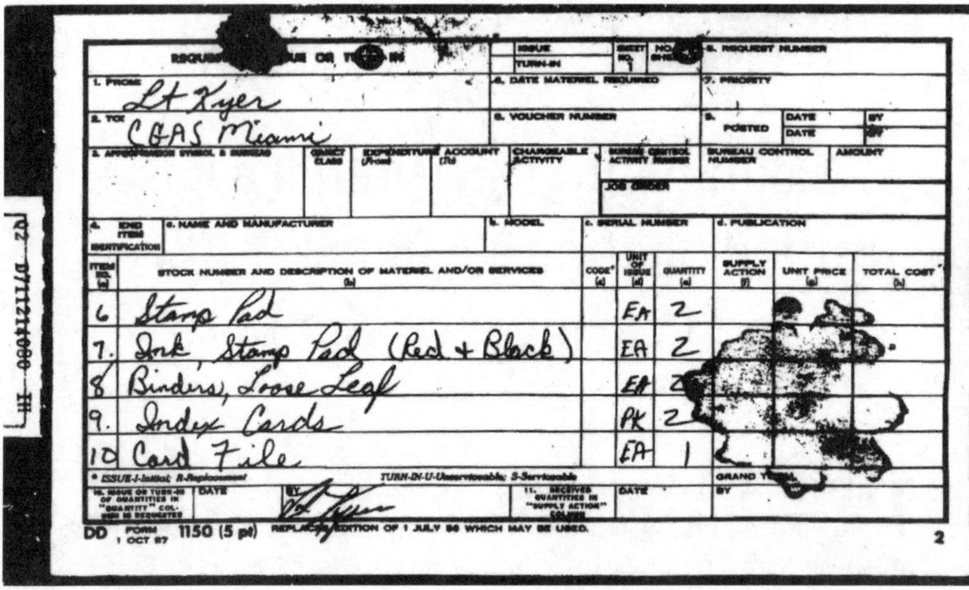

REQUISITION [illegible] ISSUE OR TURN-IN — ISSUE / TURN-IN — REQUEST NUMBER

1. FROM Lt Kyer

2. TO CGAS Miami

6. DATE MATERIEL REQUIRED — 7. PRIORITY — 8. VOUCHER NUMBER — POSTED DATE BY

3. APPROPRIATION SYMBOL & SUBHEAD — OBJECT CLASS — EXPENDITURE ACCOUNT — CHARGEABLE ACTIVITY — BUREAU CONTROL ACTIVITY NUMBER — BUREAU CONTROL NUMBER — AMOUNT — JOB ORDER

4. END ITEM IDENTIFICATION — a. NAME AND MANUFACTURER — b. MODEL — c. SERIAL NUMBER — d. PUBLICATION

ITEM NO. (a)	STOCK NUMBER AND DESCRIPTION OF MATERIEL AND/OR SERVICES (b)	CODE* (c)	UNIT OF ISSUE (d)	QUANTITY (e)	SUPPLY ACTION (f)	UNIT PRICE (g)	TOTAL COST (h)
6	Stamp Pad		EA	2			
7.	Ink, Stamp Pad (Red + Black)		EA	2			
8	Binders, Loose Leaf		EA	2			
9.	Index Cards		PK	2			
10	Card File		EA	1			

* ISSUE-I-Initial; R-Replacement TURN-IN-U-Unserviceable; S-Serviceable — GRAND TOTAL

DD FORM 1 OCT 57 1150 (5 pt) REPLACES EDITION OF 1 JULY 56 WHICH MAY BE USED. 2

A requisition form filled out by my father at the Coast Guard Station Opa Locka, FL.

The two entered into the Weapons Depot Building, and while my father distracted the person inside the building, Sturgis loaded up my father's Chevy El Camino, covered up the ammunition with a black tarp and drove off. This must have been a huge adrenalin rush, betting on only themselves to pull off a scheme that most people would not dare attempt. Emboldened by their success, my father started to visit the Air Force base often for supplies.

It was around this time that my father mentioned to my mother that he didn't want her to go into one of the bedroom closets. Being naturally curious, my mother asked why? My father opened the closet door and showed her several boxes of grenades and ammunition. My mother freaked out and started to scream, "Ed! Do you realize that we have children? Do you want them to take our children away from us?"

Minutes later Sturgis knocked at the door and said, "Ed, we have to move the stuff. I got word from someone inside that the FBI was on their way over." My father and Uncle Frank loaded up the trunk of Sturgis' car and he drove off. My father started walking away from the house, and just as he was walking away several FBI cars drove up, one of the agents approached my mother with a search warrant in his hand. He said that they needed to search the house. The FBI agents looked everywhere including our backyard.

My mother was scared and nervous. She knew what they were there for, but remained quiet about what had just happened. The FBI began questioning her. They wanted to know if she had seen my father dressed in a military officer's uniform. They wanted to know if she knew where he was, but her unshakable disposition prevented her from showing any signs of fear as she said, "No. I'm sorry, but I can't help you."

As soon as the FBI agents left, my father returned to the house. An argument broke out. Mom started to scream at Dad, asking him how he could, "put his family through this?" She wanted to know what it was that he was getting himself involved in, and why were there grenades and ammunition in the house. She wanted to know from Dad, that if everything he was doing was worth putting the family through all of this danger and secrecy.

Dad couldn't get in a word, with all the questions Mom had. When she finally settled down, he asked, "Did they find anything?"

Mom said, "No, there was nothing to find."

Dad asked, "Did you say anything to the agents?

Mom replied, "No! What was there to tell? I don't know anything."

My father ended the conversation by saying, "Let's not talk about it anymore, because the place could be bugged." My parents never talked about this incident again.

My sister's birthday, Frank Sturgis took the photo.

UNDER QUESTIONING—Norwalk Hour reporter Christo- her Byron interviews former Legionnaire Richard Chandler bove, while his former partner, Edwin B. Kaiser (center), a ellow one-time Legionnaire, looks on.—Hour photo, Bramac.

Chapter Eleven

An Adventurous Soul

A few days later my father again went out into the Caribbean, this time to the Turks and Caicos Islands, to talk to the local government there about setting up a camp for his mercenaries. He tried convincing the local government that having Communism so close to the island might lead to the overthrow of their own government. My father wanted to train men and attack Cuba from the island. The Turks and Caicos Islands was a British-owned protectorate, and the government felt that an attack from their island would only provoke a political situation that might cause an situation between the Soviet Union and the United States. The government officials told my father that they weren't interested in supporting an attack on Cuba.

That day my father and someone he met on that island went out on a "boating adventure." The engine of the boat exploded, burning my father's leg severely. He managed to dress his wounds with rags and boarded the airplane headed back to Miami. When my father arrived at the house, he was in severe pain. Mom asked what was wrong.

"Oh, it's nothing," he said, but she knew that something wasn't right.

She asked again, "Ed, tell me, what's wrong?"

He replied, "I've been bitten by a shark, and I'm in pain." She couldn't believe it.

She said, "Oh my God! Where were you bit?" He showed her a little scratch on his hand, which made her laugh. Then she looked down, and noticed some blood running down his leg and my father fell onto the floor. She helped him into the car and drove him to the hospital.

When they arrived, he complained in a loud voice "Can someone please give me a pain shot?" The doctors there examined the wound, and said that he was going to need a skin graft, and if he wanted to get better he would need to admit himself. All he really wanted was a pain shot and then go home, but the doctors tricked him.

They said, "If you want us to give you a pain shot, all you have to do is sign this paperwork." He signed it, received his pain shot, and it quickly put him to sleep. They placed him on a stretcher and rolled him back to surgery. The doctors cleaned out the burn and perform a skin graft. They then removed skin from his rear upper thigh and placed it over the wounded area.

When he woke up he realized that the doctors had tricked him. He would remain in the hospital for an additional two weeks before being finally released.

When he returned from the hospital, "Uncle Frank" Sturgis visited him at the house, and said that he and Navarro had been very busy recruiting large numbers of Cubans. They were now looking for another place to start training their men. Sturgis told my father that they needed to become better organized. That they needed to appoint officers so there could be organization within the anti-Castro group. Sturgis wanted to be the head of intelligence of the Cubanos Unidos, and Navarro's brother wanted to be second-in-command. They placed my father in charge of all the Legionnaires throughout the world.

My father was going to try yet another trip to the Turks and Caicos Islands, and asked my mother to give him a ride to the airport. When he arrived at the ticket counter, the sales person said that no tickets could be released to him. He was crushed as well as upset. He called my mother just as she returned home and said, "I need you to come and pick me up."

When she arrived she asked, "Ed, What happened?"

He replied, "They kicked me off the island."

In 1972, Sturgis developed the idea of having the men train in the Everglades and my father thought it was a great idea because the Everglades belonged to the Native Americans, and the terrain was similar to many parts of Cuba. That afternoon they all talked about the need for more ammunition and guns. This prompted my father to make another trip out to Homestead Air Force Base. This time he brought me along for the ride. When he arrived, everyone there welcomed "Lt. Kaiser" and his son Scott (me).

As we were walking around the base, a few of the soldiers stopped and asked my Dad if they could take me on a platform jump. I was extremely excited and ready for anything. The three of us climbed the wooden ladder until we reached the top of the platform. We were about sixty to seventy feet off the ground.

One of the soldiers hooked me up into a harness and counted, "Three, two, one!" and pushed me off the platform. I slid down the wire cable until I reached the end. I had such a feeling of pride and accomplishment. I was in eight-year-old heaven! The only words I could find were, "That was fun! Can I do it again?"

After the jump the sergeant standing next to my dad handed him a card that read, 'Scott Kayser, (Honorary Paratrooper). I looked at the card, and I was happy. I just couldn't wait to show everyone, especially my mother, but before putting it my pocket I whispered in my father's ear, "Dad, they spelled my name wrong."

He said, "Put it away and keep quiet." I remembered seeing my father's name spelled that way on his uniform.

I was told yet again, "Kids are to been seen and not heard".

As we started to walk towards a building, my dad said, "I want you to stay outside the office with the guys, and I'll be right back." The guys in the barracks took a liking to me and it felt good. It didn't seem as though my father was gone long. He soon returned with a bunch of papers in his hand. Now, I'm only speculating, but that paperwork he was carrying around may have been classified documents. He certainly didn't have any paperwork when he entered those offices.

It wasn't long before my Dad and I would visit the base again. On our next visit, the officers told my dad that they had a surprise for him and me. A bit nervously, we shadowed the men. One of the soldiers asked my father to follow him into the barracks where they gave me a small uniform that had the Screaming Eagle patch, a parachute patch, a rifle patch and a lighting bolt patch. I felt like I was on top of the world and my father felt relieved.

After leaving the barracks we headed over to the Armory Building. Dad took me inside and looked around for a bit. The place was huge. It had a rounded roof and it was big enough to park a few planes in it. We didn't spend more then a few minutes in there before my father decided to leave.

We were on our way back home, when dad said he needed to make a quick stop. We headed over to Rudy's Meat Market off NW

57th Avenue also known as Red Road. Rudy was dad's friend and just another uncle to me. Before we walked in, dad reminded me again, that kids were to be seen and not heard and I didn't want to get into any trouble. We all went into this small room in the back, and dad yelled out, "Cuba Libre!" meaning, "Free Cuba!"

In the room with my dad and me, were Rudy Junco, Frank Sturgis, Wilfredo Navarro, DiBattisto, Jerome Schneider, Arencibia and Ferre.

Throughout my father's life, he accumulated an extensive arrest record. He is documented as having committed crimes under the FBI file number 243-334B. These crimes included burglary and larceny, aggravated assault, assault with a deadly weapon, theft of government property, possession of drugs, breach of the peace, drinking in public, resisting arrest with violent assault and battery on police officers, impersonating an officer in the U.S. Military, impersonating a police officer, CIA and FBI agent, impersonating a government official working for the Pentagon, and passing out worthless checks. The list is extensive. My father was described as an individual who was 'armed and dangerous' and in the past, he had a card identifying him as a police officer and implied a level of influence and/or connections with the CIA, FBI, ATF and U.S. Customs.

Was my father this bad man on his own, or was he apart part of something bigger? After all, he was no longer an American citizen. So how was he was able to identify himself with all theses agencies is beyond my comprehension. My father left behind a couple of his address/phone books in addition to the handwritten letters and notes. In these books are some very interesting names that appear.

William Pawley was an active member of the Republican Party. And a close friend to former President Dwight Eisenhower, Richard Nixon and CIA director Allen W. Dulles. He took part in a poli-

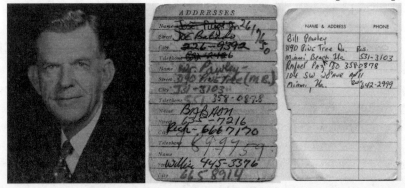

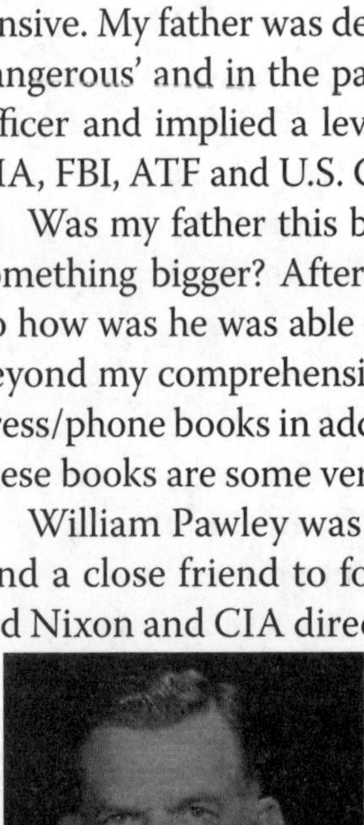

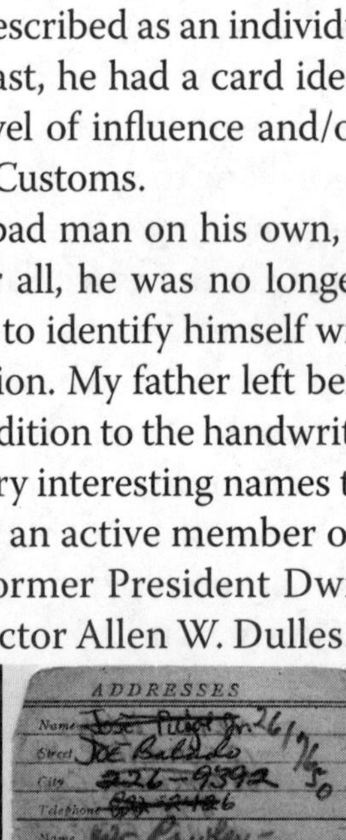

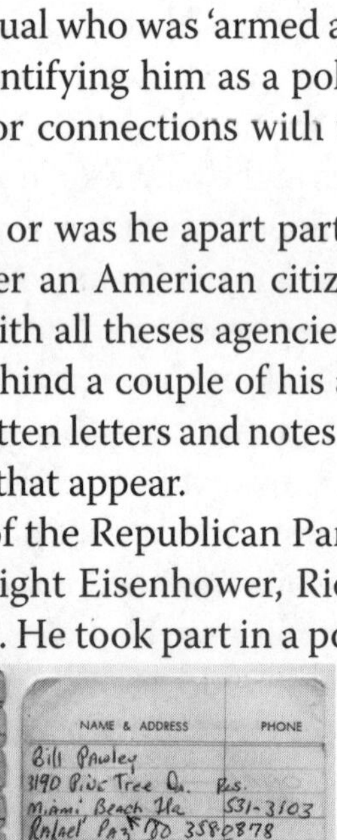

cy that later become known as "Executive Action," which was a plan to remove unfriendly foreign leaders from power.

There is enough on William Pawley to fill another entire book. The hardest part of this project writing about my father, is knowing when to stop reporting on each character in this mess.

In the winter of 1962, word was spreading that there were two Soviet officers in Cuba, who had information regarding Soviet nuclear weapons in Cuba, and who wanted to defect. William Pawley contacted Ted Shackley at JM/WAVE. Shackley decided to help Pawley organize what became known as "Operation Tilt" or the "Bayo-Pawley Mission." He also assigned Rip Robertson, a fellow member of the CIA in Miami, to help with the operation. David Sanchez Morales, another CIA agent, also became involved in this attempt to bring out these two Soviet officers.

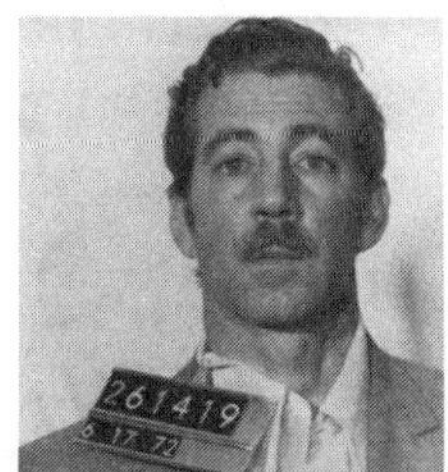

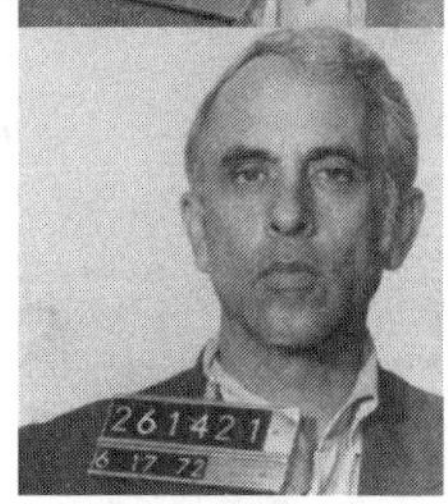

On 8th June, 1963, a small group, including Pawley, Eddie Bayo, Robertson, Virgilio Gonzalez, Eugenio Martinez, (both of Watergate infamy) John Martino, Richard Billings and Terry Spencer boarded William Pawley's Flying Tiger boat. After landing off Baracoa Cuba, Bayo and his men got into a 22-foot boat and headed for the Cuban shore.

The plan was to pick them up with the Soviet officers two days later. However, Bayo and his men were never seen again. It was rumored that Bayo had been captured and executed. However, his death was never reported by the Cuban press.

When John Kennedy received word that Pawley's group formed as an assassination team to kill Fidel Castro, John and Robert Kennedy ordered them to stand down. On the night of June 10, 1963 everyone started complaining about, how could Kennedy order us to stand down, to cease and desist, John Martino said, "what a Son of a bitch those Kennedys are."

William Pawley turned and looked at Rip Robertson and the others and said, "you don't worry John, we're going to kill that motherfucker."

The Bayo-Pawley operation has been covered in several articles and books. Many of these authors have suggested that the Bayo-Pawley affair was linked to the Kennedy assassination.

We know now that the defecting Soviet colonels never existed, that there were no Russian missiles left in place in Cuba and that the entire Bayo story was a hoax for the sole purpose of assassinating Castro.

Was their secret purpose to get CIA arms with which to kill Fidel Castro? The Bayo-Pawley mission fit nicely with Johnny Roselli's later claim that President Kennedy was assassinated by an anti-Castro sniper team sent to murder Castro, captured by the Cubans, tortured, and redeployed in Dallas. Through the handiwork of Roselli's assistant, John Martino, the CIA, *Life*, Pawley, and Senator James Eastland were all implicated. Pawley was a wealthy businessman and certainly capable of financing such a project.

His last known residence was in Miami Beach, where he died of a "self-inflicted" gunshot wound in January 1977, because he suffered from a severe case of *shingles*. Is it a coincidence that he died under questionable circumstances the same year and a month, before my father supposedly did?

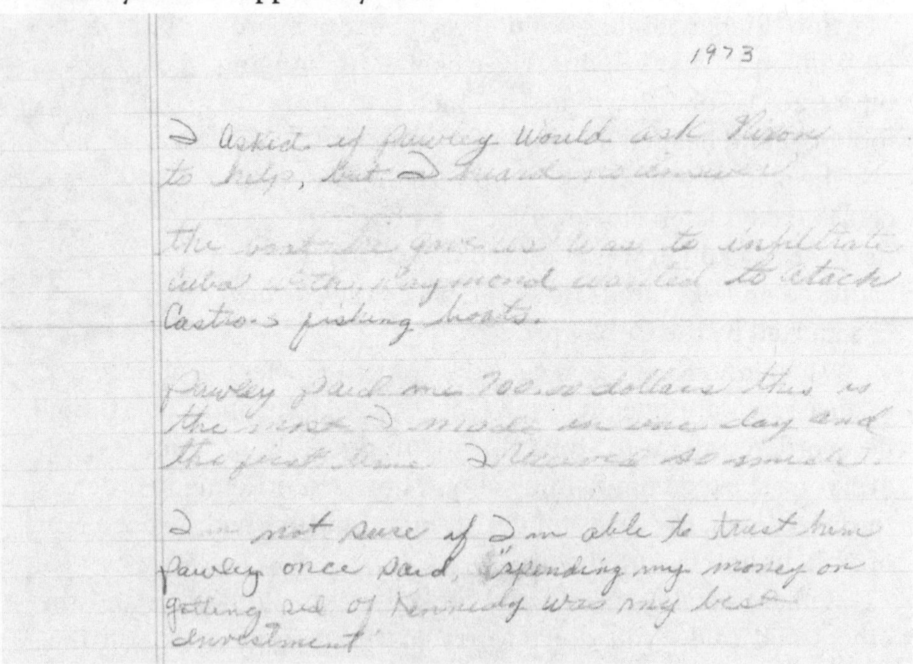

1973

I asked if Pawley would ask Nixon to help, but I heard no answer.

The boat he gave us was to infiltrate Cuba with. Raymond wanted to attack Castro's fishing boats.

Pawley paid me 700.00 dollars this is the most I made in one day and the first time I made so much.

I'm not sure if I'm able to trust him Pawley once said, "spending my money on getting rid of Kennedy was my best investment"

This letter is paraphrased, my father writes, I asked if Pawley would ask Nixon to help, but I heard no answer.

The boat he gave us was to infiltrate Cuba with, Raymond wanted to attack Castro's fishing boats.

Pawley paid me $700.00 dollars this is the most I made in one day and the first time I received so much.

I'm not sure if I'm able to trust him Pawley once said, "spending my money on getting rid of Kennedy was my best investment."

In 1971 Edwin Kaiser wearing a U.S. Army fraudulent uniform discovered some photographs, along with classified documents that linked the assassins to Dealey Plaza in Dallas. He didn't stop there, he made recordings, testified, and plead to the U.S. Government to provide safety for himself and his family.

Like many, who have come close to "whistle-blowing," my father was ready to point his finger at those who were involved, he stood fast to his findings, he believed he was the only person to have actual photos of those involved in the "Big Event." Photos of the men in Dealey Plaza. The government didn't listen, Howard S. Libengood suppressed my father's information, the government did not want to provide safety for my father and his family. Soon my father was dead.

Days after the assassination. PBRUMEN was the CIA Cryptonym for Cuba. So that document refers to Cuban intel service and Fortson, and here we go Pawley enters the picture.

Pawley, Martino and Fortson.

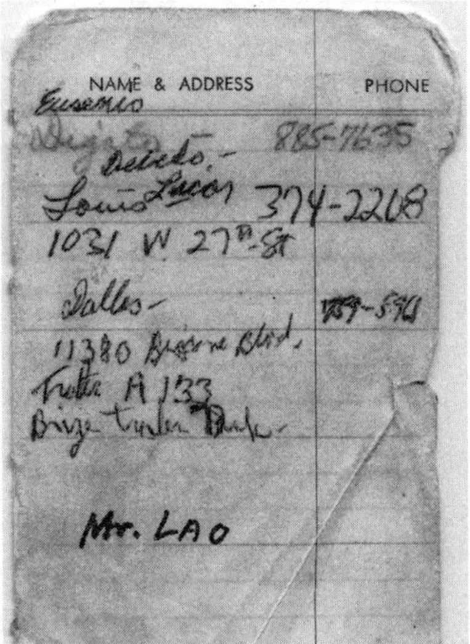

Irving Richard Poyle was handled by Oliver E. Fortson, at least some of the time including just after the JFK Assassination. This fits with Fortsons other activities.

Also found in my father's phone book is Eusenio – aka Eugenio Martinez – aka "Musculito".

Musculito said, "We Cubans have never stopped fighting for the liberation of our country. I have personally carried out over 350 missions to Cuba for the CIA. Some of the people I infiltrated there were caught and tortured, and some of them talked.

My reaction was that it was crazy to have those important pictures developed in a common place in Miami. But Barker was a close friend, and I could not tell him how wrong the whole thing was. The thing about Barker was that he trusted Eduardo totally. He had been his principal assistant at the Bay of Pigs, Eduardo's liaison with the Cubans, and he still believed tremendously in the man. He was just blind about him. "

"I wanted to overthrow Castro and unfortunately I got knocked off by the president who was helping us, Richard Nixon."

Rolando Eugenio Martinez describes himself as a frustrated ex-CIA agent. At 86 years of age, he does not regret his past as a "plumber" of "Watergate," but regrets that he lost that and many other battles. Born in Artemisa, Cuba, he had to flee in the time of Batista. He then returned home, but fled the revolution of Fidel Castro, only to return yet again and suffer another defeat in the Bay of Pigs invasion in 1961.

But what made him feeling betrayed as he described, occurred the night of June 17, 1971 at 2:30 am in the morning. Rolando Martinez, alias "Musculito," was arrested along with Virgilio Gonzalez, Bernard Barker, James McCord and Frank Sturgis inside the Democratic National Committee offices in the Watergate complex of buildings in Washington.

It was the beginning of the political-journalistic adventure. The greatest ever told. It has generated countless articles, books and movies. Yet Martinez still justified, 38 years later, the reasons for the break-in that took him to jail with his comrades "We were going to steal documents showing that Castro was financing the campaign of the Democratic candidate, George McGovern."

Martinez maintains that he and his companions were victims of a trap concocted by James McCord, one of the five "plumbers" who was formally part of the CIA. "He was an undercover agent.... He betrayed us. He was very mysterious. He told us the information we had collected was not enough and we had to repair a microphone that did not work well."

Some researchers believe Martinez was also involved in the assassination of John F. Kennedy. One source claims that Virgilio Gonzalez was the gunman in the Dal-Tex building and Martinez was his spotter.

Chapter Twelve

CUBA

The Cuban government accuses one of my father's former acquaintances, Rolando Masferrer Rojas, of over 2,000 killings. Castro's government also says that the "Flying Tigers" that Masferrer organized (most likely under William Pawley) to protect President Batista would carefully remove all the evidence after their killings, making it hard to prove their guilt.

On January 9, 1959 Masferrer said he had to abandon the island, because Fidel Castro accused him of stealing ten million dollars. He left in a boat, landing in Miami. In time, he befriended Mafia boss Santo Trafficante and union leader Jimmy Hoffa.

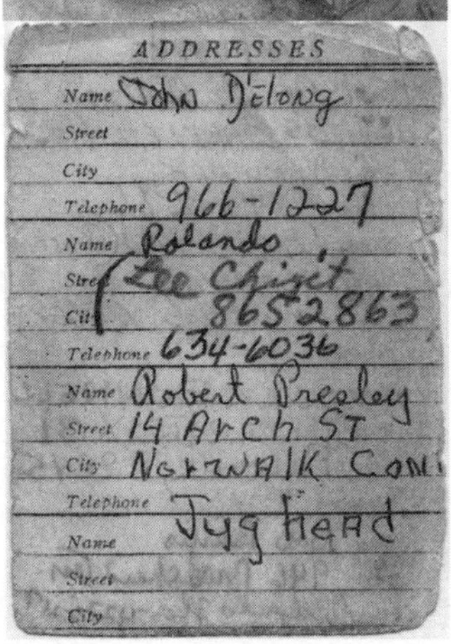

On August 21, 1970, my father told his contacts in the CIA that the Cubanos Unidos had a .50-caliber machine gun, a .30-caliber machine gun, some C-4 explosives and a quantity of small arms. The CU was planning a five-man, three-day infiltration and sabotage mission to Cuba. One of the planned tactics was to kill Cuban soldiers and cut them into pieces to terrify others. 105-18943.

Soon thereafter, my father started participating in the military training of *another* anti-Castro group, and there was a camp accident. His hand was severely burned by an explosion. He had been giving paramilitary training tactics to an anti-Castro organization headed by Rolando Masferrer.

Wilfredo Navarro was working as an informant for the FBI. And, on one occasion he went to his handlers and told them that my father was now very loosely associated with the Cubanos Unidos and seldom was at the meetings or training exercises. He said he considered my father to be untrustworthy and unreliable. Navarro told the others in CU that another independent anti-Castro organization had started using a military training camp on Highway U.S. 27 about 30 miles north of Miami. The camp was located on a large farm, reportedly owned by a retired U.S. Army general. Each Saturday about 100 Cuban exiles would go to this farm and practice military tactics under the leadership of my father. FBI 105-202233-6 and FBI 2-415.

Navarro started to spread the word about my father, and the people of CU were confused as to who my father was actually representing. The majority of the trainees believed that my father represented a U.S. government intelligence agency. Apparently, he frequently displayed a military-type telephone credit card and made several calls to U.S. military bases in Alaska and Washington DC. He also claimed to have a direct connection to someone in the Pentagon, to whom he was required to report. Navarro stated that he had personally seen a military-type telephone credit card, and heard my father make these kinds of phone calls.

This now begs the question: Exactly who and with what was my father involved? Was he working with the Pentagon? I don't truly know. The FBI? CIA? U.S. Customs? Maybe the Mafia? Or was it all of them in some manner? Although highly unlikely, at times he appeared to be a lone vigilante with a penchant for democracy and an extraordinary will.

My father left me the addresses and telephone numbers of his friends, contacts and acquaintances along with some of his hand written letters. I guess if he was murdered, he really didn't have a choice. People came to our house and took everything. Well almost everything. In these files, are the names of the most notorious assassins living in Miami, high-level covert operations administrators, operatives and various men who hold keys to any number of doors. In today's climate of espionage, with all our technology, it's hard to imagine a simpler era when one man could infiltrate, act and report with only paper and pen.

I spoke to Rolando Masferrer's nephew on the phone, his name also was Rolando Masferrer, during our conversation he mentioned that when his uncle was under investigation, and was in hiding from the FBI, my father and Navarro were supposed to get him out of the country to safe haven. During a planning session with Masferrer, Navarro and my father, the FBI raided the place, arresting Rolando Masferrer on the spot.

When Masferrer was brought in for questioning by the FBI, Masferrer opened a door and saw Navarro and my father standing just outside. This explains how Masferrer thought my father double crossed him, Masferrer said, "It was Navarro who set the whole meeting up."

After a lengthy conversation with Masferrer, I asked him point blank, "What do you think happen to your uncle?"

He replied, "It was a guy by the name of Townley, Michael Townley who killed my uncle. He was under the witness program for awhile. They wanted to keep him safe, but now he's off."

I said, "Who's they?"

"The CIA," he replied.

I asked, "So you think Townley killed your uncle?"

"Yes! Yes, he did it, all the FBI documents and files points to Townley and we're sure of it."

I asked Masferrer if he could tell me how his uncle had met my father, he said, "Through Wilfredo Calvino, yeah, it was his friend Calvino who introduced him to your dad."

I wanted to know more, but we had been talking on the phone for a half hour, and it seemed he wanted to go. So, just before we hung up I said, "Rolando, I would like to email you my father's entire phone book, and perhaps you can take a look at it, and tell me any names you might recognize?"

We both agreed, I would send him the pages, and he would get back with me. And just like with Tony Calatayud, I never did hear back from either one. I felt as though they wanted to talk to me, in fact they both said, you can call me at anytime and for what ever reason, they stopped taking my phone calls and will no longer correspond with me through emails.

Could it be because of what Tony said in our phone conversation? "There is information that is not available for publication."

What is that supposed to mean? A million questions started to run through my mind, JFK, Watergate, the need to assassinate Castro, how was my father killed, if they knew anything about it, etc. etc. etc. It was hard for me to spit a question out, but what did he mean in saying, "There is information that is not available for publication?" After all, Castro was still alive, and apparently our conversation only had to do with my father who was part of anti-Castro plots, or was there more to it?

Well, now, it is 35 years later, and you mean to tell me there's more? I'm now beginning to wonder if my father was involved in something bigger then just anti-Castro activities?

SECRET

RE: EDWIN BENJAMIN KAISER, JR.

On October 15, 1970, Specialist 4, KENNETH BARRICK, United States Army AWOL Apprehension Team, Miami, Florida, removed ADOLFO P. RODRIGUEZ from the Miami Office of the Federal Bureau of Investigation and lodged him in the South Miami, Florida Jail. u

On November 9, 1970, WILFREDO NAVARRO BEATO, head of CU, advised that KAISER now is very loosely associated with CU but the organization seldom sees him and now considers KAISER as being untrustworthy and unreliable. u

NAVARRO explained that about three months ago CU and other independent anti-CASTRO organizations started using a military training camp on Highway U. S. 27 about 30 miles north of Miami. The training camp is located on a large farm which reportedly is owned by a retired U. S. Army General. Each Saturday about 100 Cuban exiles go to this farm and practice military maneuvers and tactics. They have an odd assortment of arms but no live ammunition is used. The training is given by a Captain (first name unknown) HICKLEY and a Lieutenant PUJOL. These individuals reportedly were previously in the United States Armed Forces. u

During the past month or so CU has been relatively inactive in that it has no operating funds or money for political propaganda activities. KAISER now considers himself the leader of the training camp and has been talking critically of CU, its leadership and previous operations. KAISER is still unemployed, has no visible means of support and continues to consider himself the military leader of the persons attending the training camp. u

\- 8 -

SECRET

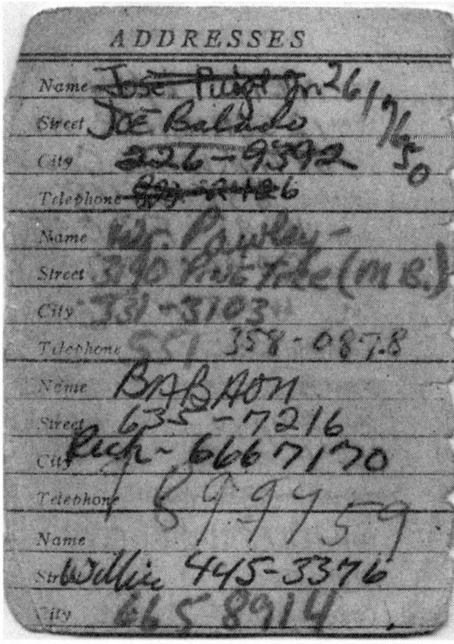

A page from my father's phone book showing a José Pujol Jr. No doubt the same Lt. Pujol mentioned as a military advisor to the combat training sessions, north of Miami on the large farm of a retired U.S. Army General. 'Joe Balado' is almost certainly an alias of Jose Pujol. Also, please note the entry directly underneath Pujol/Balado; it is William Pawley.

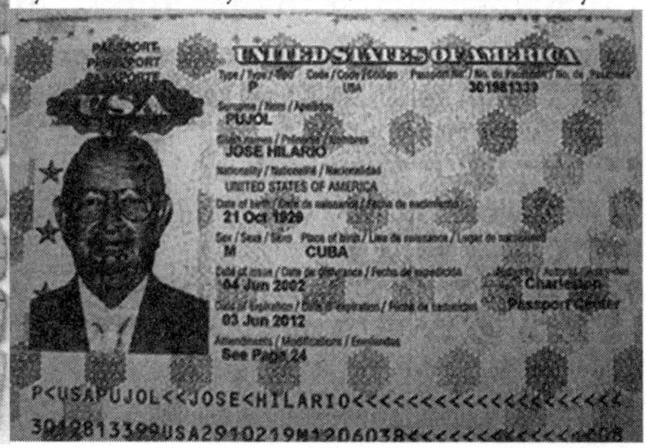

Captain Jose Hilario Pujol's United States Passport #301981339 lists his date and place of birth as October 21, 1929 in Cuba. Pujol had assisted in smuggling illegal aliens such as Luis Posada Carriles into the U.S., which could have resulted in revocation of his citizenship.

A letter from a U.S. Naval Intelligence Officer:

> I am a Naval Intelligence Commander and have worked many times with the CIA over the years. In my younger years I taught foreign languages at University of Pennsylvania and at USC in California. Fluency in those languages have been a big help in my Intelligence work, particularly in clandestine operations with the CIA.
>
> Pujol worked clandestinely for the CIA and risked his life many times for the cause of freedom of Cuba from the Communist Regime of Fidel Castro. His handler at the time was CIA Officer Grayston Lynch, who tells me that he admired Pujol and still trusts him completely. Gray Lynch is now retired, and in very serious physical condition barely able to speak. But he wanted to express to me his opinion about Pujol. I have talked to others in Brigade 2506 who admire Pujol for his heroism in the fight for freedom and democracy. I personally find Pujol to be one of the most honest, dedicated and loyal persons I have met.
>
> Sincerely,
>
> Harold Feeney
> Commander U.S. Naval Intelligence

After researching my father's phone book, and coming across several names like, Jose Pujol, Luis and Tony Calatayud, I decided to look them up and give them a call. I wanted to see if they were still alive. I needed someone I could talk to who could give me insight into my father's life. To my surprise I first located Jose Pujol through telephone information. I phoned his house and we immediately started to talk. He thought I was a reporter wanting more information. He said, "I have told you everything I already know."

I said, "But sir, I have never talked to you."

As soon as I said that he replied, "Then who are you? And what do you want?"

I took the opportunity to introduce myself, saying, "My name is Scott Kaiser, I am the son of Edwin Kaiser. I would like to talk to you about my father, who has your name in his address phone book."

After a nice long conversation he invited me over to his house. So I planned my trip to Miami – hoping to personally interview him.

Upon arriving in Miami I called Pujol to let him know I was in, he invited me over to his house. I asked him if he could tell me anything about my father, and what I heard made me proud. I learned my father always fought for freedom.

Pujol said, "Like your father we don't believe in kingdoms, dictatorships left or right, we believe in a free democracy where you don't have to live oppressed and under someone else's rulings, or fear the government, where you pay your taxes and the government is responsible to tell you what they have done with the money you pay them."

He said, "Do not hurt anybody in life if possible, but do not be afraid of dying to defend what you believe, not that you want to die, but if it comes you accept it."

But, I wanted more, I had already known that my father would never live under a communist regime government.

I wanted to know if Pujol could tell me anything I didn't know, or share in any anecdotes about he and my father, while they were fighting Castro's communist government? But, I thought I could probably get more information out of Luis Posada and others, if I could only find them.

While I was at Pujol's home, I showed him my father's phone book, with his and Posada's name in it, along with a document that my father had signed. It was a unity agreement between the Cubanos Unidos and Luis, who at the time was head of the anti-Castro group called JURE. So, I knew I needed to talk to Luis to get some good information about my father.

I asked Pujol if he knew Posada, and if Nino Diaz was still around? To my surprise Pujol pulled out his phone book and dialed Posada.

Pujol said, in Spanish, "Luis, you'll never guess who is at my home, Kaiser's son, Scott. And he would like to talk to you".

I was excited to get on the phone and asked if he would sit down with me and talk.

Luis said "Maybe, why don't you call me later." It took me three days of talking on the phone before he would finally see me.

In the meantime, Pujol had showed me a recent picture of Nino Diaz sitting at his table, and a photo of Pujol and Felix Rodriguez together.

I thought to myself, "Wow! This is great!"

I had brought along a document that said my father had shown Nino Diaz and Rodriguez some photos, and who better to ask than the guy's who have seen my father with the photos?

I exclaimed to Pujol, "Isn't Felix dead?"

He said, "No! He's still alive and well."

Wow! I was excited to hear that.

I called Nino, Felix and Luis from Pujol's house. Nino and Felix invited me over. It was going to take some time to convince Luis.

I went to Nino's house and started to ask him all kinds of questions about my father. He finally remembered who my father was, when I showed him the photo of Navarro and my father standing outside Navarro's house. I asked if he knew anything about Watergate? And what did he think of Howard Hunt? He said, Hunt was a "pendejo [idiot]."

I laughed a bit, but I wanted to know more about Watergate. Nino said, "I would need to talk to 'Musculito.'" Musculitio is Eugenio Martinez.

Nino then put me in touch with someone who had Eugenio Martinez number.

I called Martinez from Nino's house and explained to him who I was, and after talking to him for a while on the phone, he invited me over to his house. I showed him the document of my father having photo's of Sturgis, Hunt, Gordon Liddy and other's. I wanted to know who the other's were?

He said, that the other's were Barnard Barker and David Morales. I asked him, "Why would the FBI or the CIA only list the names of Hunt, Sturgis and Liddy in that document and not the other's? And, how did my father get a hold of these photographs?"

Martinez explained. He said, "Your father stole them. How else do you think your father got a hold of them?" He also mentioned that no one knew about my father being the sixth man in the Watergate burglary. But, I had been following a different line of inquiry, and my thought was: How did all this tie into JFK's assassination?

I knew my father hadn't been a part of the killing, so I asked point blank: "What did Watergate have to do, if anything, with Kennedy's assassination?

"Those were the photo's we were all looking for."

"So why is Barker's name not listed? Why only list the others if Barker was also a part of Watergate?"

"Only one reason I can think of is that Barker answered only to McCord, who was a high level CIA agent that also held a rank of Lt. Colonel."

I then called Tony Calatayud. I was really hoping to meet with him at his house, but he decided that we should meet at an IHOP. During brunch I started to ask him about my father, and what he know about my father's death.

Tony explained, "I was told by a man named Richard Poyle, who was with your father the day he was killed, that a mass fell, it broke, and hit your father on the head and knocked him into the boat. It was a mass that killed your father. But I don't believe that, I don't believe that at all. I believe that he was killed. I know he was killed."

He told me a story: "Your father and I once took a lot of guns to the Bahamas, and there we dug a big hole and covered the guns up with plastic and dirt. A year later we went back to the Bahamas and uncovered those guns and used them, when we infiltrated into Cuba with a boat the CIA gave us to use."

Time flew by, and Tony had to go. I thought we had a good time together. Tony said, "I will send you a detailed email with some more things we did." As of today, I'm still waiting on the email.

I finally met up with Felix Rodriguez at his house, there were so many things running through my mind that I couldn't think straight. I was excited, nervous and, did I mention, excited. Here I was, about to come face to face with the man who had hunted down Che Guevara.

Felix and I talked about the Cuban revaluation, and about the capture of Che. I had a few questions to ask, he said fire away. My first question was: is this your name in the document where my father shows you some photos? After he read the document I had just handed him, his answer was: "Yes, I knew your father, I think we use to call him 'Casey.'"

I asked, "Do you remember hanging out at some place near Yumura furniture in downtown Miami?"

"If you're talking about the old coffee shop, where we all use to hang out at, it was a spot for those who were a part of the company. That's were we would all meet."

I also wanted to find out the truth of Pujol's story, so I asked Felix what happened to Che's hands after he was killed. I really wanted to know if they in fact had cut them off? So, I said, Mr. Rodriquez, "I was told by someone that after Che was killed someone cut off his hands, can you confirm that?"

All he did was look at me with a smile on his face and handed me a stained gold Rolex watch.

It took me three days of convincing Luis Posada that I was my father's son. He finally got around to inviting me over to his home, as we talked about my father and many other subjects, he started into one of his stories, but I didn't have my camera running. I asked if he would repeat it, and I turned on my camera.

He told me a story about what happen in Guatemala in 1990. How Castro sent in a three man hit team into Guatemala to assassinate Posada. I asked him why would Castro want to assassinate you? He replied, "abecause I have done to many things against him".

I asked Posada about James Files, and he said on camera, "He was with the company." The company, meaning the CIA or Operation 40, either way Posada acknowledged that Files was part of the company. It certainly appeared that Posada didn't want to give me to many details on camera. I could tell he felt very nervous while I had my camera running, towards the end, I had to shut everything off so he could talk.

Barker and a few others had Secret Service credentials, that's properly why his name was not listed, I was thinking to myself could Morales also had Secret Service credentials too? That could mean that there is some truth to what E. Howard Hunt said in his deathbed confession.

I had to constantly remind Psoada, time and time again that my father worked with him, and I wasn't there to get him or anybody into any kind of trouble.

On camera, we talked about Hunt, Sturgis and many other's. Before I could ask him where he was the day Kennedy was assassinated, he immediately told me that he was at Ft. Benning Georgia when Kennedy was killed. But off camera, he told me that George H.W. Bush, Files and Bosch were all in Dallas. I was thinking to myself: how would he know this?

When I showed photos that some say are of Bosch in Dallas, sitting next to a man holding an umbrella. Posada could not confirm or deny it was Bosch. He said, "The photo looked too blurry and was inconclusive."

I showed Posada my father's address book with his name in it, and under his name was the word "Dallas" written in my father's hand. He choked up and stayed quiet for about 5 seconds. He just looked at me with this strange look on his face, then the only words that came out of his mouth was "I was there."

I questioned him, "When you say 'I was there,' is it safe to say you were in Dallas or Georgia?"

But all he did was look at me with a smile on his face.

When my father had visited the FBI office in Miami, he had told them that Rolando Masferrer was a former Cuban Senator living in exile in Miami and in the past had launched raids and invasions on Haiti and Cuba from South Florida. He said that Masferrer had an anti-Castro group of Cuban-exile/militants, who claimed they wanted to attempt an overthrow of the present Cuban government. My father voluntarily appeared at a Miami FBI office and stated that he was a part of Cubanos Unidos, which was dedicated to overthrowing the present government of Cuba, and that he had no intention of violating any United States laws.

Masferrer and a CIA Deputy Director of Plans, Richard Bissell, planned an assassination attempt on Fidel Castro as early as

December 1960. The *Miami Herald*, reported that Masferrer was leading a small group of fifty-three people, who were polishing up their killing skills at a ranch owned by multi-millionaire Howard Hughes. In 1961, Masferrer had met with recently-elected President John F. Kennedy, presumably to talk about Castro and the situation in Cuba.

Originally presented to President Eisenhower by the 5412 Committee (also known as the "Special Group") on March 17, 1960 (7½ months before the election), Eisenhower gave initial approval for a plan of covert action against Castro. After the election, these talks would bear fruit in the form of Operation Zapata or "The Bay of Pigs." CIA Deputy Director for Plans Richard Bissell, under Director Allen Dulles, would brief the young president about the CIA's plans to infiltrate Cuba on April 4th 1961.

Just three months after Kennedy was elected into office, the invasion began. Kennedy disliked Masferrer's radical and fanatical personality. The two of them never had any publicly known conversation after that. Masferrer was killed by a car bomb in 1975.

Rafael "Pilín" Mendoza – one-time president of Expreso Aereo Inter-Americano and close friend of Carlos Prio Socarras, a former President of Cuba – was a well-known figure in the *Partido Auténtico* (Cuban Authentic Party), and later was in exile. Mendoza told my father that Prio would make a $1,000 contribution to the CU, but Navarro refused the contribution for fear that Prio would attempt to take over the organization. Prio also said that Juanita Castro, Fidel's sister, told the CU leaders that she had American backing, and had offered to furnish money and arms. Again, the CU refused the offer, this time because Juanita Castro reportedly could not to be trusted and had a bad reputation in the Cuban exile community.

On January 14, 1971 it was reported that two Cuban exiles launched a massive recruiting campaign to build an army to assassinate Fidel Castro. The Navarro brothers claimed they had at their disposal, 50 million dollars to wage war against Castro's regime. This money was said to have been supplied by a group of independent millionaire industrialists. The Navarro brothers said that draftees would be sent to camps at bases already operating outside the U.S. They also said they had purchased a small island which would be used for training operations.

Nine days later, on January 25, 1971, the Navarro brothers and my father travelled from Miami to Puerto Rico. Their sole purpose was to recruit manpower. My father also brought his U.S. Army lieutenant's uniform. He was planning on visiting the Ramey Air Force Base in Aguadilla, Puerto Rico. Navarro's uncle, José "Pepin" Fortuno Navarro arranged a press conference the next day at 6:00 PM in room 2505 of the Hotel Borinquen in San Juan. Fortuno's and his friends were 100% pro-American, but for obvious reasons he could not make any public announcements, or have any overt association with the U.S. Government.

Fortuno had been in contact with the FBI office in Miami, and had provided them with information for almost a year on the Cubanos Unidos organization. His purpose was to alert FBI agents in the San Juan office that he was in Puerto Rico. In addition to the thirteen representatives of the English-speaking media in attendance, there was also the local Cuban newspaper, *Replica*, a Spanish-speaking daily. The main announcement was to announce the leaders of the Puerto Rican faction of the Cubanos Unidos, who were Eladio del Valle, José Casero and Danny Fernández. All three were unknown to the San Juan office of the FBI. The arm of the organization, as pointed out in the press conference, was to oust Fidel Castro. They wanted to assassinate him and all communists. Their goal was to regain Cuba.

Wilfredo Navarro said that representatives of the CU in Puerto Rico, Danny Fernández and José Casero had planned on coming to Miami to help Navarro promote the CU there. Navarro also made it clear that my father was the military adviser for the CU.

Navarro also contacted some right-wing organizations and anti-communist freedom fighters in Canada, New York and New Jersey, for the purpose of holding a large rally in New York City. These men and groups were supposed to join and support CU. After my dad returned from Puerto Rico, he phoned the appointed CU leaders in Puerto Rico, and told them that CU in Miami had no members, no military equipment and most importantly, no money, and that Navarro was a fraud.

Perhaps my father was saying these things, because Wilfredo was making all kinds of promises to my father that he couldn't keep. My father always would say to me, "What is a man if he can't keep his word"? Back then, your word and a handshake was a contract.

As a result of this, José Casero in Puerto Rico sent a representative to Miami to meet with my father, and then with Wilfredo. After these meetings, Casero discontinued all cooperation with the CU and with Navarro in Miami. Navarro said that he was very angry with dad and didn't trust him, but needed to keep him as a military adviser.

W. Murray of the Cubanos Unidos San Juan office said that his organization had been built with the aid of the CIA, and with the consent of the Department of Defense and the Department of State. He said that efforts had been made to avoid any possible violation of U.S. neutrality laws. In several conversations with William C. White, the Chief Assistant U.S. Attorney, Murray said the Cubanos Unidos had substantial backing in the Miami area from all sectors and groups of the Cuban exile community. At the same time, Frank Sturgis was trying to get the majority of anti-Castro groups to sign a "unity agreement."

The plan was to join all the disparate groups under one umbrella to better co-ordinate their plans and missions. The only exception was José Elías de la Torriente Ajuria who used a former Cuban Army General Eulogio Castillo in his "*Plan Torriente*." This was designed to overthrow Castro's government, and Torriente used Castillo as his military leader. Torriente had even visited Brazil, Argentina, the Dominican Republic and Venezuela to try to get aid and support for his group, and indeed had even announced in July, 1970 that there would be an invasion of Cuban within 120 days. What kind of leader announces an invasion to the potential victims?

Murray said the CU had a training camp in the Everglades where recruits were being trained by the Special Forces for an eventual invasion of Cuba. This fact was reportedly known only to the CIA and the Pentagon. Murray said they didn't need any fund-raising functions, since they were already well-financed. The money, supposedly, was coming from the CIA, also there were other training camps in Haiti and the Dominican Republic. Special Agent Patrick Murray said that while he'd never actually seen these camps, he'd been told that they did exist by CIA contacts in Miami.

Murray emphasized that the eventual work that the CU did for the liberation of Cuba from communism would be a totally Cuban operation supported by the Cuban community, and carried out by Cuban volunteers. An effort had been made by the CU to avoid enlisting of prominent Cuban revolutionaries, because the danger existed that they would be too difficult to handle. Murray again said that he was familiar with the provisions of the Registration Act and the neutrality laws of the U.S. He also emphasized that his actions in this regard would not be in violation of these laws.

On February 10, 1971 Navarro received a telephone call from Gordon DiBattisto who was then in New York. Having just arrived from Washington, DiBattisto was planning to return to Miami at noon that day. He wanted Navarro to pick him up at the airport. DiBattisto told Navarro that he had seen important people in Washington and was optimistic about the U.S. government backing the CU.

A day later Navarro was told by DiBattisto, who was back in Miami, and who had been in contact with U.S. Congressman Frank Horton. Congressman Horton said, "If the CU were to start a massive propaganda effort, the U.S. government would probably back the organization."

Frank Horton was a mainstream Republican during Kennedy's administration. He served on the Rochester City Council from 1955 to 1961 and was elected to the House in 1962. During his three decade tenure, Mr. Horton was known as a backroom dealmaker, often arranging for people from his state to be placed on influential committees. Horton began his thirty years in Congress with the Cuban missile crisis and ended it with agreements between the United States and Russia to destroy nuclear weapons. In between, he had a front-row seat to history, including the civil rights movement, the assassination of President John F. Kennedy, the race to the moon, Watergate, the creation of the Environmental Protection Agency and the Department of Energy, the tearing down of the Berlin Wall, and the fall of the Soviet Union.

Navarro said that CU planned to have a large press conference and rally in New York a week later, on February 18, 1971. DiBattisto went to New York to help my father work on the arrangements. Three days before the event, Navarro loaned my father his car and $200.00 to go to New York and finalize arrangements for the 'big rally' and press conference. My father drove to New York and got drunk, spent the money in the bars and didn't arrange any meeting with any right-wing groups. He didn't contact the press and didn't work on promoting anything.

On March 5th, Navarro said that my dad abandoned Navarro's car and returned to Miami. Before he left New York, my father called two Cuban exiles in Miami, and said that he received an order from the U.S. government telling him that Navarro needed to be eliminated right away. That he was guilty of treason. When the Cubans came to Navarro's house with guns, he was able to elude them and snuck out the back door.

This poses a few questions, why would the government want Navarro eliminated? And why was he accused of treason? Could it be because the Navarro brother's were somehow involved in the assassination of President Kennedy, rather then the Novo brothers that many researchers thought them to be? And when I was talking to Tony Calatayud and Rolando Masferrer on the phone why won't they answer any direct questions I had about the Navarro brothers? After all, they are dead. The Navarro brothers I mean, why wouldn't they tell me something more, other then to say they we're nice fellows? I bet they were.

Navarro had called DiBattisto, and said that he was flying to New York and would like to meet him there. From there, they went to Washington where they met Congressmen, Frank Horton from New York and Florida's Dante Fascell as well as Senator Claude Pepper, also from Florida. All three politicians purportedly offered to support CU. Navarro and DiBattisto also met with representatives the Department of State and the CIA but neither gave them favourable responses.

One of eleven children, Gerald Patrick "Gerry" Hemming was born in Los Angeles, California on March 1, 1937. He attended El Monte Union High School before joining the Marine Corps

in 1954. He left the Marines in October 1958, and the following year traveled to Cuba where he gave help to Fidel Castro and his revolutionary forces. In January 1959 according to him, he met Lee Harvey Oswald. Later Hemming "switched sides" and in 1961, established the Intercontinental Penetration Force or Interpen a group of anti-Castro guerrillas who trained at No Name Key, Florida, in the early 1960s. Members of this group were initially issued membership cards signed by Frank Sturgis.

These experienced soldiers were involved in training anti-Castro groups funded by the CIA in Florida. When the government began to crack down on raids from Florida in 1962, Interpen simply set up a new training camp in New Orleans, Louisiana. When this work came to an end in 1964, Hemming then moved to work in the construction industry in Miami. According to Victor Marchetti, in an article in *Spotlight*, he was also Lee Oswald's case officer at the then-secret Naval Air Facility (NAF) Atsugi in Japan, stationed there for part of 1957 and 1958 as a radar operator in the Marine Corps.

There are researchers that believe there was a combination of Interpen members and anti-Castro Cubans, who were involved in the assassination of John F. Kennedy. This included Hemming, James Arthur Lewis, Roy Hargraves, Edwin Collins, Steve Wilson, David Sanchez Morales, Herminio Diaz Garcia, Tony Cuesta, Eugenio Martinez, Virgilio Gonzalez , Felipe Vidal Santiago and William

Hemming was playing in the same sandbox as my father and Frank Sturgis. There is no doubt in my mind that they were all very familiar with each other and each other's activities.

On April 21, 1971 my father again went to Haiti, where according to Hemming, he visited Mike McLaney. Hemming said, "Kaiser was delivering an ultimatum to McLaney. A hit was going to go down and out of professional courtesy, Kaiser asked him to take sides."

Mike McLaney was a part-owner of the casino in the Hotel Nacional in Havana before Castro had overthrown Batista. His brother William had worked at the casino, and Mike was a high roller who had played golf in Palm Springs with both Joseph P. Kennedy and his son John F. Kennedy, when he was a senator. He also had ties to Baltimore Colts owner Carroll Rosenbloom, who reportedly loaned McLaney part of the money he used to buy his share of the casino.

McLaney naturally would have also been connected to Meyer Lansky and Santo Trafficante, who was the Mafia boss in Florida and pre-Castro Cuba where he operated both the Sans Souci and

Casino International, as well as holdings in seven other casinos. McLaney also owned the property near New Orleans, on Lake Ponchartrain where Hemming's group, Interpen trained. A cache of weapons for Sturgis and Hemming were seized there.

My instincts tell me that since my father was talking to Mike McLaney in Haiti, that the "hit" which he was referring, was regarding François 'Papa Doc' Duvalier. Duvalier died on April 21, 1971. Later that day, after my father had arrived home from Haiti he said to my mother, "I now have blood on my hands." But he did not elaborate, my mother thought it was another one of his shark bite stories, so she didn't ask.

On June 30, 1971 José de la Torriente, a well known person in Miami and leader of an exile group known as Plan Torriente, said that the CU had a plan where they would set up a base in Haiti for operations against Cuba. Torriente believed that his associates had discovered that this CU operation would be financed by the profits made from the sales of illegal drugs. Because of this, Torriente and his group refused any co-operation with the CU. Torriente turned this information over to the U.S. Bureau of Narcotics and Dangerous Drugs.

Torriente had retired as vice president of Collins Radio and was living in Coral Gables, Florida. In 1970, he formed Plan Torriente, which was a plan to overthrow the government of Cuba. He held rallies in various cities throughout the United States. He collected hundreds of thousands of dollars and traveled extensively throughout Latin America and Europe to raise money for an invasion of Cuba. In 1971, numerous articles appeared in the *Miami Herald* exposing Torriente as the president of a housing development, who used donated funds for personal use. Later, the Cuban exile community in Miami was severely critical of Torriente for having failed in his plan to invade Cuba. On April 12, 1974, while Torriente was watching television in his living room, he was shot and killed by an unknown assassin firing through the window.

In following the "Collins Radio trail," from JMWAVE missions off Cuba to Dealey Plaza and Oak Cliff, it is clear that a secret intelligence network that could get away with killing the President was not going to be indicted anytime soon. The ongoing cover-up best serves those within our government who continue the cover-up by supporting the Warren Commission's deluded lone gunmen theory.

When the FBI questioned the CIA about my father on July 22, 1971, Deputy Director of Plans, James Jesus Angleton prepared a memorandum titled "Ed Kaiser and (deleted)." When the CIA released these documents, it contained three pages of deletions. The only information in it was the statement, "On the basis of limited data available, this Agency's files contain no identifiable information on Ed Kaiser." In another report from Angleton, the FBI reported: "Ed Kaiser has been the subject of a criminal-type investigation by the FBI Miami office since early 1971. Kaiser allegedly wore the uniform of the U.S. Army and used fraudulent military identification to enter the premises of the U.S. Coast Guard Station in Opa Locka, Florida, where he fraudulently obtained office and medical supplies. Kaiser is reported to have entered the premises of other military bases at Homestead, Florida and San Juan, Puerto Rico, where he allegedly represented himself as a military officer and used military facilities. An investigation of this matter is continuing and, as of yet, no Federal criminal charges against Kaiser have been initiated."

Hemming told me, "You make him sound like a junkie. The guy was stealing classified documents."

In September 1971 my father said he had a battalion of men for Hemming to train. He later said he had about 150 men. But it was Hemming's impression, after talking with my father, that he probably had only five men. When talking about his attack force, which he called the Cubanos Unidos, my father talked in the future tense as to how many men he would have, rather than what he had at the present time. Hemming asked to see his operation, but it never materialized. Hemming got the impression that the whole thing was simply a "dream" of my father.

In order to attempt to convince Hemming to help him in his operation, my father told Hemming that he had a friend in the FBI, who was involved all the way. He gave Hemming the name of the FBI agent and his telephone number to verify his story. Hemming said he called the Miami FBI office and asked for the agent (name unrecalled), but was told that he was not in the office that day. Hemming later verified that the number, which my father gave him, was in fact the Miami FBI office. My father also told Hemming that he had the backing of the United States government and the FBI in his venture, though it was very secretive. My father brought Hemming to our home in Hialeah, where he met my mother and me. I was too young to remember Hemming, but my mother remembers him. She said, "How could I forget him? He was a towering guy, over six-feet in height. He was a big man, who ended up spending a week at our house in Hialeah. He ordered some magazines that came in the mail that had our mailing address on them. And I was pissed that your father would bring some bum over to our house. I ended up sending all those magazines back saying he didn't live here!"

My father's Split from Cubanos Unidos and Wilfredo Navarro

On October 18, 1971 Wilfredo Navarro said that his brother Roerme, plus Ramon Orozco, Santiago Loreto and two others had been arrested by the Dade County Department of Public Safety and charged with the theft of a 31-foot Bertram boat. They were each released on $1,000.00 bond. On December 29, 1971 Wilfredo said that he recently settled a civil lawsuit and was awarded a $15,000.00 in damages. He said the money would be used to again start Cuban revolutionary activities in an attempt to overthrow the present government.

My father had left a government-type notebook and a large quantity of pink index cards in Navarro's Continental. He eventually moved them into Sturgis' home. The notebook contained the name of a person whose name was blacked out but whose phone number was not – 305-681-3591. The notebook had a large quantity of names and telephone numbers of Cuban exile revolutionaries, who were all well-known in the Miami area. It also contained lists of military equipment either obtained by, or needed by my father's Cuban exile revolutionary group in the Everglades.

The index cards were in a box stamped, "Received May 19, 1970, Office Customs Agent-in-Charge, Miami, Florida." There were 188 pink cards, and they contained the names, descriptions and file numbers of persons arrested by the U.S. Customs on narcotics charges. Navarro said that my father admitted he stole these cards from the Customs office before they moved. My father admitted to him that he had taken the cards and had even contacted the individuals on them.

My father then told the FBI that he was no longer associated with the Cubanos Unidos. He said that he had no knowledge as to where their activities were taking place, but he felt that Wilfredo Navarro was continuing his efforts to form a raiding group to attack Cuba.

Moving arms:

Special Agent Michael L. Hall, Treasury Department, Alcohol, Tobacco and Firearms Division disclosed that in 1971, Parabellum Inc., (Marti Building, Room 305 at 290 S.W. 8th Street, Miami), had obtained a gun license, (number 5-10309) and a license for Social Security purposes, (number 59-1163062). The officers of this organization were Anselmo L. Alligero, born in Cuba and a U.S. citizen as of April 11, 1945, as president.

Alligero's father was a big politician and a wealthy tycoon in Cuba. Anselmo had, in the past co-operated with the CIA, and was known to carry a pistol in his belt at all times. Alligero's wife, Aguedia was listed as secretary and Rolando P. Masferrer was vice president. Masferrer was in jail on a gun violation. In the early stages of the organization, Masferrer had traveled extensively in South America.

Hall said that on January 26, 1972, Hemming filed corporate changes for Parabellum Inc., removing Masferrer and listing himself as vice president and operational director. Hall said that U.S. Customs had arrested Hemming in the early 1960s, and that he had been in California for a while but returned to Miami around March 1972.

Hall also said that on the original and changed corporate papers for Parabellum Inc., no mention was made of either Frank Fiorini or "Bill" Kaiser. But that he had started receiving information about Fiorini and my father beginning around March 1972 until about the second week of May 1972.

He said Fiorini and my father had made up business cards, and were representing themselves to various organizations including the Miami Dade Police Department as being employed by Parabellum Inc. Both of them were attempting to sell guns. Hall contacted Alligero and Hemming about my father and Fiorini, and they both emphatically denied that either were ever employed by Parabellum, and had no right to say so. Hemming told Hall he would contact them with instructions to stop representing themselves as officials or employees of Parabellum.

The CIA, received information on Alligero and Hemming's travel plans, the two traveled extensively in the Caribbean, South America and the Mexico areas, and were representing themselves as agents with an exclusive franchise in these areas for the Military Armament Corporation which is an organization located in Power

Springs, Georgia. There had been an apparent split between the Hemming and Alligero camps, leading Alligero and Masferrer to travel to Powder Springs. Agent Hall said, "I don't know what the connection Masferrer has with the Military Armament Corporation, but knew that one Mitchell T. Werbell III, is the president of Military Armament Corporation Powder Springs, Georgia." My father also sold arms for Mitch Werbell.

Agent Hall stated that he and his department were against the issuance of a gun license for Parabellum; however, all the requirements were met and the license issued. Therefore, his department maintained an alert concerning Parabellum. He stated that because of this alert, he cannot understand how the company manages to exist when no profit has been realized since its incorporation. Not even expenses for the maintenance of its office space, which is a one room affair with a desk and several straight back chairs. He stated, however, Alligero and Hemming do continue to travel extensively and that it appears that this organization is mainly a front for the purpose of shipping arms out of the country, or some other undercover, underground activity.

On Easter week, 1974 controversial Cuban exile leader Jose de la Torriente was shot dead. During the two years in between 1975 and 1977 the search for the killers of an anti-Castro revolutionary Rolando Masferrer came to a screeching halt due to lack of resources. He had been killed by a car bomb October 31, 1975. Jose Mulet survived a few bullet wounds in a separate shooting. No arrests were made.

Miami Mayor Maurice Ferre requested help from the U.S. Justice Department after Masferrer was killed.

JFK, Watergate and Informants:

On August 27, 1962, J.H. Wilcherster, U.S. Customs Agency, Miami, advised on that date the Hialeah Gardens, Florida police, along with Dade country Florida, Department of Public Safety, confiscated some arms belonging to Laureano Batista Falla at Scott's Motel, 8550 W. Okeechobee Road, Hialeah Gardens, Florida. The materials confiscated included one German machine gun, two M-1 rifles, some pistols and ammunition, and some medical narcotics. No arrests were made, and the arms were in possession of Sergeant Edward Clode of the Dade Country Department of Public Safety.

On August 28, 1962, a telephone call was received at the Miami office of the FBI from an individual who identified himself as Alex Rourke, a writer from New York City. Rourke said that the arms confiscated by the Department of Public Safety belonged to Laureano Batista Falla, and that the arms should be returned to Batista if some Federal agency would give Sergeant Clode permission to do so. Rourke requested the FBI to instruct Sergeant Clode to return these arms to Batista Falla. His request was declined.

The August 29, 1962, edition of the *Miami Herald* published an article stating that a small arsenal of weapons and battle field supplies, enough to equip a half-dozen anti-Castro guerrillas, had been seized in a raid on August 28, 1962, by the Dade Country Department of Public Safety. The article continued that seized in the raid were two trench guns, a carbine, three M-1 rifles, three pistols, and a German automatic rifle. Also confiscated were medical supplies, narcotics, field rations, gas masks, and camouflage equipment. The article stated the raid was made at 10:00 PM on August 27, 1962, and that five Cubans, including one woman, had been milling around the front of the motel room, but quickly fled during the excitement when the police arrived. It was also noted that Laureano Batista Falla was the leader of a dissenting faction of the *Movimiento Democtata Cristiano.* Orlando Bosch said that Batista was also apart of (MIRR) *Movimiento Insurreccional De Recuperacion Revolucionaria,* and was also acquainted with Frank Fiorini who may have stolen one of the M-1 Carbines.

Bill Stucky, wrote a press article about Interpen, he noted about an on-going investigation of Hemming. Hemming was also identified with the William Stucky, who interviewed Lee Harvey Oswald during a public broadcast in New Orleans in August 1963. According to the testimony in the Warren Commission hearings by William Stucky and Carlos Bringuier, Lee Harvey Oswald came to Bringuier's New Orleans clothing store announcing that he, Oswald, was a former Marine trained in guerrilla warfare, who wanted to join the anti-Castro guerrilla group in New Orleans. Many members of the Interpen group were ex-Marines, as was Frank Fiorini. Bringuier claims he stalled Oswald, and then several days later encountered Oswald on the streets of New Orleans passing out "Fair Play for Cuba" leaflets. The meeting led to a disturbance, and Oswald and Bringuier were arrested. Hemming was upset that one of his men was locked up.

Hemming confessed to A.J. Weberman in the early 90s saying, "That fucking Oswald, I played him like a violin."

I had a seemingly odd coincidence while researching some of the names in my father's phone book. The entry "Ed Weiser" of Weiser Enterprise is actually Weiser Industries, and it led me to a Weiser Security in Miami. After calling the offices, I was directed to a man with the last name Weiser, whose main office was in New Orleans. He told me that his father Earl L. Weiser had been a police officer in New Orleans, and that he had been the officer that stopped the fight between Oswald and Bringuier. Frank Sturgis and Richard Sanderlin also did some gunrunning through Weiser in Florida; Tampa and Miami.

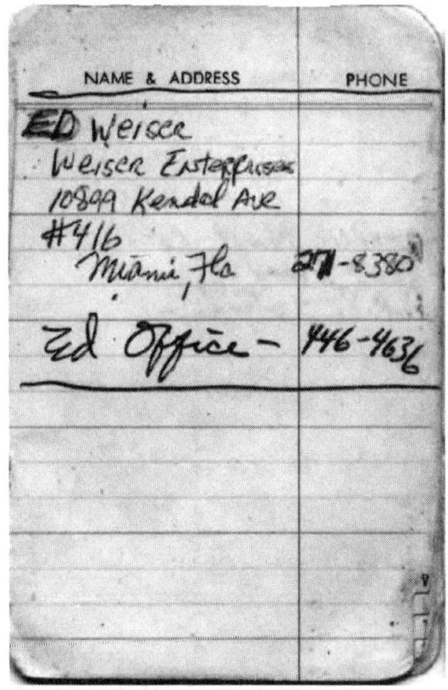

Also in my father's phone book is Alexander Roasevich, aka Alexander Rorke. Note that his phone number starts with EL-54800, he was responsible for the security of five German provinces and participated in the capture of SS men, and the first post-war roundup of Communist agents in the Allied military zones of Germany. His plane, flown by commercial pilot Geoffery Sullivan, disappeared on 24 September 1963 in route to Cuba just two months before the Kennedy assassination. His father-in-law, Sherman Billingsley, held a press conference at the Stork club offering a $25,000 reward for his return and also for the pilot.

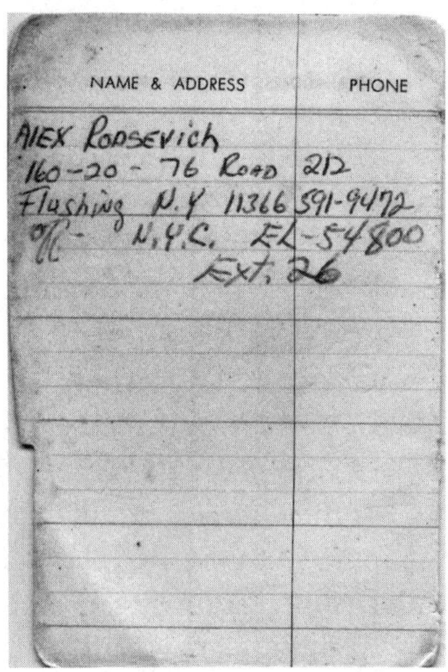

It was rumored that the CIA was involved because of Rorke's friendship with and allegiance to Kennedy. In 1975 the CIA described him a "former witting collaborator (relationship terminated)." J. Edgar Hoover wrote "No. I do not want in any way to get involved in this....H" on papers pertaining to correspondence and inquires by Billingsley. Rorke was declared legally dead in 1968.

According to Judith Vary Baker (Author of *Me & Lee*) Rorke knew Oswald, and was the pilot chosen by Oswald to fly Baker to Mexico after Oswald successful delivery of a bio-weapon to an agent there. This bio-weapon was created to kill Castro by cancer.

After Alex Rorke disappeared, Oswald was back in Dallas, where the tragedy reached its final stage. Is it possible that my father was aware and included it, and wrote it before Rorke disappeared? Given the fact that Sturgis and Rorke were good friends, it's possible.

The CIA Miami office on November 23, 1963, advised that the office of the Coordinator of Cuban Affairs in Miami had advised that the Department of the State feels some misguided anti-Castro group might capitalize on the present situation, and undertake an unauthorized raid against Cuba. They believed that the assassination of President John F. Kennedy might herald a change in the U.S. policy.

FBI sources and informants familiar with Cuban matters in Miami area advised that the general feeling in the anti-Castro Cuban community was one of stunned disbelief and, even among those who did not entirely agree with the President's policy concerning Cuba, the feeling was that the President's death represented a great loss not only to the U.S. but to all of Latin America. These sources knew of no plans for any unauthorized action against Cuba.

George H.W. Bush

The substance of the forgoing information was orally furnished to George H.W. Bush head of the CIA and Captain Williams of the Defense Intelligence Agency on November 23, 1963. At 1:45 p.m. Mr. GEORGE H.W. BUSH, President of the Zapata Off-Shore Drilling Company, Houston, Texas, residence 5525 Briar, Houston, telephonically furnished the following information to writer by long distance telephone call from Tyler, Texas.

BUSH stated that he wanted to be kept confidential, but wanted to furnish hearsay that he recalled hearing in recent weeks, the day and source unknown. He stated that one JAMES PARROTT had been talking of killing the President when he comes to Houston.

BUSH stated that PARROTT is possibly a student at the University of Houston and is active in political matters in this area. He stated that he felt Mrs. FAWLEY, telephone number SU 2-5239, or ARLINE SMITH, telephone number JA 9-9194 of the Harris County Republican Party Headquarters would be able to furnish additional information regarding the identity of PARROTT.

BUSH stated that he was proceeding to Dallas, Texas, would remain in the Sheraton-Dallas Hotel and return to his residence on 11-23-63. His office telephone number is CA 2-0395.

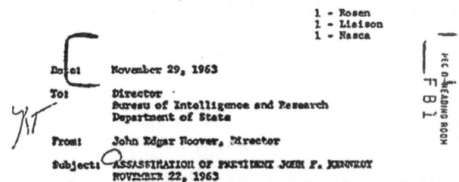

1 - Rosen
1 - Liaison
1 - Nasca

REC 0- READING ROOM
NOV 29 1 31 PM '63
FBI

Date: November 29, 1963

To: Director
Bureau of Intelligence and Research
Department of State

From: John Edgar Hoover, Director

Subject: ASSASSINATION OF PRESIDENT JOHN F. KENNEDY
NOVEMBER 22, 1963

Our Miami, Florida, Office on November 23, 1963, advised that the Office of Coordinator of Cuban Affairs in Miami advised that the Department of State feels some misguided anti-Castro group might capitalize on the present situation and undertake an unauthorized raid against Cuba, believing that the assassination of President John F. Kennedy might herald a change in U. S. policy, which is not true.

Our sources and informants familiar with Cuban matters in the Miami area advise that the general feeling in the anti-Castro Cuban community is one of stunned disbelief and, even among those who did not entirely agree with the President's policy concerning Cuba, the feeling is that the President's death represents a great loss not only to the U. S. but to all of Latin America. These sources know of no plans for unauthorized action against Cuba.

REC- 38 62-109060-1396

An informant who has furnished reliable information in the past and who is close to a small pro-Castro group in Miami has advised that these individuals are afraid that the assassination of the President may result in strong repressive measures being taken against them and, although pro-Castro in their feelings, regret the assassination.

DEC - 9 1963

The substance of the foregoing information was orally furnished to Mr. George Bush of the Central Intelligence Agency and Captain William Edwards of the Defense Intelligence Agency on November 23, 1963, by Mr. W. T. Forsyth of this Bureau.

1 - Director of Naval Intelligence

VHN:gci (12) TELETYPE UNIT

XEROX
DEC. 9 1963

I think anyone who read the preceeding document would wonder if it is discussing the George Bush we all know. I've run across the denials of Bush's spokespeople, as well as the denial of the "other George Bush at CIA in 1963" and it's admirably summarized in this Zapata Corporation entry on Wikipedia: A second FBI memorandum, written by J. Edgar Hoover, identifies "George Bush" with the CIA. It is dated 29 November 1963 and refers to a briefing given to Bush on 23 November. The FBI Director describes a briefing about JFK's murder "orally furnished to Mr. George Bush of the Central Intelligence Agency ... [by] this Bureau" on "December 20, 1963. When this second memorandum surfaced during the 1988 presidential campaign, Bush spokespersons (including Stephen Hart) said Hoover's memo referred to another George Bush, who worked for the CIA. CIA spokeswoman Sharron Basso suggested it was referring to a George William Bush. However, others described this G. William Bush as a "lowly researcher" and "coast and beach analyst," who worked only with documents and photos at the CIA in Virginia from September 1963 to February 1964, with a low rank of GS-5. Moreover, this G. William Bush swore in an affidavit, in federal court denying that Hoover's memo referred to him.

"I have carefully reviewed the FBI memorandum to the Director, Bureau of Intelligence and Research, Department of State dated November 29, 1963 which mentions a Mr. George Bush of the Central Intelligence Agency.... 'I do not recognize the contents of the memorandum as information furnished to me orally or otherwise during the time I was at the CIA. In fact, during my time at the CIA, I did not receive any oral communications from any government agency of any nature whatsoever. I did not receive any information relating to the Kennedy assassination during my time at the CIA from the FBI. Based on the above, it is my conclusion that I am not the Mr. George Bush of the Central Intelligence Agency referred to in the memorandum.'" (United States District Court for the District of Columbia, Civil Action 88-2600 GHR, Archives and Research Center v. Central Intelligence Agency, Affidavit of George William Bush, September 21, 1988.)

In 1960 Richard Nixon recruited an "important group of businessmen headed by George Bush Sr. and Jack Crichton, both Texas oilmen, to gather the necessary funds for the operation." Nixon is talking about "Operation 40," the group that Warren Hinckle and William Turner described in *Deadly Secrets*, as the "assassins-for-hire" organization.

In a speech given by John F. Kennedy, a threat was made to tear the CIA into a thousand pieces. Would it be a coincidence that George H.W. Bush had front row seats to Kennedy's assassination? Several researchers have speculated that George H.W. Bush is in pictures taken at Dealey Plaza that day. It is also widely accepted that George H.W. Bush's Zapata Oil Company was a CIA front for the Bay of Pigs invasion.

It also makes a lot of sense to me that they were all potentially involved in the assassination of President John F. Kennedy regardless of who my father was directly referencing.

NK-1 Norfolk, Va May 12- EX-CUBAN REBEL COMES HOME
Frank Fiorini who once fought for Castro is shown wit
his wife,Juanita,left, and father Anthony,center at h
father's home in Norfok . Fiorini, who lost his citiz
ship earlier this month is in Washington today to fig
revocation of his pilot's license and cancellation of
a B-25 bomber registered in his name byt the FAA.
AP WIREPHOTO lbm51200cg 1960

Chapter Thirteen

My Father's Associates Implicated in the Assassination of JFK

Special Agent, Barry Carmody indicated that after a good deal of searching he had been able to identify, locate, and interview an Officer Massey regarding an alleged conversation between he and a Mr. White. Mr. White had alleged in December, 1963, that he had witnessed a meeting between Santo Trafficante, Frank Sturgis and Frank Ragano during which the assassination of President Kennedy was discussed. White alleged that he advised Officer Massey to forget about it, or he and his entire family could be killed.

There have been a handful of suspicious deaths of people trying to get interviews, or those who may have seen something that some did not want known. Time may have passed by, and if there was once a group responsible for the assassination, and cover-up, they are either dead, or feel safe enough that no one is going to find anything. Still the facts that were first given, don't add up. The reports are not accurate, and anyone who seemed to have a different version such as an eyewitness, has been either shot dead or killed in an automobile accident. Now a death can be explained away or over looked, but when there is a number of suspicious deaths of so called witnesses, or people of interest it makes one wonder.

The most important witness in the center of the whole assassination of JFK, Mr. Oswald, was himself killed in front of millions. This had to have been planned right up to the shot fired into Oswald's gut. The lame excuse that Jack Ruby, a nightclub owner, was over come with grief and anger is just that ... lame! So answer me this, knowing there would be outrage and people looking to take revenge, why was it that Oswald was led right into a crowd, no Secret Service, no bullet proof vest for Oswald, and no other visible armed officers or even military? Why wasn't Oswald surrounded? No one should have even been aware of the time, or where the transport of Oswald to court would be. This was National Security, and what I find very troubling is that no one really focused on security. Oswald was setup – a patsy – and it appears some cops may have also had a hand.

Frank Sturgis and Edwin Kaiser knew Santo Trafficante who also resided in Miami. Sturgis worked with Trafficante after he no longer performed any casino operations in Cuba. Frank Sturgis met with Trafficante on Flagler Street in Miami. He was there to conduct some business. Sturgis called himself the "Chief of Intelligence" of the "Cubanos Unidos."

(Source comment: Many Cubans believe that Fiorini and Kaiser were affiliated with the Mafia. This group formed a non-profit organization in Tallahassee, Florida to aid Cubans; they printed bonds and sold them locally to businesses and Cuban refugees. It seems apparent that a "*con*" game was going on.)

My Father and the Planned 1972 Democratic Convention Riots:

Both the 1972 Republican and Democratic Convention were scheduled during that summer in Miami Beach, Florida. In a "Secret, Eyes Only" memorandum prepared for USDC Judge William M. Hoeveler, Gerry P. Hemming said: "during January 1972, I was contacted by FBI Agent Robert James Dwyer in reference to assisting in a Miami FBI project involving Edwin Kaiser and Frank Sturgis that motivated a 1972 meeting with Alcohol, Tobacco and Firearms Miami Supervisor Hale for backstop briefing."

Sturgis was at the time a White House/Special Operations Group operative and was later arrested at the Watergate complex in June 1972. In April 1976, Hemming told Dick Russell, "There were some plans for the convention. I talked to some of the people participating in it, who later participated in the Watergate thing. They wanted to start a shoot-out using the Yippies and the Zippies and the other hard core commies. The people I spoke to were going to put some equipment in their hands and in the hands of some local vigilantes to start a shoot-out. They said this would finally straighten out Washington as to where the priorities were on overcoming the domestic communist menace."

Hemming stated to researcher A.J. Weberman, "I get a phone call from Bob Dwyer. I hadn't talked to him in months, since the

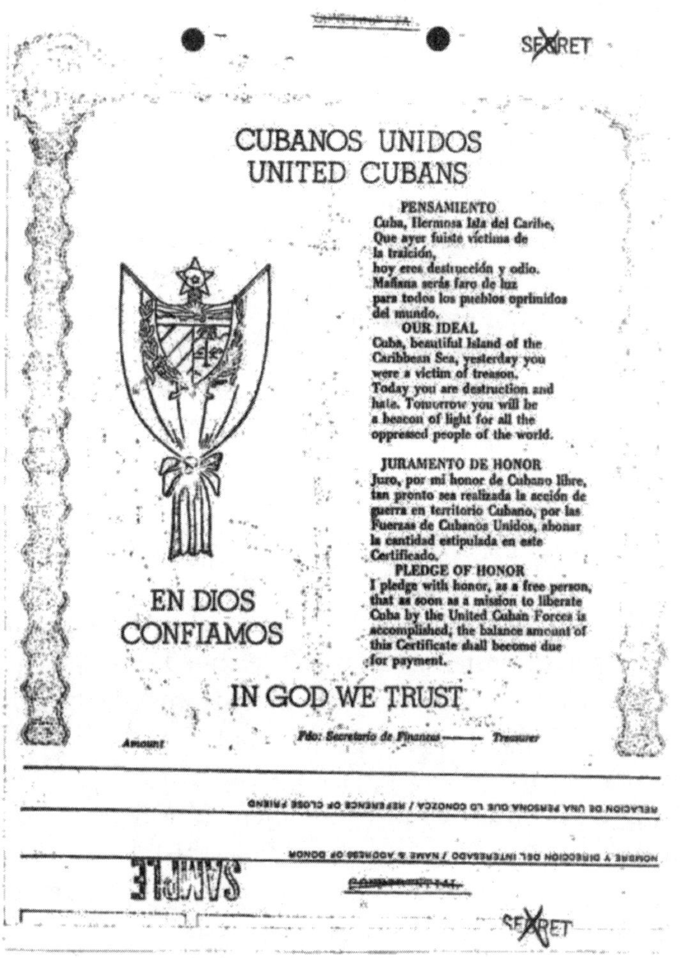
SECRET

CUBANOS UNIDOS
UNITED CUBANS

PENSAMIENTO
Cuba, Hermosa Isla del Caribe,
Que ayer fuiste víctima de
la traición,
hoy eres destrucción y odio.
Mañana serás faro de luz
para todos los pueblos oprimidos
del mundo.

OUR IDEAL
Cuba, beautiful Island of the
Caribbean Sea, yesterday you
were a victim of treason.
Today you are destruction and
hate. Tomorrow you will be
a beacon of light for all the
oppressed people of the world.

JURAMENTO DE HONOR
Juro, por mi honor de Cubano libre,
tan pronto sea realizada la acción de
guerra en territorio Cubano, por las
Fuerzas de Cubanos Unidos, abonar
la cantidad estipulada en este
Certificado.

PLEDGE OF HONOR
I pledge with honor, as a free person,
that as soon as a mission to liberate
Cuba by the United Cuban Forces is
accomplished, the balance amount of
this Certificate shall become due
for payment.

EN DIOS
CONFIAMOS

IN GOD WE TRUST

Amount
Fdo: Secretario de Finanzas —— Treasurer

SAMPLE

SECRET

Nixon compound thing. Some of [Antonio] Veciana's boys had a scheme to have a Cuban Comar fire a STIX missile at the compound. There was a similar plan to attack Guantanamo during the Bay of Pigs. They were gonna take out Nixon and put [Spiro] Agnew in power. I told Dwyer that to me it was all a provocation, and would end up in arrests, and I'm the fucking guy standing in the middle. [Steve] Czukas shows up at my home to discuss this. [Kevin] Shanley should have been there.

"Czukas asks me to withdraw my license to export weapons to the Guatemalan Congress. A quarter of a million dollar deal. When I told my partner, he said, 'That lying cocksucker wanted me to give weapons to Sturgis, who was over here earlier and spilled the fucking beans.' Czukas was always the domineering bad type of cop asshole who was going to put us all away. He was a company motherfucker.

"I told my partner, 'You know Bob Dwyer. He called me the other day with the same shit. They're trying to set us up.' Whatley shows up, I was using Bernardo De Torres office at the time. He shows up with his cousin - here's an ex-felon carrying a badge and a gun. His cousin was a Lieutenant in the Sheriff's Department in Jefferson City, Colorado. We meet at the Holiday Inn Motel at the airport. I said, 'I'll demonstrate the weapons to you.'

"I call Bernie and tell him to leave the weapon in the office I'll come over there. We fired it into a phone book behind the office. We demonstrated the silencer and the whole thing. Whatley wanted me to sell them to him under the table. I told him to get a letter from the Jefferson City Chief of Police saying he needed machine guns. We considered this a provocation. The first question that comes up in my mind is 'Why aren't they going to Powder Springs Georgia and talking to Werbell?'

"They wanted more than one machine gun. My guess was that they were going to give them to Frank. They need silenced weapons so that somebody in the crowd of demonstrators, maybe Kaiser, could crank off a few rounds. The guys would be told 'Shoot some demonstrators in the back, drop your weapons, and get the fuck out of there!' Now other people with silenced weapons would be taking out direct targets. No one would hear this.

"The weapons dropped would be the same caliber. They didn't want 45 caliber Mac 10's, they wanted nine millimeter. The nine millimeter round was a sonic round. We had to half load the powder to keep it below supersonic so that the silencer would work effectively. A 45 round is subsonic. They wanted a nine millimeter because they were going to have thrown down pieces that were the same caliber. The 45 rounds look like it was government issued to Cubans.

"If the demonstrators were found with German World War II souvenirs, Lugers and P-38s, this is all pawn shop weapons, readily available. Sturgis was trying to use Kaiser as his cut out. Sturgis was famous for waving 'bye-bye' at the airport. I don't think STURGIS would be anywhere near the scene. That he got caught (laughs) in the Texas School Book Depository is ... everybody said finally the motherfucker did something instead of sending others to do it and what do you know? He got caught."

Chapter Fourteen

My Father and Watergate

Prior to Watergate, E. Howard Hunt and Frank Sturgis would often meet at our house to discuss plans for their time in Washington. Hunt who was working as a "plumber" under Nixon at the time, thought there had to be very incriminating evidence against the crew that had participated in the "Big Event." Sturgis had tried to recruit my father for Watergate. My mother overheard a conversation, while the two were standing by the back door in our kitchen, Frank mentioned to Hunt, "No one could steal like Kaiser ..."

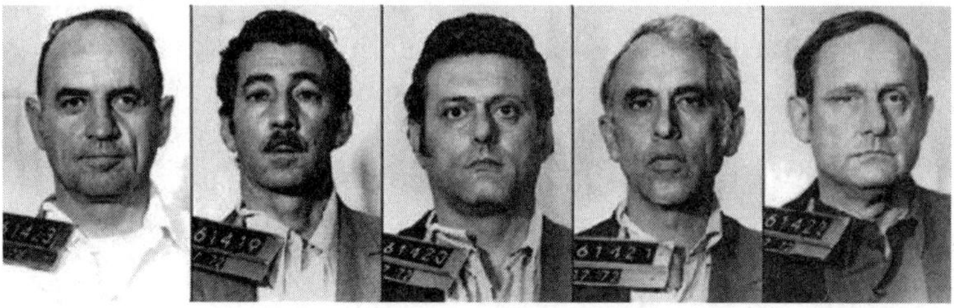

In June 1972, James McCord, Virgilio Gonzalez, Frank Sturgis, Eugenio Martinez and Barnard Barker were all arrested while burglarizing the headquarters of the Democratic National Committee at the Watergate Building in Washington DC. Sturgis told Andrew St. George that while in prison, "I will never leave this jail alive if what we discussed about Watergate does not remain a secret between us. If you attempt to publish what I've told you, I am a dead man."

When Dallas County Deputy Constable Seymour Weitzman heard shots coming from the nearby grassy knoll, he rushed there to find veteran CIA asset Bernard Barker, posing as a Secret Service agent. No Secret Service agents had been assigned to cover the grassy knoll and all accompanied President Kennedy to the hospital

- Bernard L. Barker – a Realtor from Miami, Florida. Former Central Intelligence Agency operative. Barker was said to have been involved in the Bay of Pigs incident in 1961.

• Virgilio R. Gonzalez – a locksmith from Miami, Florida. Gonzalez was a refugee from Cuba, following Castro's takeover.

• James W. McCord – a security coordinator for the Republican National Committee and the Committee for the Re-election of the President. McCord was also a former FBI and CIA agent. He was dismissed from his RNC and CREEP positions the day after the break-in.

• Eugenio R. Martinez – worked for Barker's Miami real estate firm. He had CIA connections and was an anti-Castro Cuban exile.

• Frank A. Sturgis – another associate of Barker from Miami, he also had CIA connections and involvement in anti-Castro activities.

Those Indicted by a Grand Jury on September 15:

• G. Gordon Liddy – from Washington, counsel to the Finance Committee to Re-elect the President, a former FBI agent, former Treasury official, and former member of the White House staff. During the investigation, Liddy refused to answer questions and was fired from his job.

• Everett Howard Hunt (Eduardo) – A former White House consultant, a known Plumber in Nixon's employ, tasked with preventing information from leaking to the press, CIA employee, conspirator in the Watergate burglary. Hunt was also a writer of espionage novels and had worked on declassifying the Pentagon Papers.

Nixon said, "Hunt will uncover a lot of things. You open that scab, there's a hell of a lot of things...

This involves those Cubans, Hunt, and a lot of hanky-panky that we have nothing to do with ourselves ... this will open up that whole Bay of Pigs thing ...

It's going to make the CIA look bad, it's going to make Hunt look bad, and is likely to blow the whole Bay of Pigs thing..."

FBI Report Excerpt:

On June 19, 1972, Special Agent Robert James Dwyer happened to be in contact with Edwin Kaiser, known as a long-time friend and associate of Frank Fiorini. Edwin Kaiser is a resident of Hialeah, Florida and was questioned about Frank Fiorini. Kaiser admitted being a friend and associate of Fiorini, but stated he had absolutely no knowledge of Fiorini's activities or about Fiorini's

The Senate of the United States

Mr. Edwin B. Kaiser, Jr.
6585 West 8th Lane

Hialeah, Florida

16—75321e-1 U.S. GOVERNMENT PRINTING OFFICE

19 73

For attendance as a witness before the Select Committee on Presidential Campaign Activities under authority of S. Res. 60, agreed to Feb. 7, 1973.

7/24-26/73 Witness fee, 1½ days at $ 25 per day, 37.50

Transportation from Miami, Florida to Washington, D.C. and return air fare in the amount of $151.27 paid under seperate cover voucher

Departed Miami, Florida 6:15 p.m. 7/24/73 37.50
Returned Miami, Florida 12:21 a.m. 7/26/73

Administrative Assistant xxxxx

Payee's Copy

associates related to the burglary of the Watergate Building of June 17, 1972. Kaiser stated on the night of June 16, 1972. he was involved in an argument with Wilfredo Navarro and an unidentified Hialeah Gardens Police Officer was a witness.

Wilfredo Navarro was also questioned by SA Robert James Dwyer of the FBI, and he too mentioned that he was a friend of Frank Fiorini, but had no knowledge whatsoever of Fiorini's activities, or the others that were arrested. Navarro admitted he was with Edwin Kaiser in Hialeah Gardens, talking with a Hialeah Gardens Police Detective on the night of June 16, 1972. Foot Note: [FBI MM 139-328 page 135.].

The fact that the officer is referred to as an unidentified Hialeah police officer, raises suspicion in my mind. It is very convenient that there happened to be a local officer of the law, who was apparently not worth corroborating my father and Navarro's alibis. Please remember this was a "police detective," who was employed by the city that was home to the largest CIA base of operations in the U.S., outside of Virginia.

A Sixth Burglar in the Watergate Break-Ins?

On June 19, 1972 Special Agent Kenneth D. Scheiwe was telephonically contacted at the Ft. Lauderdale FBI office by Mike Wales, who was an investigative reporter for the *Sun Sentinel*, a Pompano Beach newspaper. Wales said he had information that a sixth man was involved in the burglary of the Democratic Party National Headquarters in Washington, DC on June 17, 1972, and that this sixth man had not yet been identified. Wales stated he knew that one "Bill" Kaiser had been good friends of Frank Fiorini for several years, suggested Kaiser as a possible suspect for being a sixth man involved, and further stated that he is not aware of the whereabouts of Kaiser.

The following is an excerpt of a letter written by Edwin Kaiser. In it, he mentions that six men were involved in the Watergate break-in burglary, not five as has always been the official story. Was my father a sixth burglar in the Watergate break-in? I can only offer some documented testimony, and a written account in my father's hand.

This is somewhat paraphrased:

"Five of the six men involved in Watergate were from the Bay-of-Pigs. 6 out of 6 from Miami. All involved at one time or another with Cuba or her problems. It is my belief that if we had more Americans with the love they have and have shown, and the want to do, not talk about doing something, but doing it for this Country, to work as this 6 men try to work, we Americans would be better off. As I said before, I only knew one of them. I only wish I had the pleasure to know them all. {(crossed out with pen) I have information on a exchange.} Tuesday 26th July – Ramone Orosco.

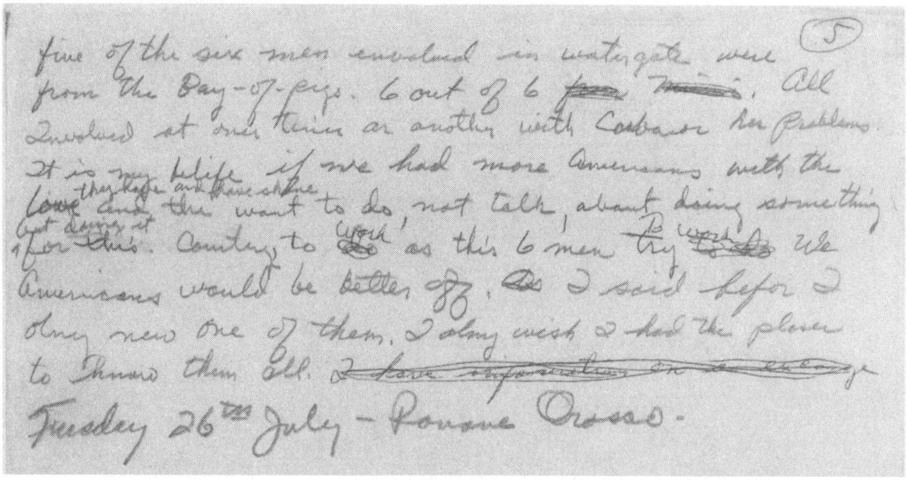
5

five of the six men involved in watergate were from the Bay-of-pigs. 6 out of 6 ~~[illegible]~~ ~~[illegible]~~. All Involved at one time or another with Cuba or her Problems. It is my belief if we had more Americans with the Love they have and have shown and the want to do, not talk about doing something but doing it for this. Country, to work as this 6 men try ~~[illegible]~~ We Americans would be better off. ~~[illegible]~~ I said befor I olny new one of them. I olny wish I had the plesur to Know them All. ~~I have information on a exchange~~

Tuesday 26th July – Ramone Orosco.

On June 20, 1972, the following background information was furnished to FBI Special Agent, George E. Davis by MM 1550-ks (a.k.a. Ricardo Anibal Morales Navarete), who is well acquainted with many Cuban exile leaders in Miami, and concerning whom every effort should be made to protect the identity of one "Bill" Kaiser.

It sounds to me that they making the statement that special care should be taken to not blow my father's cover to Navarrete. Navarrete is speculated to have been part of Operation 40 and was thought to be an informant for the FBI, CIA, DEA and U.S. Customs throughout his nefarious career. He was often referred to as, "The Monkey."

Navarrete further advised his FBI contact that Eugenio Rolando Martinez, also known as "Musculito," age about 42, from Vidado, Cuba, arrived in the United States in 1959, and became employed by the CIA from 1959 until 1968 as a boat captain. He made dozens of trips to Cuba carrying infiltration teams on his power boat. In about 1968 he was laid off by the CIA, and for a short period of time he was associated with the anti-Castro group headed by

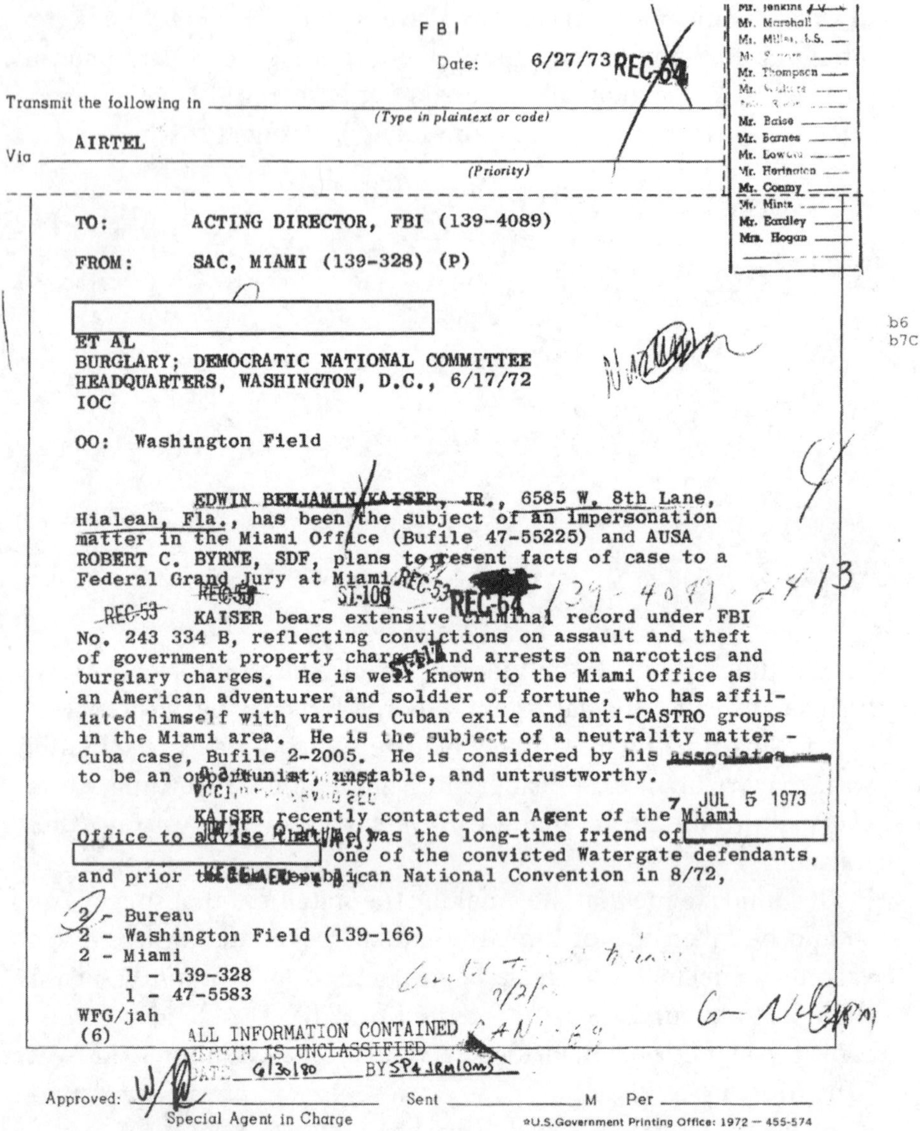

FBI

Date: 6/27/73 REC-64

Transmit the following in ______ (Type in plaintext or code)

Via AIRTEL ______ (Priority)

Mr. Jenkins
Mr. Marshall
Mr. Miller, E.S.
Mr. Thompson
Mr. Baise
Mr. Barnes
Mr. Lowery
Mr. Herington
Mr. Conmy
Mr. Mintz
Mr. Eardley
Mrs. Hogan

TO: ACTING DIRECTOR, FBI (139-4089)

FROM: SAC, MIAMI (139-328) (P)

[redacted]
ET AL
BURGLARY; DEMOCRATIC NATIONAL COMMITTEE
HEADQUARTERS, WASHINGTON, D.C., 6/17/72
IOC

b6
b7C

OO: Washington Field

EDWIN BENJAMIN KAISER, JR., 6585 W. 8th Lane, Hialeah, Fla., has been the subject of an impersonation matter in the Miami Office (Bufile 47-55225) and AUSA ROBERT C. BYRNE, SDF, plans to present facts of case to a Federal Grand Jury at Miami.

REC-53 REC-64 139-4089-2413

KAISER bears extensive criminal record under FBI No. 243 334 B, reflecting convictions on assault and theft of government property charges and arrests on narcotics and burglary charges. He is well known to the Miami Office as an American adventurer and soldier of fortune, who has affiliated himself with various Cuban exile and anti-CASTRO groups in the Miami area. He is the subject of a neutrality matter - Cuba case, Bufile 2-2005. He is considered by his associates to be an opportunist, unstable, and untrustworthy.

7 JUL 5 1973

KAISER recently contacted an Agent of the Miami Office to advise that he was the long-time friend of [redacted] one of the convicted Watergate defendants, and prior to the Republican National Convention in 8/72,

2 - Bureau
2 - Washington Field (139-166)
2 - Miami
1 - 139-328
1 - 47-5583
WFG/jah
(6)

ALL INFORMATION CONTAINED
HEREIN IS UNCLASSIFIED
DATE 6/30/80 BY SP4 JRM/OMS

Approved: ______ Special Agent in Charge Sent ______ M Per ______

*U.S.Government Printing Office: 1972 — 455-574

Jose De La Torriente of Miami. This mutual association presents a possible connection with my father. In the more recent past Euginio Martinez became associated with Bernado Barker in real estate. Wilfredo Navarro was into real estate as well. Martinez had the reputation according to this source, of being courageous, daring, dependable and a very loyal individual, in whom all knowledgeable anti-Castro action men had complete confidence. His immediate commanding officer in the CIA had been James McCord.

This tie between Wilfredo and Barker in real estate dealings is a second conduit for my father's connection to the Watergate burglars and the JFK assassination that preceded it.

Virgilio Gonzalez, also known as "Villo" was a professional locksmith of indeterminate age, probably 45 to 55, and was an old friend of former Cuban President, Carlos Prio Socarras and Bernard Barker. He had served in the United States Air Force during World War II and was shot down over Germany, becoming a prisoner of war. After the war he returned to Cuba and served as a sergeant in the Cuban Bureau of Investigations during the Prio regime. During the late 1940s Barker became involved in gangster activities in Cuba.

In 1959, a CIA agent using the code name "Eduardo" (most likely E. Howard Hunt) introduced Barker to Frank Fiorini (aka Frank Sturgis) who was "in charge" of an anti-Castro Cuban operation at the Bay of Pigs. Barker had begun working as a translator for the CIA, and he introduced Manuel Artime to Frank Bender.

Frank Bender, whose real name was Gerry Droller, had been born in Germany just after the beginning of the 20th century. He fled Nazi Germany during the war and had worked with the Maquis, the resistance movement in France. It was probably here where Droller/Bender had been spotted by the OSS (Office of Strategic Services), run by William "Wild Bill" Donovan. After the war he was recruited into the CIA, and he reorganized post-war West Germany and worked to strengthen German-American relations.

Bender was later assigned to Formosa (Taiwan), working with Chiang Kai-Shek. He was also involved with the ousting of Jacobo Arbenz in Guatemala, and while there worked with Richard Bissell, E. Howard Hunt, David Atlee Phillips, David Morales and William Pawley ... all names which figure prominently in the JFK assassination, the anti-Castro Cuban movement and/or Watergate. While influential, Droller/Bender did rub many CIA agents and operatives the wrong way, mostly because his politics weren't as far to the right as the Hunt-Bissell-Pawley group.

Frank Sturgis wanted to appoint Manuel Artime as the new head of the Cuban government. Bernard Barker had a sister named Rosa, also known as "Tita," who was the widow of Arturo Fique and of Fausto Gomez, each of whom had been killed in the Congo. Rosa had disclosed that "Eduardo" (Hunt) was then working with the White House.

Navarrete advised that Frank Fiorini had the reputation among the Cuban exile activists of being a most untrustworthy, discredited, unsavory gangster who would not hesitate to kill. The Miami source felt that Martinez would never become involved in any operation with Fiorini unless he were ordered to do so by someone of high authority in whom he had complete confidence.

The Miami source also said that in his opinion, the chain of command in this operation would most likely have been 'Eduardo' to McCord to Barker to Martinez to Gonzalez to Fiorini. Later that afternoon, June 20, 1972 the Miami source furnished the following additional information:

Barker had a nephew, Fausto Gomez, Jr., age 19, the son of Rosa. Gomez Jr., who had disclosed that Barker invited Rosa to work as a switchboard operator at the Fontainebleau Hotel in Miami Beach, so that she could listen to conversations of delegates attending the Democratic National Convention. Barker's real estate partner, Andres Amoedo, a Cuban exile, had the dubious reputation of being a sharp salesman by selling swamp land to unsuspecting buyers.

FBI informant code number "MM1550-KS" assigned to one Ricardo Morales (full name 'Ricardo Anibal Morales Navarette') said he did not recognize the photo of McCord, but he did identify photos of Barker and Martinez as Cuban exiles who had been involved in CIA-inspired operations against Cuba. He recognized Gonzalez as a Cuban locksmith and Fiorini (Sturgis) as an American mercenary of disrepute.

With further regards to Gonzalez, Morales Navarette said that two or three months earlier, Gonzalez established his own locksmith business in Miami located in the area commonly called "Centro Commercial Cubanos" ... next door to the Yumura Furniture Store. Gonzalez then offered his services to professional thieves, furnishing lock-picking equipment and providing silencers for handguns.

This is a excerpt directly from the CIA files: The Deputy Director for Operations for the CIA reference's and cites "subject Ed Scott, alias Casey, Casid and Kaiser CIR-316/02055-73 and dated August 15, 1973, the following information was provided by (name unknown) from having personal contact with Ed Scott in Miami on 29 July, 30 and August 3, 1973. The CIA further cites it is unable to identify Ed Scott based on the available data. Should the FBI be able to provide further identifying information we will be glad to recheck our records. In the interim it is suggested that you query the Department of the Army concerning information dated September 27, 1960 on one Eduardo Teofilo Scott who may or may not be identifiable as the same subject."

> On July 29, 1973 an American who has identified himself as Ed Scott (Kaiser) telephoned (name unknown Someone who was in Jail in CUBA and has been recently released) at the address of Mrs. (name unknown) in Miami, Mr. (name unknown) is currently staying at his sister-in-laws house. Scott (Kaiser) said that he and (name unknown) had mutual friends and that he needed to see (name unknown) right away at the Cuban shopping center on NW 22 Avenue and 11th Street which the Cubans named "Centro Commercial Cubanos."
>
> Scott (Kaiser) who was waiting in front of a small coffee shop located in the shopping center. Upon (name unknown) arrival Scott suggested that they go into the Yumura furniture store where he introduced (name unknown) to one of its owners, a Sergio Gonzales, who was in prison in Cuba with (name unknown).
>
> According to (name unknown) Gonzales was supposed to have served six years as a political prisoner and is a former head of the 30th of November revolutionary activities for years, that his group was about to do something big in Cuba, and asked (name unknown) if he could get him some arms. (name unknown) told Scott (Kaiser) that he was arrested for attempting to leave Cuba illegally, and he was not involved with any group and did not want to discuss this any further.
>
> Scott (Kaiser) said that he could tell (name unknown) the location of the Russian military camps in Cuba, the location of all the prisons in Cuba, and asked if (name unknown) thought the prisoners would escape if freed by a group, if a group infiltrated into Cuba, would the people of Cuba help them? He also asked what the Cubans needed in way of arms, food etc., to change the present situation in Cuba.
>
> Scott (Kaiser) asked (name unknown) about the current conditions in Cuba, the length of his prison sentence, if (name unknown) would be willing to join Scott's

group, Scott (Kaiser) asked (name unknown) if he knew anything about a large amount of drugs being smuggled by small boats with Cubans from the United States.

Scott (Kaiser) also asked (name unknown) if the American government had talked to him since his return to the United States from the Islands. Scott (Kaiser) said that he would like to take (name unknown) to an office where a girl would take down information from (name unknown) by typewriter and a tape recorder.

Scott (Kaiser) then took (name unknown) out to his car, a dark green 1970 or 71 Ford Galaxy, opened the trunk and showed (name unknown) a large number of round things, resembling sticks , wrapped in tin foil. Scott (Kaiser) told (name unknown) they were dynamite. (name unknown) was unable to note the license plate number on the car.

Scott (Kaiser) would not tell (name unknown) where he obtained (name unknown) telephone number, but (name unknown) later found out that it was given to Scott (Kaiser) by a Cuban friend, by the name of Felix Rodriguez (fun) who is now employed at the coffee shop counter in the shopping center.

Scott (Kaiser) told (name unknown) that he was called to Washington recently in connection with the Watergate case. Scott had an attaché case containing tapes, index cards and photostatic copies of photos of Frank Sturgis, Gordon Liddy, E. Howard Hunt, and others which he showed to (name unknown).

Scott (Kaiser) said that he made a number of references to an Aldo Vera, Lanz Diaz, Higinio "Nino" Diaz and other persons. (name unknown) said he steadfastly refused to cooperate with Scott (Kaiser) and told Scott (Kaiser) that the only thing he could tell him is what went on in prison because he knew nothing about what went on outside of the prison walls.

On July 30, 1973 Mr. Saldivar (fun) father of Eugenio Saldivar, visited (name unknown) at (name unknown) sister-in-law's apartment. Mr. Saldivar and (name unknown) then went to have coffee at the aforementioned shopping center and saw Scott (Kaiser) there with some of his "cronies" and Armando, who is not further identified, but was exiled in the Uruguayan Embassy in Havana in 1962.

The group started a normal conversation with (name unknown) and after they drank their coffee, Scott (Kaiser), in an effort toward trying to be funny, according to (name unknown) took an old Cuban $100 bill out of his pocket to pay for the coffee. The group insisted that (name unknown) have lunch with them but (name unknown) declined with the excuse that he had a doctor's appointment.

On the morning of August 3, 1973 (name unknown) again visited the Cuban shopping center to purchase some items and again encountered Scott (Kaiser). An unidentified Cuban at the shopping center that day called Scott "Casid" (Kaiser). Scott (Kaiser) told (name unknown) that he was very busy these days and showed (name unknown) a large boat near the shopping center which Scott (Kaiser) said he was fixing up in preparation for a trip soon. Scott (Kaiser) invited (name unknown) to come see him the following day where he was working on the boat.

The boat that Scott was working on is located in back of the Cuban shopping center on NW 22nd Avenue (name unknown) said it reportedly is worth about $75,000 and is owned by a Mr. Richard Cabrera, nickname Cayo, whose means of livelihood is unknown to (name unknown).

In a note to this agency dated August 6, 1973 (name unknown) said that "they", sources not named, told him that Scott is also known by the name of Kaiser, and that Scott, or Kaiser, has spread the story around the Cuban colony that he is a member of the CIA; that he fought in the Indo-China war; that he was a member of the French Foreign Legion, and that he was wounded many times in World War II. Scott (Kaiser) said that he and Armando were going to Washington again to be questioned in the Watergate matter.

Scott is a personal friend of Armando Fernandez, who is about 45 years old, who reportedly is in jail in Cuba at the present time and claims to be or to have been associated with the CIA. Reportedly Fernandez, together with Carlos De Armas who is about 50 years old, were arrested in Cuba on or about July 20, 1973 for having gone to Cuba to bring out the family of Armando Fernandez and some other people. According to (name unknown)

> the families who were to have left Cuba illegally on the return trip with these three were also arrested in Varadero where the families lived.
>
> (name unknown) said that the person called "El Pirate" allegedly had been in jail in Cuba previously but got out and came to Miami and that these three persons used to hangout in the Yumura furniture store in the shopping center on NW 22nd Avenue.

We know from the above that "Scott" was actually my father. He was using my name as his alias. The question is, who was the unknown person my father was talking to?

Both my father and this unknown person, seem to have the same friends, and they both arrived at the shopping center on NW 22 Avenue and 11th Street in downtown Miami.

Sturgis lived off NW 25 Avenue and NW 122 street in Miami, and this shopping center wasn't far from where he lived – only ten minutes by car. The coffee shop, located next to the Yumura furniture store, was the place where Cuban radicals would hangout. My father brought me there on many occasions. I would play in the back of the store, throwing rocks into the canals, while the men conspired.

My father often met Uncle Frank and others there to drink Cuban coffee, eat Cuban pastries and discuss business. I believe that one of the many "unknown names" redacted in this CIA document was Frank Sturgis. The smoking gun is when the "unknown name" (aka Sturgis) said he steadfastly refused to cooperate with "Scott," and told Scott the only thing he could tell him is what went on in prison, because he knew nothing about what went on outside of the prison walls.

I think my father was on to something in wanting to know if this unknown person had talked to the U.S. Government. I also believe that when my father took the more direct approach, by gathering information about this person with a typewriter and recorder, it must have somehow scared this person into completely shutting down, and telling my father that the only information he could give him, was the time he spent behind prison walls.

The CIA may have wanted to further diffuse Frank's involvement with Watergate, but most importantly his possible involvement in the assassination of John F. Kennedy. Frank Sturgis and Wilfredo Navarro both testified to the Rockefeller Commission.

The FBI had another informant, code-numbered "MM1115-KS" (this is a different source than Navarette, and I surmise that it is my father), and this informant speculated that the burglary and wire-tapping of the Democratic National Headquarters in Washington may have been the outgrowth of rival political factions among Cubans struggling for power in the Republican Party.

Sturgis has also said there was incriminating evidence that they had tried to retrieve. Some have pointed to that information as being photographic evidence of suspects in the assassination of President John F. Kennedy, similar "evidence" that I had been told my father carried around in his attaché' case.

Whether this evidence and/or (photographs) were of the shooters in situ or just pictures of them out of context was never divulged. If my father told the FBI, even in strictest confidence, that he had photographic evidence pointing to suspects other than Lee Oswald, anybody could see that it could have placed him in a very dangerous situation.

He would have had the FBI, obeying the directive from J. Edgar Hoover to toe the line on the "single assassin" theory on one side, and the possible assassination conspirators on the other – with my father in the middle. The very definition of being between a "rock and a hard place."

Could it be that the photos my father was carrying in his attaché case may have possibly been of those involved in the Kennedy assassination? Had he been carrying those photos around for quite some time, or could he have obtained those photos prior to or during the Watergate break ins?

Why would my father be showing them off to Aldo Vera, Higinio "Nino" Diaz and others around August 23, 1973? If they were photos of individuals in Dealey Plaza on November 22, 1963, were those photos, my father's "get-out-of-jail-free" card? In other words, "you mess with me, and I'll blow this whole thing wide open"? Could this be the reason why he never spent enough time in jail to see any real prison time?

Even between a "rock and a hard place," a bright or a gutsy guy can play both sides against each other, without getting crushed. Photographic evidence of a conspiracy could act as a "Sword of Damocles" over the collective heads of the conspirators. At the same time, keeping the FBI on notice by threatening to release the proof, and thereby blowing up Hoover's nice tight "lone nut" package.

My father was both bright and gutsy, and if this is indeed true, I wouldn't have put it past him to be able to play both sides at the same time.

I now have more questions then I have answers. And, who was Eduardo Teofilo Scott?

For example, if my father and Navarro were good friends, why then would he want to assassinate him?

If my father and Frank Sturgis were good friends, why then would he be showing off Frank's, Hunt's, Liddy's and other photos to everyone?

To whom is the word "others" referring when my father referenced having photos of additional people?

Could my father have been the one who stole photos from the Watergate Building resulting from the break-ins to the (DNC) Democratic National Committee before they were discovered?

You see my quandary here. Almost every time a simple question gets answered, another three questions arise, and become all the more complicated. It's worse than crabgrass!

In a May 7, 1977 interview, Frank Sturgis said, "The reason why we broke into the Watergate building was because Richard Nixon was interested in stopping the news leaks related to the photographs of our role in the assassination of President John F. Kennedy."

Nixon, who was VP to Eisenhower was a powerful figure in supporting the Bay of Pigs as well as forming Operation 40. All the Cubans had high hopes with Nixon when he became president in 1969. The Cubans believed they would now have a president that would use U.S. military power to invade Cuba and do away with Castro once and for all.

Nixon would frequently ask Richard Helms to view all the documents on the Bay of Pigs. Nixon believed the CIA was hiding something, Nixon believed the Bay of Pigs fiasco was a direct result of Kennedy's assassination hence the reason Nixon said to Haldeman "Look, the problem is that this will open the whole, the whole Bay of Pigs thing." Tell Richard Helms to ask the FBI to stop their investigations into Watergate. Nixon couldn't go to Helms and ask him directly because he knew he would not have his way with Helms, and Helms would not release those classified documents to his boss the "Commander in Chief."

Nixon would not take Helms' insubordance lightly. Nixon would pull the CIA out of Cuba shutting down all CIA infiltration's. Two attempts on Nixon's life had failed, it appeared as though my father was going to be Sturgis' cut out and used as a pasty. Hemming said, "The guy had Oswald tattooed a crossed his forehead".

Two assassination plots against Nixon failed, Watergate did not, according to Eugenio Martinez, he was among the thirty remaining frogmen station in Moa Bay Cuba infiltrating for the CIA when Nixon shut it all down. Mr. Martinez was also a willing participant burglar at Watergate.

Nixon had always referred to Kennedy's assassination using the code "Bay of Pigs." When Castro took power after the overthrow of the Fulgencia Batista regime, Castro had promised the U.S. that he would hold free elections. He backed out of that promise and aligned himself with the Soviet Union. The CIA took this political slap in the face and devised a plan to invade the south of Cuba at the Bahía de Cochinos (Bay of Pigs). They would land unseen and unopposed and then would convince the Cubans living there to join them in the march to Havana to overthrow Castro.

The top three at the CIA: Allen Dulles (Director), Charles Cabell (Deputy Director) and Richard Bissell (Deputy Director of Plans) had approached President Dwight Eisenhower in mid-March of 1960 with a plan to invade Cuba and topple Castro. The ship-borne invasion was to take place at the town of Trinidad, about 170 miles southeast of Havana. When this landing site was rejected by the State Department the fall back site of Bahía de Cochinos was selected.

In the meantime, Richard Nixon, who was running for the Presidency against John Kennedy, became involved and was soon convinced that if the CIA could pull off the whole thing before the November elections, he would win by a landslide. The CIA didn't pull it off, Nixon lost the election, and the top three had to brief Kennedy on the invasion plans.

While Kennedy didn't exactly like the plan, he allowed the CIA to continue on but warned that there would be no military support of any kind. As history records, the invasion was a horrific failure with more than a hundred killed and over a thousand captured. While Kennedy – only in office for three months – accepted public responsibility for the failure, Dulles, Cabell and Bissell were all fired. It was a learning experience for the new president on the difference between the perceived powers and the actual powers of the presidency.

Ever after, Nixon always associated the Bay of Pigs invasion with Kennedy and after his assassination, he used 'Bay of Pigs' as his internal code word for Kennedy's assassination.

Indeed, in his memoir, *The Ends of Power*, former White House Chief of Staff H.R. "Bob" Haldeman cites several conversations in which President Nixon expressed concern about the Watergate affair becoming public knowledge and where this exposure might lead. Haldeman wrote:

> In fact, I was puzzled when he [Nixon] told me, "Tell Ehrlichman this whole group of Cubans [Watergate burglars] is tied to the Bay of Pigs."
>
> After a pause I said, "The Bay of Pigs? What does that have to do with this [the Watergate burglary]?"
>
> But Nixon merely said, "Ehrlichman will know what I mean," and dropped the subject.

My father said that Frank Fiorini would come over to the house in Miami, practically everyday prior to Watergate, trying to get him involved. Fiorini told my father, the Thursday before the break-in, that he was going to Washington DC on a high level mission for the CIA and for President Richard Nixon. Fiorini wanted to know if my father would accompany him.

It is common knowledge now that President Nixon had a tape recording system in the Oval Office at the White House. What isn't generally discussed is that Nixon had the system installed and operational in February 1971.

For over two years, until the middle of July 1973, as many as nine Sony reel-to-reel tape records whirred away, picking up Oval Office conversations, unknown to all visitors and much of Nixon's staff as well. Only members of his "inner circle" knew about the system and were therefore more circumspect when talking with the President in the Oval Office.

It wasn't just the strategically placed lavaliere microphones around the room that picked up conversations. The telephone was also set internally so any call to or from the President was recorded, including many conversations with former President Lyndon B. Johnson.

A tape recorded three days after the Watergate break-in, was given to Rose Mary Woods, Nixon's secretary, to transpose. She "accidentally" erased 18½ minutes of one of the most crucial tapes in the nation's history.

Woods once said, "The buttons said on and off, forward and backward. I caught on to that fairly fast. I don't think I'm so stupid as to erase what's on a tap."

She later admitted that while transposing the tape, she answered a phone call and kept her foot on a button which effectively re-recorded over the Oval Office conversation. She also said that the "other" 13½ minutes was not her fault. The taped meeting had been between Nixon and his Chief of Staff, H.R. 'Bob' Haldeman. Did this tape implicate President Nixon, revealing that he had attempted to cover up the break-ins?

Nixon led Haldeman to surmise in his memoirs that when Nixon mentioned "the whole Bay of Pigs thing," he was actually referring to the Kennedy assassination. Haldeman claimed that Nixon stated, "This whole group of Cubans, [the Watergate burglars] is tied to the Bay of Pigs. Haldeman questioned Nixon about the connection. He said, "The Bay of Pigs? But what does the Bay of Pigs have to do with this? [the Watergate break ins]?

Nixon merely said, "[Assistant to the President for Domestic Affairs, John] Ehrlichman will know what I mean; and Nixon then dropped the subject."

Haldeman said, "After our staff meeting the next morning I accompanied Ehrlichman to his office and gave him the President's message. Ehrlichman's eyebrows arched, and smiled. 'Our brothers from Langley? He's suggesting I twist or break a few arms?'

"Ehrlichman's leaned back in his chair, tapping a pencil on the edge of his desk. 'All right, he said, message accepted.'"

President Nixon called Ehrlichman into the Oval Office and wanted all the facts and documents the CIA had on the Bay of Pigs. In short, Nixon wanted a complete CIA report on the whole project. The President wanted to know: just how much the CIA knew, and when they knew it.

Haldeman also said that almost half a year later, Ehrlichman was in his office and said, "Those bastards in Langley are holding back something. They just dig their heels and say the President can't have it. Period! Imagine that? The Commander-and-Chief wants to see the documents relating to a military operation, and the spooks say he can't have it. There're protecting something and it must be pure dynamite."

President Nixon then gave CIA Director Richard Helms a direct order to turn over those CIA documents in regards to "The Bay of Pigs." It is known that Helms met with President Nixon in the Oval Office for a long meeting. When Helms left, Ehrlichman returned to the Oval Office.

Haldeman also said in his memoir that the very next day, Ehrlichman, who had met with Nixon after the Helms-Nixon meeting said that Nixon was beside himself and was more furious than he has ever seem him. "He was absolutely speechless."

President Nixon was seldom at a loss for words and most of the "inner circle" of Haldeman, Ehrlichman, John Dean and the others were attorneys or businessmen, and they would never be at a loss for words.

In Haldeman's book, he said that, "Nixon has just told me that I'm now to forget all about those CIA documents, and in fact, I am to also cease and desist from trying to obtain them. It seems that in all those Nixon references to the Bay of Pigs, he was actually referring to the Kennedy assassination."

Journalist Daniel Schorr, who was always disappointed that he had only made number seventeen on Nixon's famous "Enemies List," targeted the Nixon White House all during Watergate. According to Schorr, in an outgrowth of the Bay of Pigs, the CIA made several attempts on Fidel Castro's life. The Deputy Director of Plans at the CIA at that time was Richard Helms. Unfortunately for Helms, Castro knew of many of the assassination attempts beforehand.

On September 7, 1963 a few months before Kennedy was assassinated, Castro made a public speech in which he said, "Let Kennedy and his brother Robert take care of themselves, since they, too, can be the victims of an attempt which will cause their death".

After his meeting with Helms in the Oval Office, why did President Nixon order his staff to no longer pursue the CIA's paper trail? Was there something that Helms told Nixon in that meeting, which caused the President to back off? Or, as some researchers now believe, did Helms blackmail President Nixon into leaving the CIA alone under threat of a possible presidential assassination? Could Helms simple have said something like, "Mr. President, we can always schedule another presidential motorcade in Dallas if this nosing around my agency doesn't stop."

President Nixon was already so paranoid that he suspected most, if not all, of his staff were plotting against him, either by leaking to the press, or by turning state's evidence when questioned by the prosecutor looking into Watergate. Nixon once said, "It's likely to blow the whole Bay of Pigs wide open." Was he talking about the CIA assassination attempts on Fidel Castro, a CIA operation that may have triggered the Kennedy tragedy, and which Richard Helms desperately wanted to hide.

Again, directly after the Watergate break-ins, rumors were spreading that there were six burglars and not the five that were caught and jailed. There were four break-ins at the Watergate building and it was only the last one where the "Watergate Five" were nabbed. Was it possible that my father was a participant in an earlier burglary or burglaries, or even the notorious June 17, 1972 act?

Mike Wales, a Pompano Beach *Sun Sentinel* investigative reporter, as noted before, cited a reliable source claiming six men were involved in the break-ins, and the sixth man's name was Bill Kaiser.

In Wale's book *Ed Arthur's Glory No More: Underground Operations from Cuba to Watergate*, I found the following interesting passage. Keep in mind there is no index in the book, and there are a few spelling errors. On page 153-154, I found the mention of a man named "Bill Kaiser."

> Shortly before Watergate, Jerry Patrick Henning turned up in Miami, announcing to one and all that he was through with the "business" (probably gun-running) and was going "loaded with heat," meaning he was carrying a gun. Curiously, Frank Fiorini also turned up in Miami with the same story. He was going straight too. No more involvement with the anti-Castro Cubans, he told intimates. No more running around the Caribbean! He would now settle down with his wife and become a model citizen.
>
> Another of [Mitch] Werbell's agents in the South American field, and a close friend of Frank Fiorini, was Bill Kaiser, a soldier-of-fortune like Fiorini and Werbell, who vanished from his Miami haunts a few days after the Watergate burglary hit the front pages of the *Miami Herald*. Kaiser later surfaced in Port au Prince as a guest at Mike McLaney's Casino International. A Miami

> federal agent told the author the FBI wanted very badly to have a chat with the elusive Kaiser, hinting that he had played a role in the Watergate break-in.
>
> A third man involved with Werbell and Fiorini was Murray Middleman of Philadelphia, whose connections remain a mystery. But Jim and Jerry Buchanan, Ed Arthur's old compadres, do not remain a mystery, although just what they were doing the night of the Watergate break-in is anybody's guess and might be of interest to federal officers. Both Jim and Jerry were long-time friends of Fiorini, having worked with him and Arthur in the early days of the anti-Castro movement. Both were in Costa Rica with Fiorini.

In May 1973 my father contacted a Miami FBI agent and told him that he was a long time friend of Frank Sturgis, (aka Frank Fiorini), one of the convicted Watergate defendants. My father told the agent that prior to the Republican National Convention in August, 1972, Sturgis had invited him to participate in a planned riot at the convention.

Sturgis later told him that the plan for the riot was off, but that something bigger was being planned. Then Sturgis mentioned to my father the name of a nationally known figure – a businessman not a politician – who was in charge of planning the financing and direction of this new operation. According to my father, this individual was an unknown name in the Watergate investigation. My father, at the time of contact, said he would furnish this information in exchange for the following three conditions by the government:

1. The safety of his family.
2. Employment security at his present job, a service attendant at the Shamrock service station, 5501 Okeechobee Road in Hialeah.
3. An opportunity to apply for state and federal pardons.

Airtel To: SAC, Miami (139-328) 7/2/73

From: Acting Director, FBI (139-4089)

REDACTED

ET AL.

BURGLARY OF DEMOCRATIC NATIONAL COMMITTEE HEADQUARTERS, WASHINGTON D.C., 6/17/72

Who was this man who was, "a nationally known figure that was a businessman, not a politician who was going to be in charge of planning and financing this new operation?"

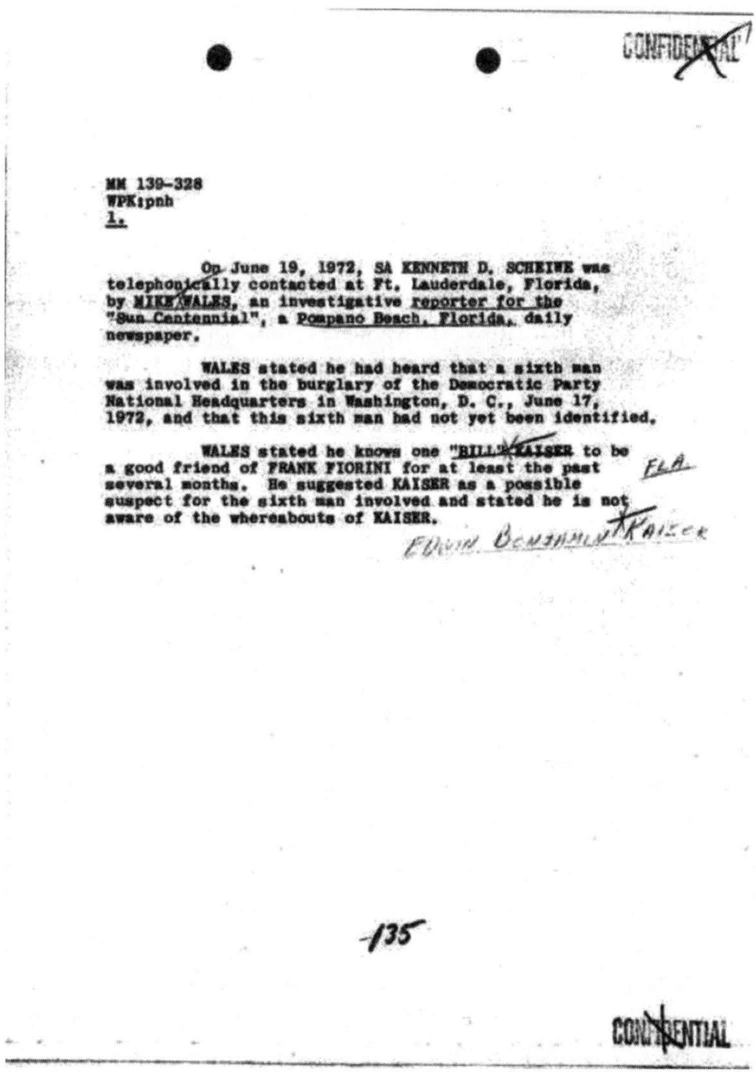

CONFIDENTIAL

MM 139-328
WPK:pnh
1.

On June 19, 1972, SA KENNETH D. SCHEIWE was telephonically contacted at Ft. Lauderdale, Florida, by MIKE WALES, an investigative reporter for the "Sun Centennial", a Pompano Beach, Florida, daily newspaper.

WALES stated he had heard that a sixth man was involved in the burglary of the Democratic Party National Headquarters in Washington, D. C., June 17, 1972, and that this sixth man had not yet been identified.

WALES stated he knows one "BILL" KAISER to be a good friend of FRANK FIORINI for at least the past several months. He suggested KAISER as a possible suspect for the sixth man involved and stated he is not aware of the whereabouts of KAISER.

FLA.

Edwin Benjamin Kaizer

-135

CONFIDENTIAL

It could have been any number of individuals, but during the course of my research, only two people stood out as possible, if not probable suspects. There were only two people I found in my father's phone book that had the resources to do this. There were only two people that kept surfacing and re-surfacing, as I was researching this information. The only the two people most likely to have the money and influence to carry out a project like this were: Howard Hughes, a very well known internationally billionaire, businessman, aviator and later recluse, who had CIA and other high-level government ties for years. Hughes needs no thumbnail sketch, as his exploits have been chronicled for decades. Or maybe William D. Pawley, who is a lesser known name. A former U.S. Ambassador to both Peru and Brazil, a close friend of CIA Director Allen Dulles. A man who took part in the project which became known as "Executive Action," the CIA-directed plan to remove unfriendly foreign leaders from power. Pawley also served in Panama, Guatemala, Nicaragua and Cuba after the Second World War, and played a role in Operation PBSUCCESS, the CIA plot to overthrow Guatemalan President Jacobo Arbenz.

There is one more interesting name that appeared in my father's phone book and I'm not totally certain where to place him: Holmes Tuttle, a behind-the-scenes king-maker who had fourteen successful auto dealerships in California and Arizona. Tuttle was instrumental in the positioning of candidates and securing seed money for the right wing of the Republican party, from 1952 to 1984. Tuttle was considered a "Funding Father" and was a member of President Reagan's "Kitchen Cabinet." A group of unofficial advisors, who screened cabinet candidates and helped to direct policy. Tuttle's phone number and address was in my father's address book.

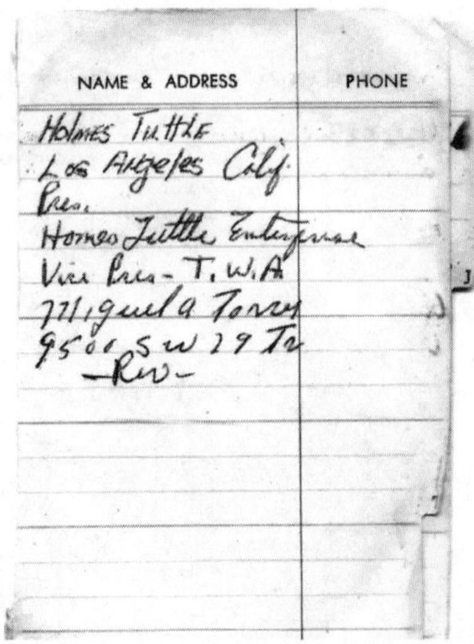

In Los Angeles, in 1964, Tuttle along with two other conservative California businessmen threw a fundraiser for the presidential campaign of Barry Goldwater. Because Goldwater could not make it to the thousand-dollar-a-plate dinner, Holmes called his old friend Ronald Reagan to make a speech. He had once sold a car to Reagan in 1946, and now called on him for help in a pinch. Reagan stole the show, and Tuttle and his friends helped Reagan win the governorship of California and eventually the U.S. Presidency in 1980.

If my father had not been associated with any covert agency and our government was not aware of my father's dealings, then why would he have any of these names in his little black book? That question cannot be answered. It does however make one wonder about my father's contacts and dealings.

Here is some background on George H.W. Bush's involvement in the whole Cuban Thing:

In 1953, Bush got money from Brown Brothers Harriman and, with partners Hugh and Bill Liedtke, formed Zapata Petroleum and by the late 1950s they were all millionaires. Bush bought subsidiary Zapata Off-Shore from his partners and went into business on his own in 1954. By 1958, the new company was drilling on the Cay Sal bank in the Eastern Gulf of Mexico.

These islands had been leased to Nixon supporter and CIA-contractor Howard Hughes the previous year and were later used as a base for CIA raids on Cuba. The CIA was using companies like Zapata to stage and supply secret missions attacking Fidel Castro's Cuban government in advance of the Bay of Pigs invasion. The CIA's codename for that invasion was "Operation Zapata."

In an interesting sidelight ... in 1981, all Securities and Exchange Commission (SEC) filings for Zapata Off-Shore between 1960 and 1966 were destroyed. In other words, the year Bush became Vice President, important records detailing his years at the drilling company disappeared.

To complete the trifecta of coincidence about Bush, in 1969, Zapata sought to acquire a controlling interest in the United Fruit Company, but was outbid by AMK Corporation.

In 1931, Howard Hughes built the Texas Theater – then the largest suburban theatre in Dallas – in the Oak Cliff section of the city. Part of a large chain of movie houses, it was this theater where Lee Oswald was arrested on November 22, 1963. The closeness of both men to the CIA makes it all but certain that the Texas Theater would have been a clandestine meeting place.

Numerous efforts were made to interview my father, both at home and at his workplace. During this time, he had been hospitalized for leg surgery. He did contact the Miami FBI office and agreed to be interviewed on June 26, 1973. He showed up while my mother waited outside in the car. My father was also accompanied by an attorney (most likely Ruben Ellis), who was waiting outside the FBI office for my father to arrive. The attorney was introduced to my father by Gaeton Fonzi, who Frank Sturgis had advised my father he talk to. Ruben Ellis was also Frank Sturgis' attorney.

My father said that he had changed his mind about furnishing information to the FBI. He said that he had already given it to a member of the Watergate Committee and was awaiting action from that source. The person mentioned by my father, was later identified by my father as Jack Anderson, a newspaper columnist with many dubious sources and affiliations.

Newspaperman Jack Anderson, long time associate of Frank Sturgis and the Diaz bothers, with newsman David Hartman, and Gordon Liddy.

Anderson had been talking with Frank Sturgis and the Diaz brothers for many years. He had convinced Uncle Frank that he should come forward with information concerning his involvement in covert CIA sponsored activities. Anderson believed that Uncle Frank's time was up, and that the very powers that counted on him to carry out their dirty work over the years, were the same people that were most likely going to terminate his life ... and do so in the near future.

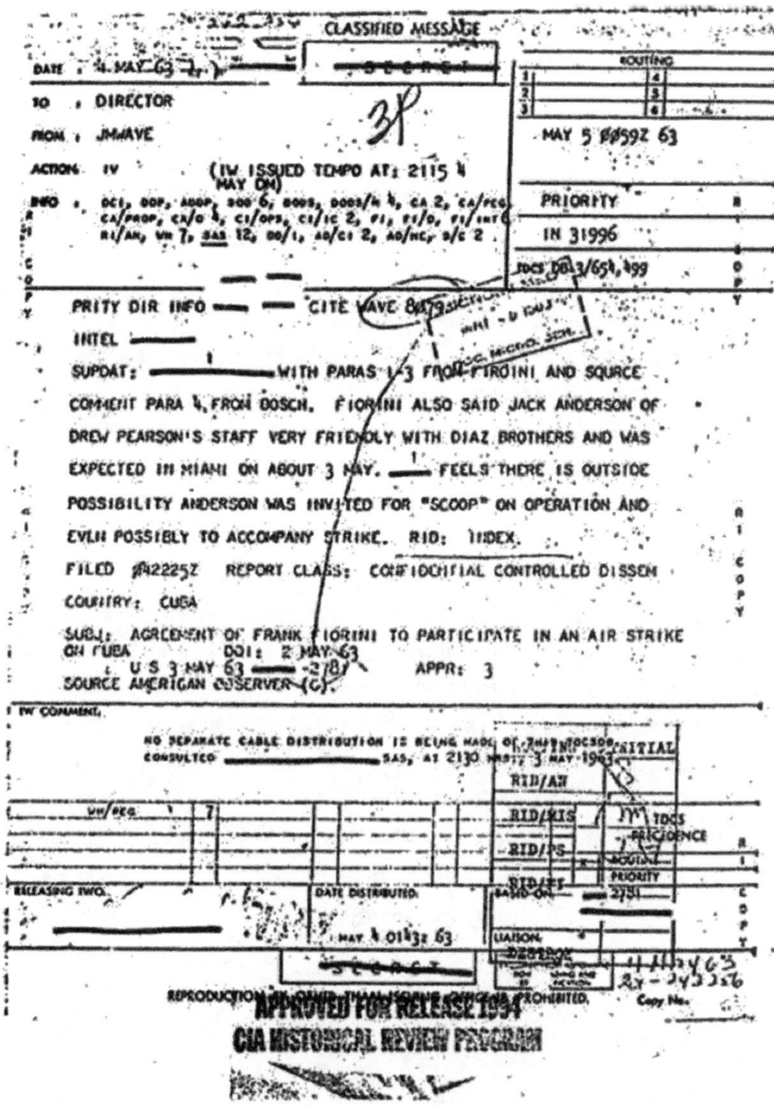
CLASSIFIED MESSAGE

SECRET

DATE : 4 MAY 63

TO : DIRECTOR

FROM : JMWAVE

ACTION : IV (IW ISSUED TEMPO AT: 2115 4 MAY ON)

INFO : DCI, DDP, ADDP, 6, ... CA 2, CA/PEG, CA/PROP, CI/O 4, CI/OPS, CI/IC 2, FI, FI/D, FI/INT 6, RI/AN, WH 7, SAS 12, ... 2

ROUTING

MAY 5 00592 63

PRIORITY

IN 31996

TDCS DB-3/654,499

PRITY DIR INFO [redacted] CITE WAVE 8479

INTEL [redacted]

SUPDAT: [redacted] WITH PARAS 1-3 FROM FIORINI AND SOURCE COMMENT PARA 4, FROM BOSCH. FIORINI ALSO SAID JACK ANDERSON OF DREW PEARSON'S STAFF VERY FRIENDLY WITH DIAZ BROTHERS AND WAS EXPECTED IN MIAMI ON ABOUT 3 MAY. [redacted] FEELS THERE IS OUTSIDE POSSIBILITY ANDERSON WAS INVITED FOR "SCOOP" ON OPERATION AND EVEN POSSIBLY TO ACCOMPANY STRIKE. RID: INDEX.

FILED 042225Z REPORT CLASS: CONFIDENTIAL CONTROLLED DISSEM

COUNTRY: CUBA

SUBJ: AGREEMENT OF FRANK FIORINI TO PARTICIPATE IN AN AIR STRIKE ON CUBA DOI: 2 MAY 63

: U S 3 MAY 63 [redacted] -2787 APPR: 3

SOURCE AMERICAN OBSERVER (C).

IW COMMENT:

NO SEPARATE CABLE DISTRIBUTION IS BEING MADE OF THIS TDCSDB. CONSULTED [redacted] SAS, AT 2130 HRS, 3 MAY 1963.

RID/AN — RID/MIS — RID/PS — RID/FI — TDCS PRECEDENCE — ROUTINE — PRIORITY

RELEASING IWO — DATE DISTRIBUTED: MAY 4 0143Z 63 — BASED ON: — LIAISON

SECRET

REPRODUCTION BY OTHER THAN ISSUING OFFICE IS PROHIBITED. Copy No.

APPROVED FOR RELEASE 1994
CIA HISTORICAL REVIEW PROGRAM

May 5th 1963 document stating that Jack Anderson was possibly invited by Diaz brothers to get a scoop on upcoming, proposed Cuban raids.

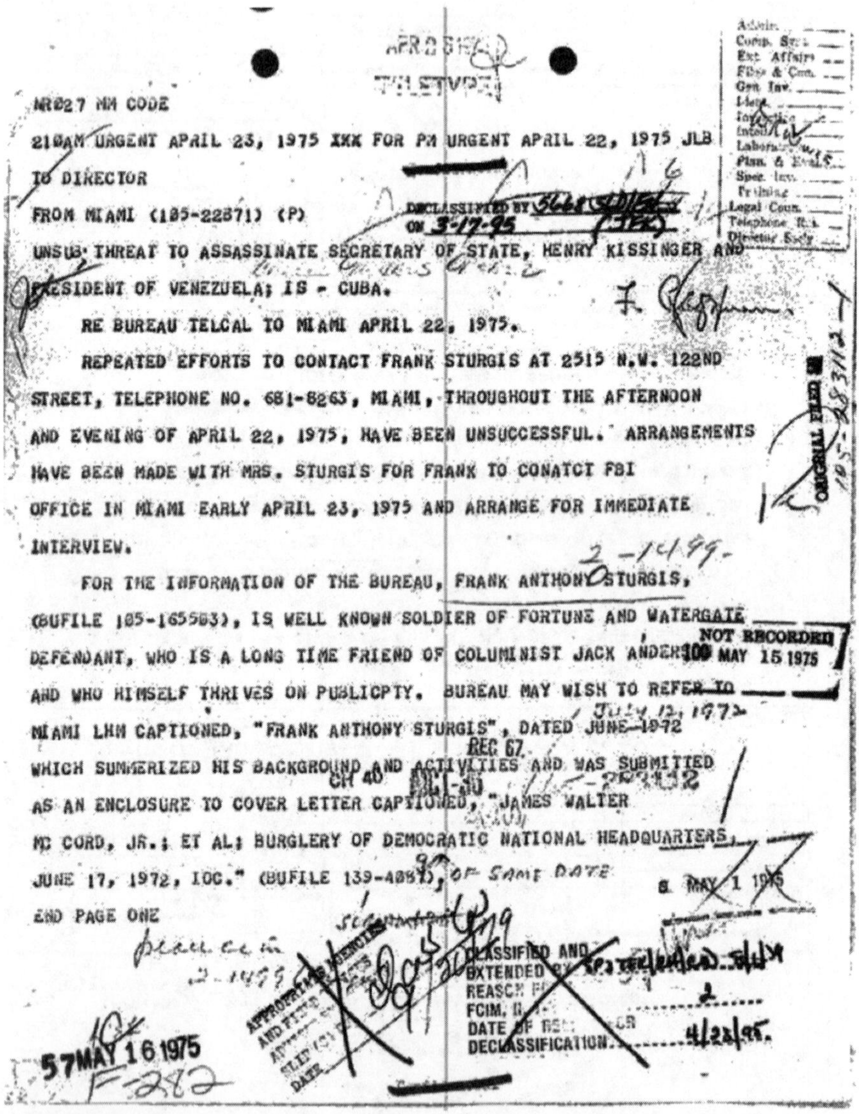

TELETYPE

NR027 MM CODE

210AM URGENT APRIL 23, 1975 XXX FOR PM URGENT APRIL 22, 1975 JLB

TO DIRECTOR

FROM MIAMI (105-22871) (P)

UNSUB: THREAT TO ASSASSINATE SECRETARY OF STATE, HENRY KISSINGER AND PRESIDENT OF VENEZUELA; IS - CUBA.

RE BUREAU TELCAL TO MIAMI APRIL 22, 1975.

REPEATED EFFORTS TO CONTACT FRANK STURGIS AT 2515 N.W. 122ND STREET, TELEPHONE NO. 681-8263, MIAMI, THROUGHOUT THE AFTERNOON AND EVENING OF APRIL 22, 1975, HAVE BEEN UNSUCCESSFUL. ARRANGEMENTS HAVE BEEN MADE WITH MRS. STURGIS FOR FRANK TO CONATCT FBI OFFICE IN MIAMI EARLY APRIL 23, 1975 AND ARRANGE FOR IMMEDIATE INTERVIEW.

FOR THE INFORMATION OF THE BUREAU, FRANK ANTHONY STURGIS, (BUFILE 105-165583), IS WELL KNOWN SOLDIER OF FORTUNE AND WATERGATE DEFENDANT, WHO IS A LONG TIME FRIEND OF COLUMINIST JACK ANDERSON AND WHO HIMSELF THRIVES ON PUBLICPTY. BUREAU MAY WISH TO REFER TO MIAMI LHM CAPTIONED, "FRANK ANTHONY STURGIS", DATED JUNE 1972 WHICH SUMMERIZED HIS BACKGROUND AND ACTIVITIES AND WAS SUBMITTED AS AN ENCLOSURE TO COVER LETTER CAPTIONED, "JAMES WALTER MC CORD, JR.; ET AL; BURGLERY OF DEMOCRATIC NATIONAL HEADQUARTERS, JUNE 17, 1972, IOC." (BUFILE 139-4089), OF SAME DATE

END PAGE ONE

DECLASSIFIED BY [illegible] ON 3-17-95

NOT RECORDED 100 MAY 15 1975

REC 67

CLASSIFIED AND EXTENDED BY [illegible] REASON FCIM, II DATE OF REVIEW FOR DECLASSIFICATION 4/22/95

57 MAY 16 1975

April 1975 document that may have showed concern over the affiliation of Frank Sturgis with Jack Anderson and the subsequent leaks of sensitive Watergate information that may occur as a result.

Chapter Fifteen

Members of Operation 40

Operation 40 was the part of the covert attacks generated by the CIA to destroy the Cuban Revolution. It was drawn up in 1959 on the orders of the Eisenhower administration.

After the Bay of Pigs defeat in April 1961, the CIA recouped its men. It reiterated its confidence in them and assigned them new missions, maintaining the objectives that gave rise to Operation 40.

Allen Dulles (April 7, 1893 – January 29, 1969) was the first civilian and the longest serving (1953–1961) Director of Central Intelligence, and a member of the Warren Commission. Dulles had established Operation 40.

Some researchers say that it was given this name because originally there were 40 agents. Others believe that the name was derived from a room with the number 40 at the Langley CIA headquarters.

The group was designed to assassinate unfriendly foreign officials that posed a threat to the United States, as well as its own members if one was found out to be a double agent. Later the organization was expanded to 70 agents in all. My father's acquaintances in this group were Frank Sturgis, Gerry Hemming, Aldo Vera, Felix Rodriguez, Pedro Lanz Diaz and David Sanchez Morales.

My father while running around with members of Operation 40, who were implicated or convicted in many infamous deeds, could have learned about their involvement in these actions. I believe he was fighting against Communism and for the cause of Cuban liberation with all his heart, but while doing so became privy to information regarding historical events such as the Bay of Pigs, the JFK assassination, Watergate, and others.

He was heavily recruited by Uncle Frank to participate in the Watergate break-ins. It is officially stated that he refused. We are still uncertain of his level of his involvement. My mother knew my father had taken off on one of his trips to Washington with Frank, but my mother had no idea what for. All he said was, "I'm going to Washington with Frank, I'll be back." My mother wanted to know why he was going to do in Washington with Frank, but he didn't say another word and left.

Chapter Sixteen

My Father's Many Aliases

My father used many tactics to navigate the endless seas of secrecy. He had so many different names, I am not sure how he kept track of which name he was using with his different contacts.

Scott, Ed Kaiser	(Alias)
Casid, Scott	(Alias)
Casey, Scott	(Alias)
Casio, Scott	(Alias)
Bill Kaiser	(Alias)
Edwin Keyser	(Alias)
Scott Eduardo	(Alias)
Howard Scott	(Alias)
Gordon Scott	(Alias)
Ed Schmidt	(Alias)
Jerome Schneider	(Alias)
Eduardo Teofilo Scott	(Alias)

This next passage serves as an example of how deep my father's peers went into the abyss.

I am trying not to swim in theory, but there is one that is too tempting not to address. That is, that the Novis/Novo Brothers of whom Marita Lorenz spoke of during her testimony to Mark Lane, could actually have been the Navarro Brothers. It would seem to make sense given their shared company. The fact that Wilfredo Navarro testified before the Rockefeller Commission with Frank Sturgis (there is no mention of the Novis/Novo brothers), the fact that Sturgis knew the Navarro brothers in the early 1960s, and according to Sonia Kaiser's testimony, Wilfredo Navarro was a right winger who knew Sturgis since the early 1960s.

In the book *Bloody Treason*, the fact Hemming said, it wasn't the Novo/Novis brother's that left Miami in the caravan. Also, the fact that my father put a hit out on Wilfredo Navarro meant my father knew something that upset him very much, and Navarro was targeted for "treason" by the U.S. Government.

Attorney Mark Lane Questions Witness Marita Lorenz in the Trial, Hunt v. Liberty Lobby.

From *Plausible Denial*:

Lane: During and before November of 1963, did you work on behalf of the Central Intelligence Agency in the Miami area?

Lorenz: Yes.

Lane: Did you work with a man named Frank Sturgis, while you were working for the CIA?

Lorenz: Yes, I did.

Lane: Was that in Miami, during and prior to November 1963?

Lorenz: Yes.

Lane: What other names, to your knowledge, is Frank Sturgis known by?

Lorenz: Frank Fiorini, Hamilton; the last name, Hamilton. F-I-O-R-I-N-I.

Lane: Was Mr. Fiorini or Mr. Sturgis, while you worked with him, also employed by the Central Intelligence Agency?

Lorenz: Yes.

Lane: During that time were payments made to Mr. Sturgis for the work he was doing for the CIA?

Lorenz: Yes.

Lane: Did you ever witness anyone make payments to him for the CIA work which you and Mr. Sturgis were both involved in?

Lorenz: Yes.

Lane: Who did you witness make payments to Mr. Sturgis?

Lorenz: A man by the name of Eduardo.

Lane: Who is Eduardo?

Lorenz: That is his code name; the real name is E. Howard Hunt.

Lane: Did you know him and meet him during and prior to November 1963?

Lorenz: Yes.

Lane: Did you witness payments made by Mr. Hunt to Mr. Sturgis or Mr. Fiorini on more than one occasion prior to November of 1963?

Lorenz: Yes.

Lane: Did you go on a trip with Mr. Sturgis from Miami during November of 1963?

Lorenz: Yes.

Lane: Was anyone else present with when you went on that trip?

Lorenz: Yes.

Lane: What method of transportation did you use?

Lorenz: By car.

Lane: Was there one or more cars?

Lorenz: There was a follow-up car.

Lane: Does that mean two cars?

Lorenz: Backup; yes.

Lane: What was in the follow-up car, if you know?

Lorenz: Weapons.

Lane: Without asking you any of the details regarding the activity that you and Mr. Sturgis and Mr. Hunt were involved in, may I ask you if some of that activity was related to the transportation of weapons?

Lorenz: Yes.

Lane: Did Mr. Hunt pay Mr. Sturgis sums of money for activity related to the transportation of weapons?

Lorenz: Yes.

Lane: Did Mr. Sturgis tell you where you would be going from Miami, Florida, during November of 1963, prior to the time that you traveled with him in the car?

Lorenz: Dallas, Texas.

Lane: He told you that?

Lorenz: Yes.

Lane: Did he tell you the purpose of the trip to Dallas, Texas?

Lorenz: No; he said it was confidential.

Lane: Did you arrive in Dallas during November of 1963?

Lorenz: Yes.

Lane: After you arrived in Dallas, did you stay at any accommodations there?

Lorenz: Motel.

Lane: While you were at that motel, did you meet anyone other than those who were in the party traveling with you from Miami to Dallas?

Lorenz: Yes.

Lane: Who did your meet?

Lorenz: E. Howard Hunt.

Lane: Was there anyone else who you saw or met other than Mr. Hunt?

Lorenz: Excuse me?

Lane: Other than those

Lorenz: Jack Ruby.

Lane: Tell me the circumstances regarding your seeing E. Howard Hunt in Dallas in November 1963?

Lorenz: There was a prearranged meeting that E. Howard Hunt deliver us sums of money for the so-called operation that I did not know its nature.

Lane: Were you told what your role was to be?

Lorenz: Just a decoy at the time.

Lane: Did you see Mr. Hunt actually deliver money to anyone in the motel room which you were present in?

Lorenz: Yes.

Lane: To whom did you see him deliver the money?

Lorenz: He gave an envelope of cash to Frank Fiorini.

Lane: When he gave him the envelope, was the cash visible as he had it in the envelope?

Lorenz: Yes.

Lane: Did you have a chance to see the cash after the envelope was given to Mr. Fiorini?

Lorenz: Frank pulled out the money and flipped it and counted it and said "that is enough" and put it in his jacket.

Lane: How long did Mr. Hunt remain in the room?

Lorenz: About forty-five minutes.

Lane: Did anyone else enter the room other than you, Mr. Fiorini, Mr. Hunt, and others who may have been there before Mr. Hunt arrived?

Lorenz: No.

Lane: Where did you see the person you identified as Jack Ruby?

Lorenz: After Eduardo left, a fellow came to the door and it was Jack Ruby, about an hour later, forty-five minutes to an hour later.

Lane: When you say Eduardo, who are you referring to?

Lorenz: E. Howard Hunt.

Lane: When did that meeting take place in terms of the hour; was it daytime or nighttime?

Lorenz: Early evening.

Lane: How soon after that evening meeting took place did you leave Dallas?

Lorenz: I left about two hours later; Frank took me to the airport and we went back to Miami.

Lane: Now, can you tell us in relationship to the day that President Kennedy was killed, when this meeting took place?

Lorenz: The day before.

Lane: Is it your testimony that the meeting which you just described with Mr. Hunt making the payment of money to Mr. Sturgis took place on November 21, 1963?

Lorenz: Yes.

(Note: Marita Lorenz returned to her home in Miami that same night, but said Frank Sturgis later told her what she had missed in Dallas on Nov. 22, 1963: "We killed the President that day.")

David Sanchez Morales, aka "El Indio," worked for the CIA under the cover of Army employment. He was involved in PBSUCCESS, the CIA's 1954 overthrow of the Guatemalan government, and rose to become Chief of Operations at the CIA's large JMWAVE facility in Miami. In that role, he oversaw operations undertaken against the regime of Fidel Castro in Cuba.

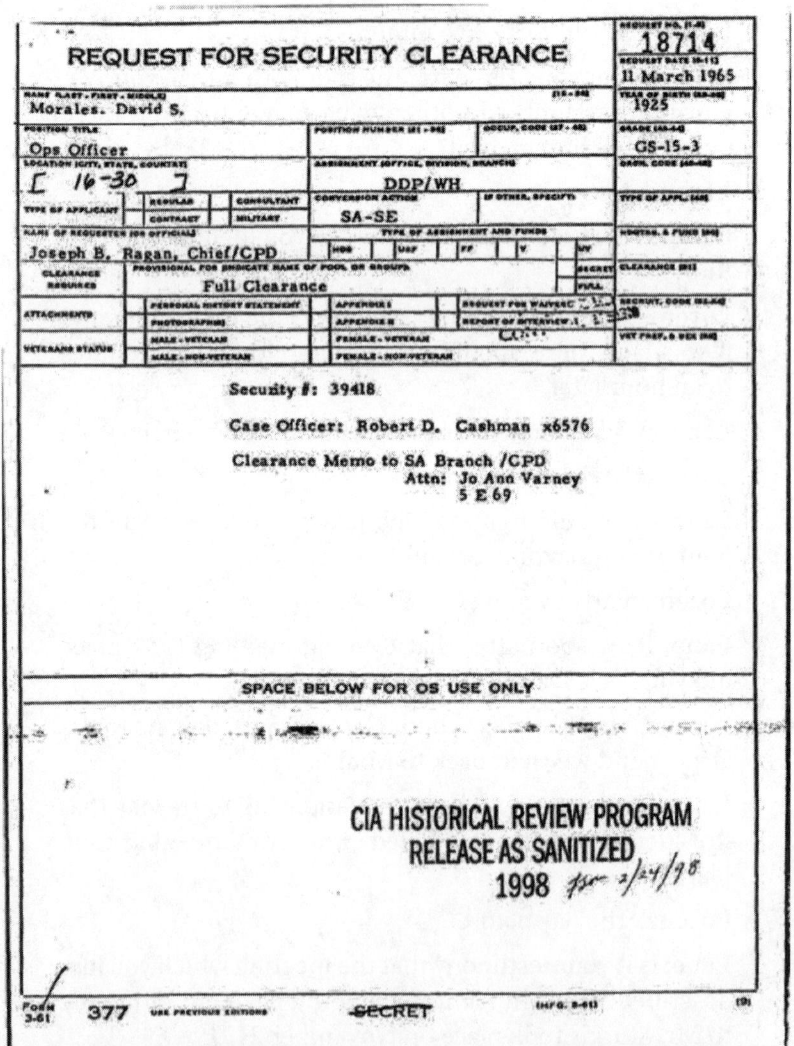

REQUEST FOR SECURITY CLEARANCE

Request No.: 18714
Request Date: 11 March 1965
Name (Last - First - Middle): Morales. David S.
Year of Birth: 1925
Position Title: Ops Officer
Grade: GS-15-3
Location (City, State, Country): [16-30]
Assignment (Office, Division, Branch): DDP/WH
Type of Applicant: Regular / Contract / Consultant / Military
Conversion Action: SA-SE
If Other, Specify:
Name of Requester (or Official): Joseph B. Ragan, Chief/CPD
Type of Assignment and Funds: HQS / UAF / FF / V / UV
Clearance Required: Provisional (Indicate name of pool or group) — Full Clearance — Secret / Full
Attachments: Personal History Statement / Photographs / Appendix I / Appendix II / Request for Waiver / Report of Interview
Veterans Status: Male - Veteran / Male - Non-Veteran / Female - Veteran / Female - Non-Veteran

Security #: 39418

Case Officer: Robert D. Cashman x6576

Clearance Memo to SA Branch /CPD
Attn: Jo Ann Varney
5 E 69

SPACE BELOW FOR OS USE ONLY

CIA HISTORICAL REVIEW PROGRAM
RELEASE AS SANITIZED
1998

Form 3-61 377 Use previous editions SECRET

Morales was involved in other covert operations of the CIA, reportedly including plots to assassinate Fidel Castro, training intelligence teams supporting the Bay of Pigs invasion of Cuba, the CIA's secret war in Laos, the controversial Operation Phoenix in Vietnam, and the hunting down of Che Guevera in Bolivia.

After Morales' retirement in 1975 he returned to his native Arizona, and died of a heart attack in 1978. HSCA investigator Gaeton Fonzi traced Morales to Wilcox, Arizona shortly after Morales' death, and talked to his lifelong friend Ruben Carbajal and a business associate of Morales' named Bob Walton.

Walton told Fonzi of an evening, after many drinks, when Morales went into a tirade about Kennedy and particularly his failure to support the men of the Bay of Pigs. Morales finished this conversation by saying "Well, we took care of that son of a bitch, didn't we?" Carbajal, who had been present at the confession, corroborated it.

Morales was also named by Howard Hunt as a participant in the JFK assassination. Carbajal described the long line of cars and men in dark glasses who paid their respects at the funeral of Morales, whose tombstone reads simply: "David S. Morales, SFC U.S. Army, World War II Korea, 1925-1978."

Morales operated under deep cover for insiders like David Phillips, Bradley Ayers, and John Martino. The released CIA records on Morales are a faint outline of the files the CIA must maintain.

In November 2006, a BBC *Newsnight* program alleged that film footage showed that David Morales, George Joannides, and Gordon Campbell were present at the Ambassador Hotel when Robert Kennedy was murdered. Subsequent research by Mel Ayton and a more thorough investigation by David Talbot and Jeff Morley has failed to uphold these identifications.

Howard Hunt said, " Sturgis and Morales and people of that ilk, stayed in apartment houses during preparations for the "Big Event". Their addresses were subject to change so that where a fellow like Morales had been one day, you'd not necessarily associated with that address the following day. In short, it was a very mobile experience. While in prison Hunt mentioned the "Big Event," referring to the assassination of President John F. Kennedy.

Marita Lorenz was asked about those who drove in the caravan to Dallas with her? She named Pedro Díaz Lanz , Frank Sturgis, Orlando Bosch, Lee Harvey Oswald (Ozzie) and two unnamed Cuban brothers.

Pedro Díaz Lanz was a Cuban pilot who helped supply weapons to Fidel Castro in the Sierra Maestra mountains, and then became the first chief of the Revolutionary Air Force before breaking with the Cuban leader. He shot himself in 2008 at the age of 81.

PAGE 3 RUEAIIA 4261 : C R E T
IMPRESSION THAT MONTERO'S ALLEGATIONS WERE BASED ON A RECENT CABLE FROM THE CUBAN MINISTRY OF FOREIGN AFFAIRS.

3. WE HAVE NO OTHER FACTUAL INFORMATION CONCERNING MONTERO'S ALLEGATIONS. WE BELIEVE THAT THE BASIS FOR MONTERO'S STATEMENT WAS, PROBABLY, AN ARTICLE WHICH APPEARED IN THE NEW YORK DAILY NEWS ON 20 SEPTEMBER 1977. THIS ARTICLE QUOTED MARITZA L O R E N Z AS SAYING SHE, ORLANDO B O S C H, FRANK S T U R G I S, PEDRO D I A Z LANZ, TWO UNNAMED CUBAN EXILE BROTHERS AND LEE HARVEY O S W A L D FORMED AN ASSASSINATION SQUAD WHICH WENT TO DALLAS TO ASSASSINATE PRESIDENT KENNEDY. WE KNOW OF NO INFORMATION IN OUR FILES TO SUBSTANTIATE THAT ALLEGATION.

4. DIAZ IS A FORMER CHIEF OF THE CUBAN REBEL AIR FORCE. HE IS NOT NOR IS THERE ANY RECORD THAT HE HAS EVER BEEN AN AGENCY ASSET, ALTHOUGH HE COULD HAVE BEEN DEBRIEFED BY US WHEN HE CAME OUT OF CUBA.

5. THERE HAVE BEEN VARIOUS PRESS ARTICLES IN THE PAST, ALLEGING THAT LORENZ WAS A CIA AGENT. SHE IS NOT AN AGENT OR EMPLOYEE OF THIS AGENCY NOR IS THERE ANY INFORMATION INDICATING THAT SHE EVER WAS AN

In the above document, two unnamed Cuban exile brothers are fingered as having been involved in the JFK assassination squad. My father was associated with Wilfredo and Roerme Navarro, two Cuban exile brothers that were thick as thieves and close associates of Frank Sturgis long before my father knew any of them.

Díaz Lanz, "was a patriot, a man who had the dignity to give all for the liberty of Cuba," his brother Eduardo Díaz Lanz told a local radio station. According to Eduardo, Pedro had warned him months in advance that he preferred to take his own life rather than "fall into the abyss."

Photo of Pedro Díaz Lanz and my father (Edwin Kaiser) 1973.

Prominent members of the Cuban exile community who also first helped and then broke with Castro, praised Díaz Lanz 's contribution to the anti-Castro cause.

Huber Matos Benitez, a revolutionary commander who broke with Castro and spent twenty years in Cuban prisons accused of treason, said of Díaz Lanz, "He was a man of firm ideas who contributed decisively to a revolution that we once considered redeeming of Cubans' rights, and that is why he became one of the early victims of Fidel Castro's betrayal."

Born in Havana on November 8, 1926, Pedro Díaz Lanz came from a family deeply involved in Cuban history. His grandfather belonged to the Cuban rebel forces known as 'Mambises' that fought Spanish colonial soldiers and his father was a high-ranking officer in the Cuban army until 1930. Díaz Lanz told friends he was a great-grandchild of a sister of José Martí who was a hero of Cuba's independence from Spain.

He graduated from college in 1944 and then studied aviation mechanics. In 1946, when he was 20 years old, Díaz Lanz began flying and soon became a commercial co-pilot for the Cuban airline Aerovias Q, which flew passengers and cargo between Havana and Miami.

Upset with Cuba's political impasse after Fulgencio Batista's coup in 1952, Díaz Lanz met Frank País, leader of an urban resistance movement in Santiago de Cuba. Later Díaz Lanz came into contact with Castro, who assigned him to obtain and supply weapons to the anti-Batista movement from abroad using his commercial pilot job as a cover. The first clandestine arms shipment for Castro's rebel forces was flown from Punta Arenas, Costa Rica, to a hamlet deep in the Sierra Maestra mountains on March 20, 1958. Piloting a cargo plane also carrying Matos, the Díaz Lanz mission was carried out successfully, delivering five tons of weapons and ammunition to the rebels.

Pedro Díaz Lanz also carried military supplies from Venezuela. It is estimated that seventy percent of the weapons delivered to Castro's rebels and their allies were airlifted by Díaz Lanz. When Castro's revolution triumphed in early January 1959, Díaz Lanz was arranging another arms shipment from Costa Rica, and he immediately flew to Santiago de Cuba to rendezvous with rebel forces.

Appointed immediately as chief of the new Revolutionary Air Force, Díaz Lanz traveled to Camaguey to try to persuade Batista's military pilots that their lives would be respected by the new regime.

At that time, Castro promised they could remain in the new armed forces and that any prior action would be considered as legitimate obedience to orders. "The pilots believed this and many of them flew to camp Columbia, the main military base in Havana."

Díaz Lanz recalls in a statement in 1988. "Who would have thought that only a few months later, they would be arrested and tried on orders from the joint chiefs-of-staff head, Raul Castro and, sentenced, disregarding the prior amnesty process promised by Fidel Castro himself." The pilots' case marked the beginning of the his loss of confidence in the Castro revolution.

Castro annulled an initial legal proceeding against the pilots, which found them innocent and ordered a new proceeding. In the end many received sentences of up to thirty years in prison, though some witnesses claimed that thanks to Díaz Lanz's intervention, their lives were saved.

Opposed to communist influences in government posts, Díaz Lanz was removed from his job and then left Cuba on June 29, 1959 aboard a sailboat. After drifting for days, he landed in Miami on July 4, 1959, and testified before the U.S. Congress about Castro's intention to turn Cuba into a communist country under the Soviet Union.

On October 21, 1959, he flew back to Cuba dropping thousands of leaflets over Havana denouncing the revolution's turn to Communism. When he flew over the Cuban capital, he drew indiscriminate gunfire from Castro's soldiers. The next day Castro accused Díaz Lanz of "bombing" Havana and linked the episode to Comandante Huber Matos, who by then had been detained in Camaguey under sedition charges.

At a rally a few days later, an angry throng demanded that both Matos and Díaz Lanz be executed by a firing squad. Matos denied any link to a conspiracy, though Díaz Lanz had previously told Matos about a private conversation, where Castro reportedly said, "We are going to have problems with Huber."

In exile, Díaz Lanz along with Frank Sturgis, founded the Cuban Constitutional Crusade in 1959. He also joined sabotage missions to Cuba that had been organized by the CIA. He was a member of Operation 40, a group of prominent anti-Castro activist assassins, in 1961. The Cuban government considered him a dangerous enemy, and even claimed he was involved in the Kennedy assassination.

Díaz Lanz wrote some years ago in *El Nuevo Herald* a Spanish Miami newspaper, "We believe in a Cuba without victors or vanquished, without hatred or rancor, where all work for all. We believe in the respect for someone else's right, in liberty and justice. [The] Beautiful dream that which all embraced and for which many gave their lives. But the dark night of greed and ambition covered our beautiful island."

Gathering Information

A Letter to CIA/FBI from (illegible) Ed Scott alias Casey, Casio and Kaiser. July 5th, 1973

> James E. Flannery was a CIA agent stationed in Bolivia from 1961 to 1964, Mexico from 1964 to 1965, and the Dominican Republic from 1965 to 1969. Kaiser also gave the Senate Select Committee on Campaign Activities this information. Sturgis refuted Ed Kaiser's Executive Session testimony: "Sturgis stated he was never approached by anyone concerning the demonstrations against the VVAW at the Republican Convention. He recalls having no such conversation with Edwin Kaiser, he said he considered Kaiser to be a good source of information for the Cuban related activities but had reason, nonetheless, to suspect Kaiser's credibility." [Sturgis Exec. Sess. Test. 7.27-28.73 as cited in SSCIA Minority Staff Report]

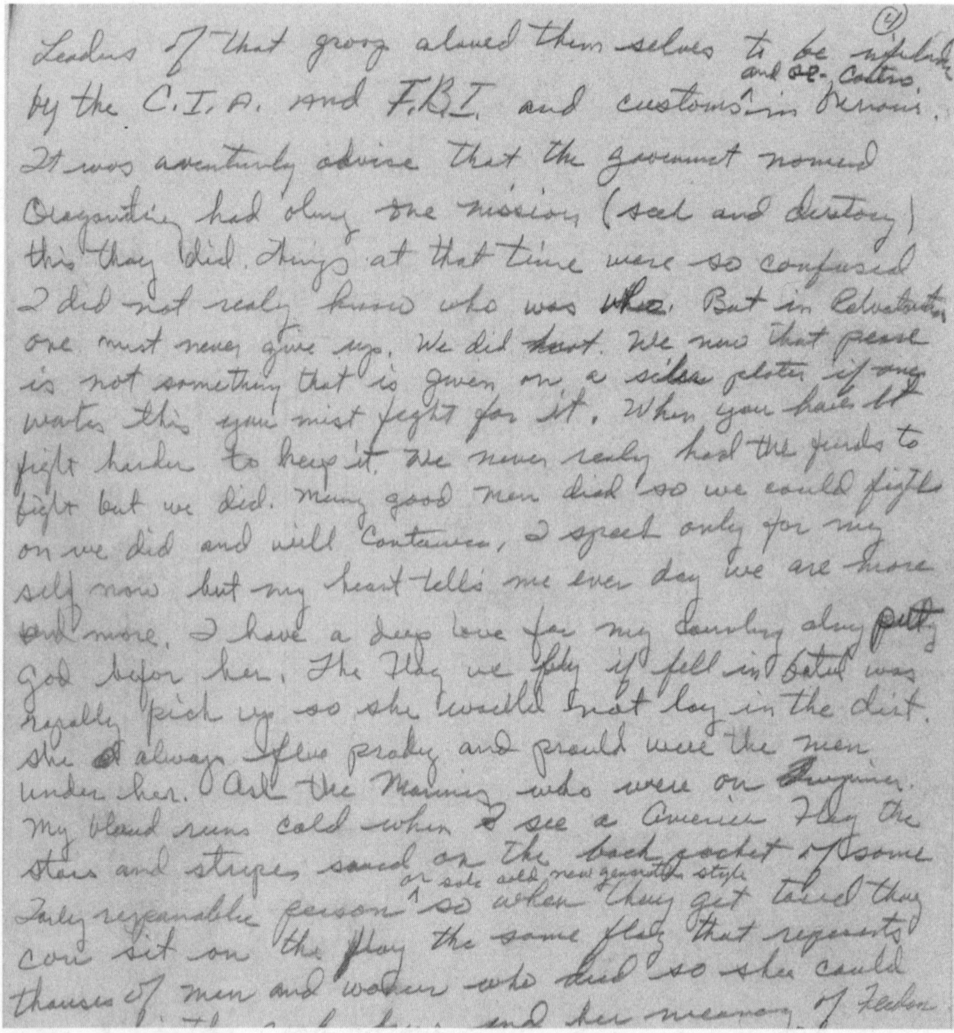

Leaders of that group allowed themselves to be infiltrated by the CIA and FBI and customs and G-2 Castro It was eventually advised that the government named organization had only one mission (seek and destroy) this they did. Things at that time were so confusing I did not really know who was who. But in Revaluation one must never give up. We did not we knew that peace is not something that is given on a silver platter if one wants this you must fight for it. When you have it fight harder to keep it. We never really had the funds to fight but we did. Many good men died so we could fight on we did and will continue, I speak only for myself now but my heart tells me every day we are no more. I have a deep love for my country only God before her. The flag we fly if fell in battle must be rapidly pick up so she would not lay in the dirt she always flew proudly and proud were the men under her. Ask the many who were on its journey, my blood runs cold when I see a American flag the stars and strips sowed on the back pocket or so called new generation style of some fairly respectable person so when they get tortured they can sit on the flag the same flag that represents thousands of men and women who died so she could wave on the coat hinge and her meaning of freedom for all and the respect she should be given. I ask myself what happen to the respect. My only assumption ----------

Chapter Seventeen

Psychological Warfare against Russians in Cuba

On August 20, 1973, the Miami field office of the FBI sent the Director a highly deleted teletype. The only words released were, "Changed and Conspiracy – Ring Case, 00: Miami." [FBI 26-425217-36 2 pages] In August 1975, my father arranged for an illegal arms shipment to a Nicaraguan anti-Castro training base, and frequently talked of uniting the White Russian refugees for military operations against Cuba.

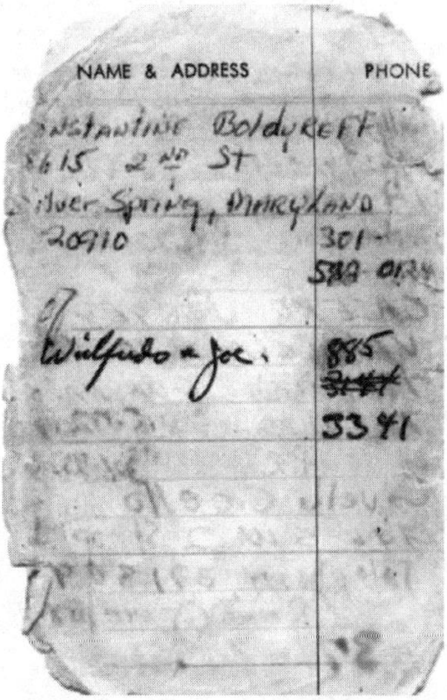

Constantine Boldyreff was the founder of NTS (National Alliance of Russian Solidarists) and a senior leader of the group. His wartime career is shrouded in secrecy, but it is clear that the CIC (Counter Intelligence Corps) believed that in late 1944, Boldyreff helped administer gangs of Russian laborers for the Waffen-SS.

Boldyreff is a case in point of the manner in which the intervention of U.S. Intelligence agencies shepherded the migration of liberation propaganda out of the fallen wartime ministries of Berlin and into the living rooms of America. Mr. Boldyreff states that World War III can be prevented by an immediate and vigorous psychological attack aimed at the enemy's weak spot, saying, "We can win the Cold War in Russia".

Boldyreff was sending anti-Communist propaganda radio broadcasts in Russian to Cuba.

In July of 2014, Antonio "Tony" Calatayud, Cuban exile activist and Miami radio commentator was arrested for a fraudulent scheme to buy distressed real estate that allegedly bilked the buyers of $1 million.

Chapter Eighteen

Friends?

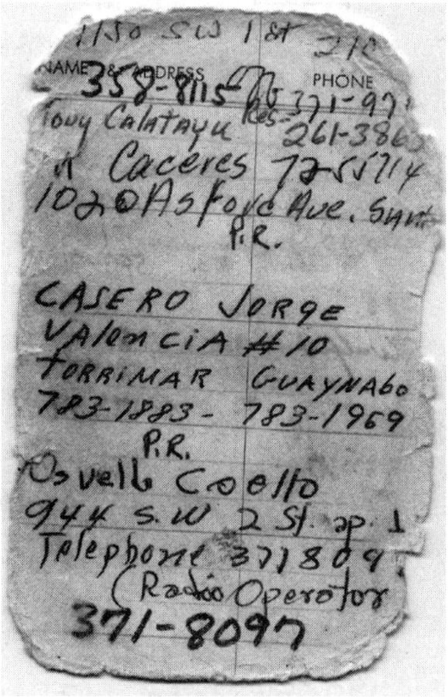

My father's phone book page includes the names of Tony Calatayud and Osvaldo Coello, "Radio Operator."

During the research of this book, I was able to track Tony Calatayud down. He was one of the very few people from my father's notes that is still alive and was willing to say a few words regarding my father and his occupation. The following is a transcription of our telephone conversation:

Tony Calatayud Sr.: Hello!

Scott Kaiser: Hello Tony!

TC: (In Spanish) Yes, how are you?

SK: How are you, I'm doing good Tony this is Scott Kaiser

TC: Fine, fine, Ahhh, Tony Jr. Ahhh, told me that you were going to call me, how are you?

SK: I am doing good brother, I'm doing fantastic, listen I have a friend of mine that is on the line with us, his name is Brett, he's helping me write a book about my father (in Spanish) your name was in the address book of my father and I was contacting everybody if they could help me with the good and the bad and the ugly things about my father.

TC: Well he was a nice fellow a very brave one, Ahhh? A gentlemen, a gentlemen and a tough guy. He was a gentlemen and a tough guy at the same time. He had a lot of military capacity, Ahhh? He told he was Ahhh? He was a member, he had been a member of the

Foreign Legion in France (laughs) in North Africa. He was a husky guy, very physical, very strong and with a lot of opinions, a lot of opinions, a friendly guy.

SK: Yeah, he wanted to help the Cuban people and he hated Fidel Castro.

TC: Yes for sure and he Ahhh? Well leave some Ahhh? Some things that are still not available for, for publication, but I can tell you that Ahhh? He was instrumental in to many responsible Ahhh? Para-military activities, Ahhh? Out against Castro government and Ahhh? I met him.

SK: Anything you can tell me that has not been publicized that you could help me with my book? Ahhh? Because I told Tony Jr. that as soon as my book comes out, he's the first person I'm going to call, so he could maybe even help us, because we want to do it before the Bay of Pigs 50th anniversary this April.

TC: What I can do, what I can do in my opinion for the benefit for your book is to send you an email, some kind of a statement, mention about him, how I met him, through whom I met him, my opinion about him as much as I can say about any military activities, military activities we were involved together, Ahmm? Some of his relationship with Frank Sturgis and me too.

SK: I also talked to Masferrer's nephew and I talked to him on the phone, Ahhh? Properly, maybe two months ago and he wrote me a beautiful email, he told me how Masferrer (in Spanish) You know Rolando Masferrer right?

TC: What's his first name?

SK: Rolando, Rolando Masferrer!

TC: Oh! Oh! Rolando Masferrer, sure, sure, with whom did you talk to?

SK: I was talking to the nephew.

TC: Oh the nephew OK Ahha.

SK: Yeah, I was talking to the nephew to Rodolfo's son,

TC: Rodolfo, OK, OK.

SK: Yeah, I was talking to him on the phone two months ago and he was telling me some good things he also sent me an email, so

I'm contacting everybody that I can contact right now out of the phone book that my father had left behind, Mmmm? That were all his friends and people he knew.

TC: What I'm going to do is to try to find out José Casero's telephone number, if Ahhh? Because he is a friend of mine and Ahhh? Tony Jr. told me that his name is to be on the list, José Casero?

SK: I have a lot of people!

TC: Have you contacted, have you contacted José Casero?

SK: No!

TC: José Casero is living now in Miami he was living in Puerto Rico. I did have available his phone number right now but I admit I misplaced it, but I can try to get a hold of him so he can talk to you, and you can talk to him, but Ahhh? for example, Tony Jr. mention the Navarro's brother's.

SK: Ahha!

TC: Oh! They died, the two of them?

SK: Yeah! They died in a car accident. I have a picture of, Ah, Wilfredo Navarro at my thirteenth Birthday!

TC: Oh my God! Don't tell me, well they were nice fellows, nice fellows. What I can do is send you an email or whatever kind of a statement is placing my opinion about your father what I knew about him and his relationship with other people and some ah small ah anecdote. Let me tell you there was a lot of obscures Ahhh? Situation your father when he died, he died supposedly accident.

SK: Yeah! I know it wasn't no accident.

TC: He was killed, in my opinion he was killed.

SK: Yeah! I know he was killed, I know.

Brett Karis: Hey can you tell us what your thoughts are on how he died?

TC: Well they, they, they, ah, ah, ah, as much as I remember at that time they say that he was involved going ah, ah, ah some kind of ah Para-military operation, command operation, whatever he was on the sea and ah there was a mast of a boat that came down and hit him and killed him, but I don't, I do not believe that. He was killed.

I don't remember the guy, that guy that was involved in the operation with him but it was kind of an obscured and ah suspicious guy as much as I remember.

SK: Do you know who the guy was?

TC: He was not a tough, he was not a tough guy.

SK: Do you know who he was?

TC: No I don't remember, many, many years, but it was a Cuban. It was a very obscure surrounding that guy, I'm talking about an operation, an operation, an actual man that worked with him on the boat, he was the one who say there was an accident, in my opinion he was killed, he was executed.

BK: Sir, what is your opinion on why he was killed?

TC: I read on some police record about, there is a report about if they say it was an accident they have to make a report to the police.

BK: Yes, because even the official report is different then the story you just said so I think that what you just said is properly more of the truth, more actuate, do you know why he was killed? Can you speculate on why you think they murdered him?

TC: I (pause) do (pause) not (pause) remember exactly, the problem is that he was ah, he was involved in too many things at the same time he was to adventurous, he was playing an adventurous game and that game.

SK: Tony, Tony (in Spanish) "Do you know what my father had"?

TC: What?

SK: A briefcase, photos of Sturgis, Hunt and Gordon Liddy. And I have a document saying all that information.

BK: Wait, wait, wait, hold on, hold on, wait! You just jumped to the photographs. Where did that come from? Why did you bring that? Scott you brought that up didn't you?

SK: I brought that up because what Tony was doing, saying that, Tony was saying you know the reason why he may have been killed was because he was very adventurous.

BK: Yeah he was too adventurous.

SK: He was into a lot of things.

TC: He know too many things! He knew too many things. Remember he was a very close partner of ahhh, Frank Sturgis and Frank Sturgis even now is in the list of the possible operation relating to the killing of John F. Kennedy.

BK: Yes! Correct.

TC: So were talking about a big involvement you know, not that I believe they were involved but ahhh? But it was a cloak and dagger group very mysterious people, very sharp people with their actions, he was a solider of fortune. Frank was a solider of fortune, in the best, in the best way of saying that he was a nice fellow. A very trained guy, you never had any problems with him. I will tell you some anecdote about your father, he told me that one time he was such, mmm, such capable military that if he, if he wanted, if I wanted he would go to my bed one of these nights and just wake me up ahhh? Because he can go inside my house in any moment at any time out of no particular reason. I remember I was a young guy he was a young guy too an I stand up and say, "if you ever go inside my privacy of my house I'll kill you right there and you father said, "I believe you, and I'm your friend." (Everyone is sharing in some laughs) He was trying to tell me how capable he was military to do any job, I never had any problems with him, he was a tough guy but a friendly gentlemen. I remember, I remember, I remember now, you used to live in Hialeah. I remember, I remember I saw you once I went to your house, I believe it was your birthday, in my opinion, there was some kind of BBQ. I was there, I was there and I remember your mother.

We closed our conversation with exchanging emails, Tony mentioned that he would get back with me on sending me some information. That day never came. I suppose we hit a nerve with this subject matter and someone close to Tony advised him to not be in contact with us any further.

Osvaldo Coello

OPENING CRITERIA COMMENTS CIA JMWAVE DIRECTOR CABLE REQUEST POA ON OSVALDO EVARISTO COELLO DIAZ 10/21/61 1 JMZIP PAPER TEXTUAL DOCU-

MENT SECRET OPEN IN FULL OPEN 07/10/98 JFK64-7:FBI RIF#: 104-10262-10048 (10/21/61) CIA#: 80T01357A

Osvaldo Coello is a National Association of Cuban Radio-Telegraph Operators-In-Exile, essentially a trade craft association. However, he claimed contacts with clandestine operations against Cuba, and stated a willingness to work for the liberation of Cuba. His paramilitary experience helped with an undercover radio operation while aboard the ship "Barbara" in April 1961.

During the Bay of Pigs, he was the first to be advised by radio, while serving on the ship Barbara, that Kennedy had just called off any air support. He also may have been a radio operator in connection with the assassination of President John F. Kennedy in Dallas on the November 22, 1963.

During the 26 of July Movement, Castro and many of his followers went to Batista's prisons, and Coello became Castro's head radio operator in communications and covert operations.

After the release of Castro and his men, they regrouped in the mountains of Cuba. They would then try a second time to overthrow the government of Cuba, this time it would be more successful with the help of the CIA, Pedro Diaz Lanz and Frank Sturgis.

Little did the CIA know they would be double crossed by Fidel Castro himself. Castro met with Sturgis and others in Miami before the 1959 coup in Cuba to perpetuate and formulate a plan of attack. Coello also played a key roll in the 1959 coup for Castro. Once Castro took power and declared his allegiance to Russia, many defected to the United States, among these was Coello who later offered his services to the CIA.

Osvaldo Coello became the CIA's top radio man, as he would listen in on Cuban intelligence and could decipher and translate Castro's plans, ideas and correspondences that he had with Cuban intelligence.

During the 1961 Bay of Pigs, Coello was the main radio operator on the ship Barbara. On April 15, 1961 eight B-26 bombers carried out their airstrikes to destroy the Cuban air force, but the effort was only partially successful. The CIA awaited orders to launch a next air strike to finish off Castro's air force base, but no orders were received, and the second air strike opportunity was inadvertently canceled. The first person to receive word by radio from the CIA would be Coello, he was notified that the second air strike would not be ordered by President Kennedy. Kennedy made it specifically clear that the American military would not intervene with Cuba.

Osvaldo Coello role as a top level radio operator for Fidel Castro, led him to work for the CIA that ultimately resulted in his experience in the failed Bay of Pigs. While attending a Cubanos Unidos meetings Osvaldo Coello said, "We got even with Kennedy didn't we?" This information was provided to me an ex-member of Cubanos Unidos, whose identity remains a secret. I guess the powers-that-be are still very much here, as they were nearly 50 years ago.

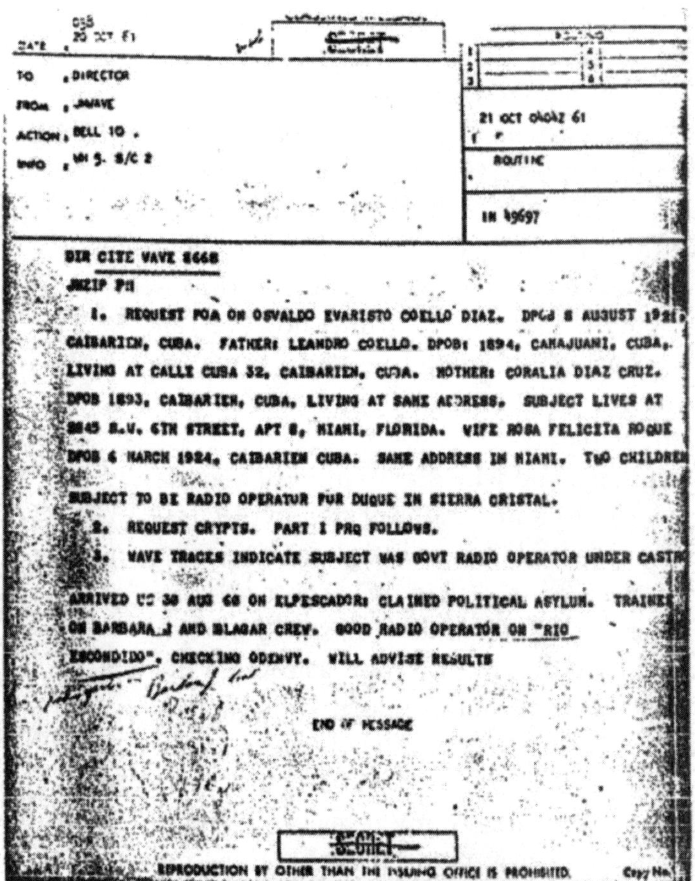

DATE : 20 OCT 61

TO : DIRECTOR

FROM : JMWAVE

ACTION : BELL 10

INFO : WH 5, S/C 2

21 OCT 0402Z 61

ROUTINE

IN 49697

DIR CITE WAVE 8668

JMZIP PH

1. REQUEST POA ON OSVALDO EVARISTO COELLO DIAZ. DPOB 8 AUGUST 1921, CAIBARIEN, CUBA. FATHER: LEANDRO COELLO. DPOB: 1894, CAMAJUANI, CUBA, LIVING AT CALLE CUBA 32, CAIBARIEN, CUBA. MOTHER: CORALIA DIAZ CRUZ. DPOB 1893, CAIBARIEN, CUBA, LIVING AT SAME ADDRESS. SUBJECT LIVES AT 8845 S.W. 6TH STREET, APT 8, MIAMI, FLORIDA. WIFE ROSA FELICITA ROQUE DPOB 6 MARCH 1924, CAIBARIEN CUBA. SAME ADDRESS IN MIAMI. TWO CHILDREN

SUBJECT TO BE RADIO OPERATOR FOR DUQUE IN SIERRA CRISTAL.

2. REQUEST CRYPTS. PART I PRQ FOLLOWS.

3. WAVE TRACES INDICATE SUBJECT WAS GOVT RADIO OPERATOR UNDER CASTRO

ARRIVED US 30 AUG 60 ON ELPESCADOR: CLAIMED POLITICAL ASYLUM. TRAINED ON BARBARA J AND BLAGAR CREW. GOOD RADIO OPERATOR ON "RIO ESCONDIDO". CHECKING ODENVY. WILL ADVISE RESULTS

END OF MESSAGE

SECRET

REPRODUCTION BY OTHER THAN THE ISSUING OFFICE IS PROHIBITED. Copy No.

CIA HISTORICAL REVIEW PROGRAM
RELEASE IN FULL 1998

Is it any wonder why Osvaldo Coello's name and occupation was in my father's address book? If anyone was capable of carrying out orders to maintain radio surveillance on the day President Kennedy was assassinated it would be someone like Coello, even the CIA admitted to his performance as a "Good" Radio Operator.

Luis Posada

Luis Posada is found in my father's phone book as Louis Licor. Posada is a known terrorist whom the United State's government has refused to extradite to Venezuela. His work had reached deep into the undercover shadowy world of the CIA covert actions against foreign countries, especially against the Cuban Revolution. How ironic that the word "Dallas" is found under Luis's name?

I am certain that this is how my father met and knew Luis Posada aka Luis Licor. In Florida, Posada also trained member of JURE, Junta Revolucionaria Cubana, a group which aimed to infiltrate Cuba. My father who was head of the Cubanos Unidos also signed a unity agreement with JURE. Cubanos Unidos actually planned and/or carried out destruction that is still classified to this day.

According to Tony Calatayud there were several raids into Cuba, but this information has not been made available for publication, he said. He planned on releasing this information to me for the very first time, however, all our means of communication (phone and emails), stopped, after I had emailed him copies of my father's phone book.

This might explain why the Miami FBI Security Supervisor in Miami was interested in discussing my father's possible knowledge with the FBI Security Supervisor in Dallas. What information did my father have on the individuals who were in Dallas that fateful day. But it seems as though the FBI in Dallas just blew off this information by stating it would require three months of investigation and a subpoena. (Subpoena who)?

Through the course of my research, I decided to go through every name thoroughly in my father 'phone book. I found names like Ewdero, Frank Ferennie, Lee, Bill Pawley, Tony Calatayud,

Jose Pujol Jr. and many more. I then began to research their names, numbers and address's, calling some and asking them questions.

Most if not all of the numbers had long been disconnected, however, tracking down some of these individuals through information was quite easy. I sometimes wondered why these numbers hadn't been resold? I assumed that all the numbers were area code 305.

I came across the name Louis Licor, and called that number – it was a dead end. I tried Lecor, it was driving me nuts trying to figure out the name. I call Miami information to see if this person was still around under any name. This particular name bothered me so much was because of the word "Dallas" that my father had written under it.

All the other names were pretty obvious as to who they were, but this one had me stumped, so I asked my mother about this person, she said, "Why does that name sound familiar?" After giving her sometime to think about it, she told me that my father made mention about a Cuban airplane that was bombed in 1976 and that this bombing took place just before my father's friend, Aldo Vera,

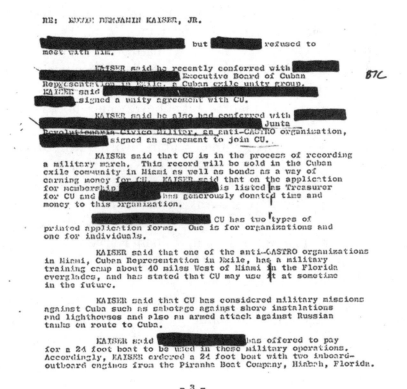

RE: [illegible] BENJAMIN KAISER, JR.

[redacted] but [redacted] refused to meet with him.

KAISER said he recently conferred with [redacted] Executive Board of Cuban Representation in Exile, a Cuban exile unity group. KAISER said [redacted] signed a unity agreement with CU. b7C

KAISER said he also had conferred with [redacted] Junta Revolucionaria Civico Militar, an anti-CASTRO organization, [redacted] signed an agreement to join CU.

KAISER said that CU is in the process of recording a military march. This record will be sold in the Cuban exile community in Miami as well as bonds as a way of earning money for CU. KAISER said that on the application for membership [redacted] is listed as Treasurer for CU and [redacted] has generously donated time and money to this organization.

[redacted] CU has two types of printed application forms. One is for organizations and one for individuals.

KAISER said that one of the anti-CASTRO organizations in Miami, Cuban Representation in Exile, has a military training camp about 40 miles West of Miami in the Florida everglades, and has stated that CU may use it at sometime in the future.

KAISER said that CU has considered military missions against Cuba such as sabotage against shore instalations and lighthouses and also an armed attack against Russian tanks en route to Cuba.

KAISER said [redacted] has offered to pay for a 24 foot boat to be used in these military operations. Accordingly, KAISER ordered a 24 foot boat with two inboard-outboard engines from the Piranha Boat Company, Hialeah, Florida.

- 3 -

was killed in Puerto Rico. She said, that my father thought that Louis or in this case Luis had something to do with the bombings.

There is evidence that Luis Posada Carriles was connected to the assassination of President John F. Kennedy, and was in Dealey Plaza that day. He spent nine years in prison in Venezuela for having masterminded the mid-air bombing of a Cuban civilian airliner in 1976, killing all 73 people aboard. That is the year that George H.W. Bush became head of CIA. The CIA has been accused of bribing Venezuelan prison guards to arrange Posada's escape in 1985. Posada was also arrested and convicted in Panama in 2000 for entering the country with the intent of killing Fidel Castro, who was attending an Ibero-American summit meeting at the time.

Anti-Castro Cuban exiles, the CIA and organized crime figures being involved in the Kennedy assassination has long been a surmise. Even though the official government position remains that Lee Harvey Oswald was a lone assassin, the majority of Americans and the rest of the world don't buy it. When the House Select Committee on Assassinations (HSCA) was formed by Congress, it found in its final report that: "President John F. Kennedy was probably assassinated as a result of a conspiracy."

CIA Covert Operations against Cuba from 1959 to 1962 and the pilot Posada's role in Operation 40 are all connected to the Kennedy assassination. Who in 1963 had the resources to assassinate Kennedy? I would think that most if not everyone who was associated with my father had the means and motives. Among them were Orlando Bosch and Felix Rodriguez, both involved with the Bay of Pigs and trained by the CIA as assassins in Operation 40.

Operation 40 personnel had the training and the sharp-shooting ability necessary to carry out the assassination of President Kennedy. Some more notable members of Operation 40 were David Morales, David Phillips, Howard Hunt, William Harvey, William "Bill" Pawley, Frank Sturgis and Gerry Hemming. Many of these men are found in my father's address book.

One thing is certain, the United States Government will never let Posada be questioned about his activities in an open forum where he could incriminate key members of the government, their ruling class or their political operatives.

Aldo Vera Serafin

Aldo Vera Serafin was a founding member of The Fourth Republic, an anti-Castro movement.

The CIA arranged for Michael Townley to be sent to Chile under the alias of Kenneth Enyart. He was accompanied by Aldo Vera Serafin of the Secret Army Organization (SAO). The SAO was a right-wing militant group based in San Diego. The organization was active from 1969 to 1972. They targeted individuals and groups who spoke against the Vietnam War, especially those who organized public demonstrations and distributed anti-war literature such as the Vietnam Veterans Against War (VVAW).

James Files said that it was Vera who snitched on him to the FBI, Vera said "that Files was one of the shooters in Dealey Plaza." Maybe that's why Luis Posada went to pay Vera a visit in Puerto Rico? Aldo Vera was also apart of the Cubano Unidos and a friend of my father's.

A Miami-Dade judge has awarded $94.6 million in damages to the family of Aldo Vera, Sr. who was a former senior Havana police official murdered in Puerto Rico by a car bomb in 1976.

Circuit Court Judge Robert N. Scola, Jr. on signed an order awarding the judgment to the Vera family in the latest wrongful death claim against the Cuban government in a South Florida courtroom. Although large, the amount pales in comparison with the almost $253-million award given by a Miami-Dade jury April 4 to the family of Rafael del Pino Siero, a former Fidel Castro friend who died in a Cuban prison in 1977.

To Director CIA (185-267092)

Subject: Edwin Benjamin Kaiser Jr.

Dallas (185-5511) From Miami (185-22264) CONFIDENTIAL

Re: Bureau Airtel August 16, 1974, to Dallas, and telephone call August 21, 1974, by Security Supervisor (name unknown) Dallas, to Miami.

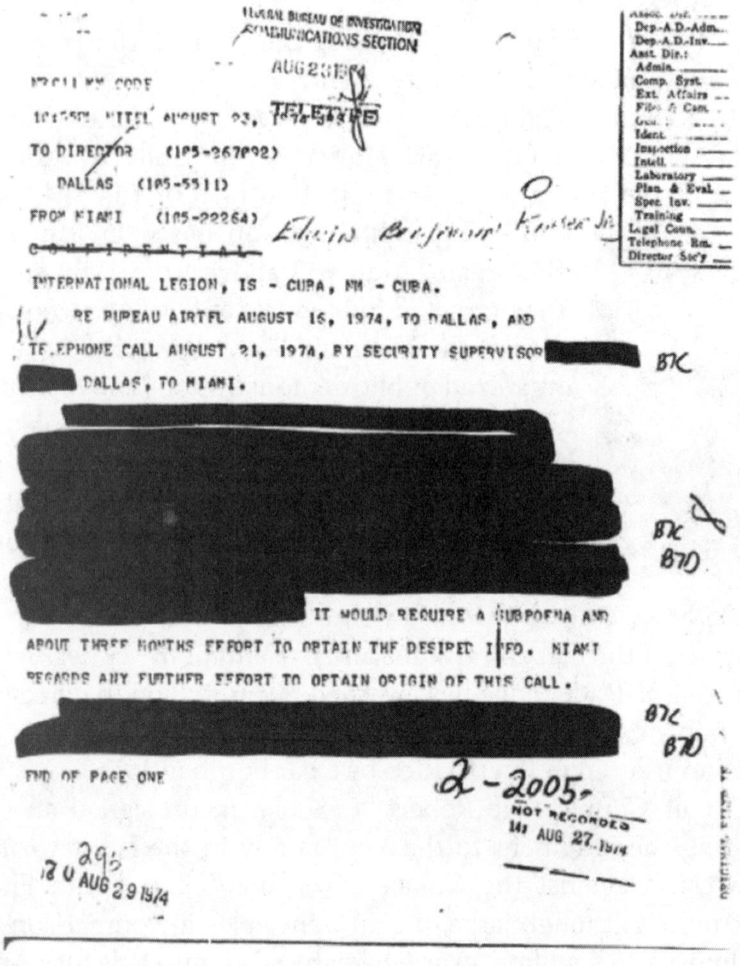

FEDERAL BUREAU OF INVESTIGATION
COMMUNICATIONS SECTION
AUG 23 1974
TELETYPE

Assoc. Dir.
Dep.-A.D.-Adm.
Dep.-A.D.-Inv.
Asst. Dir.:
Admin.
Comp. Syst.
Ext. Affairs
Files & Com.
Gen. Inv.
Ident.
Inspection
Intell.
Laboratory
Plan. & Eval.
Spec. Inv.
Training
Legal Coun.
Telephone Rm.
Director Sec'y

NR011 MM CODE

10:55PM NITEL AUGUST 23, 1974

TO DIRECTOR (105-267092)

DALLAS (105-5511)

FROM MIAMI (105-22264) Edwin Benjamin Kaiser Jr.

~~CONFIDENTIAL~~

INTERNATIONAL LEGION, IS - CUBA, NM - CUBA.

RE BUREAU AIRTEL AUGUST 16, 1974, TO DALLAS, AND TELEPHONE CALL AUGUST 21, 1974, BY SECURITY SUPERVISOR [redacted] B7C [redacted] DALLAS, TO MIAMI.

[redacted] B7C B7D IT WOULD REQUIRE A SUBPOENA AND ABOUT THREE MONTHS EFFORT TO OBTAIN THE DESIRED INFO. MIAMI REGARDS ANY FURTHER EFFORT TO OBTAIN ORIGIN OF THIS CALL.

[redacted] B7C B7D

END OF PAGE ONE

2-2005

NOT RECORDED
141 AUG 27 1974

29
70 AUG 29 1974

After several lines of scrubbed blackout information: "It would require a subpoena and about three months effort to obtain the desired info. Miami regards any further effort to obtain origin of this call."

As far as I know, my father was never in Texas. Then again, most everything in which my father was involved was not known to my mother. I only know what he told me before he died, and from accompanying him on certain tasks. Why would the Dallas CIA offices contact the Miami CIA offices with respect to my father? The memo could be in relation to any number of things or instances. There is one scenario that sticks out, and that is my father knew something.

Chapter Nineteen

Kissinger

In May 1975, my father told Sturgis that they planned to set up a phony assassination attempt on the life of Henry Kissinger, and make it appear as if the Cuban communists were responsible. This way they could then have an excuse to wage war on known Cuban communists in the United States. Sturgis thought that it

was a good idea, since Kissinger had played a dominant role in the United States foreign policy. He also pioneered the détente with the Soviet Union, orchestrated the opening of relations with the People's Republic of China and negotiated the Paris Peace Accords. Kissinger also played a role in the bombing of Cambodia and other American interventions abroad. Sturgis considered Kissinger a communist "lover" and to be the one leaking information to the press during the Nixon era.

Approximately four or five months later, my father again phoned Sturgis and told him that things were going "really big." He wanted Sturgis to do some gun running for him, which Sturgis refused.

My father said, "If you meet me at the Newark Airport and I hand you $2,000, will you consider?" To which Sturgis said, "No." My father said that he was "going to make a big hit" and indicated they were going to assassinate someone.

Sturgis asked the identity of the person they were going to kill, but my father would not tell him. My father said, "It's as far as you go. Does that give you a hint?"

Sturgis later told the FBI office that he did not know where my father was. He felt that my father may have gone back to Alaska

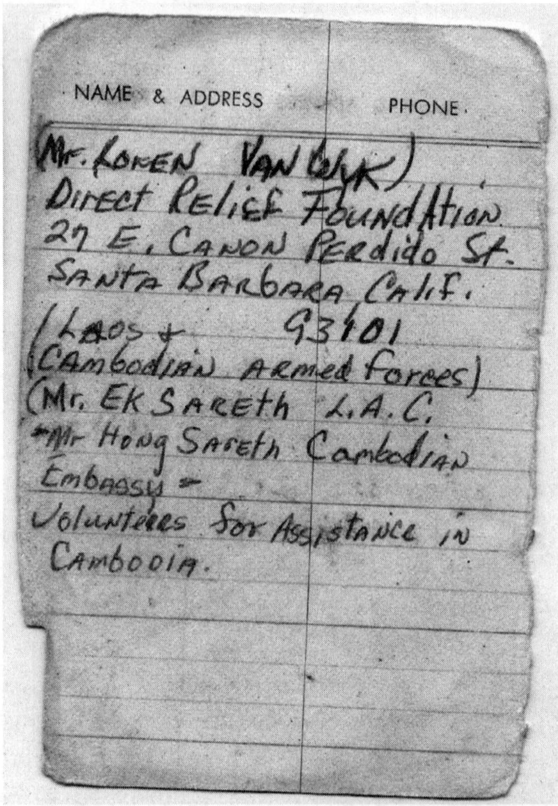

NAME & ADDRESS PHONE

(Mr. Loren Van Dyk)
Direct Relief Foundation.
27 E. Canon Perdido St.
Santa Barbara Calif.
(Laos + 93101
(Cambodian armed forces)
(Mr. Ek Sareth L.A.C.
*Mr Hong Sareth Cambodian
Embassy -
Volunteers for Assistance in
Cambodia.

where he was friendly with an Army Sergeant. Sturgis additionally described my father as a "crazy, paranoid, mental individual, who would kill, with no doubt, and is considered a dangerous individual."

Sturgis hadn't known that my father was arrested in Miami for carrying a gun. Sturgis said, "Kaiser always carried a .45-caliber hand pistol."

Sturgis said that onetime my father said, "When you contact me, use the name Ed Schmidt." He gave Sturgis the telephone number 305-443-0232. He told Sturgis if he were to ask for "Ed Schmidt," the person answering would be able to tell him where my father was at any time. He impressed upon Sturgis to use only the name of "Ed Schmidt" and not "Ed Kaiser," if he called this number.

OPTIONAL FORM NO. 10
MAY 1962 EDITION
GSA FPMR (41 CFR) 101-11.6
UNITED STATES GOVERNMENT

Memorandum

TO : ACTING DIRECTOR, FBI

DATE: 2/27/73

FROM : SAC, MIAMI (163-954) (RUC)

SUBJECT: EDWIN BENJAMIN KAISER
FPC
OO:Bureau

Re Miami letter to Bureau 1/24/73.

[redacted]

In the absence of specific requests for additional investigation, this matter is considered RUC.

2 - Bureau
1 - Miami
PCC:sl
(3)

REC-40
SI-114 47-55225-4

EX-PROC.

17 MAR 1 1973

61 MAR 1 2 1973

Buy U.S. Savings Bonds Regularly on the Payroll Savings Plan

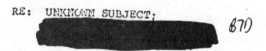

RE: UNKNOWN SUBJECT; [redacted] B7D

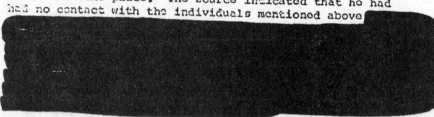

The source was unable to furnish any additional information relative to the individuals set forth above and he has no information whether this alleged plot will ever take place. The source indicated that he had had no contact with the individuals mentioned above [redacted]

B7C
B7D

Copies of this memorandum are being furnished to the United States Secret Service and United States Coast Guard, Miami, Florida.

This document contains neither recommendations nor conclusions of the FBI. It is the property of the FBI and is loaned to your agency; it and its contents are not to be distributed outside your agency.

2*

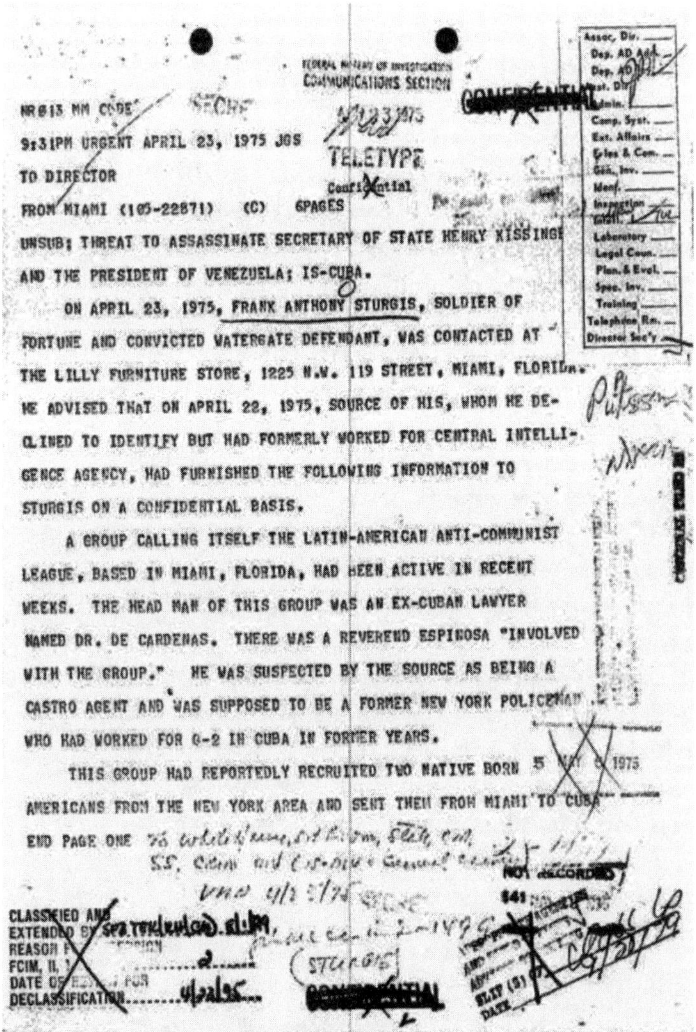

FEDERAL BUREAU OF INVESTIGATION
COMMUNICATIONS SECTION

CONFIDENTIAL

NR013 MM CODE SECRET

9:31PM URGENT APRIL 23, 1975 JGS

TELETYPE

TO DIRECTOR

Confidential

FROM MIAMI (105-22871) (C) 6PAGES

UNSUB; THREAT TO ASSASSINATE SECRETARY OF STATE HENRY KISSINGER AND THE PRESIDENT OF VENEZUELA; IS-CUBA.

ON APRIL 23, 1975, FRANK ANTHONY STURGIS, SOLDIER OF FORTUNE AND CONVICTED WATERGATE DEFENDANT, WAS CONTACTED AT THE LILLY FURNITURE STORE, 1225 N.W. 119 STREET, MIAMI, FLORIDA. HE ADVISED THAT ON APRIL 22, 1975, SOURCE OF HIS, WHOM HE DECLINED TO IDENTIFY BUT HAD FORMERLY WORKED FOR CENTRAL INTELLIGENCE AGENCY, HAD FURNISHED THE FOLLOWING INFORMATION TO STURGIS ON A CONFIDENTIAL BASIS.

A GROUP CALLING ITSELF THE LATIN-AMERICAN ANTI-COMMUNIST LEAGUE, BASED IN MIAMI, FLORIDA, HAD BEEN ACTIVE IN RECENT WEEKS. THE HEAD MAN OF THIS GROUP WAS AN EX-CUBAN LAWYER NAMED DR. DE CARDENAS. THERE WAS A REVEREND ESPINOSA "INVOLVED WITH THE GROUP." HE WAS SUSPECTED BY THE SOURCE AS BEING A CASTRO AGENT AND WAS SUPPOSED TO BE A FORMER NEW YORK POLICEMAN WHO HAD WORKED FOR G-2 IN CUBA IN FORMER YEARS.

THIS GROUP HAD REPORTEDLY RECRUITED TWO NATIVE BORN AMERICANS FROM THE NEW YORK AREA AND SENT THEM FROM MIAMI TO CUBA

END PAGE ONE

5 MAY 6 1975

NOT RECORDED

CLASSIFIED AND EXTENDED BY
REASON
FCIM, II,
DATE OF REVIEW FOR DECLASSIFICATION

CONFIDENTIAL

SECRET

PAGE TWO MM 105-22871 [redacted]

SEVERAL WEEKS AGO IN A BOAT ON CLANDESTINE OPERATION. THEY HAVE SINCE RETURNED TO MIAMI, BUT THE REASON FOR THE TRIP WAS UNKNOWN. IT WAS ALSO REPORTED THAT DR. DE CARDENAS HAD BEEN ATTEMPTING TO OBTAIN U.S. PASSPORTS FOR FOUR NATURALIZED CUBAN AMERICANS, IDENTITIES UNKNOWN. HE WAS ALSO TO TRY TO GET VENEZUELAN VISAS FOR THESE INDIVIDUALS.

DURING EVENING MEETINGS IN RECENT WEEKS, THE GROUP HAS DISCUSSED MANY THINGS. WHEN IT WAS REPORTED THAT HENRY KISSINGER WAS TRAVELING TO VENEZUELA, THE GROUP HAD DISCUSSED VARIOUS PLANS FOR CREATING SOME KIND OF AN INTERNATIONAL INCIDENT DURING KISSINGER'S VISIT IN VENEZUELA WHICH WOULD TEND TO DISCREDIT HIM AND THE PRESIDENT OF VENEZUELA.

AS A RESULT OF THESE REPORTED DISCUSSIONS, THE SOURCE HAD BEEN LED TO BELIEVE THAT POSSIBLY THESE PLANS MIGHT RESULT IN AN ASSASSINATION ATTEMPT ON KISSINGER WHEN HE WAS VISITING IN VENEZUELA.

STURGIS EXPLAINED THAT THIS SOURCE WAS UNABLE TO FURNISH ANY OTHER DETAILS IN CONNECTION WITH THIS INFORMATION AND NO OTHER MEMBERS OF THE GROUP WERE IDENTIFIED. STURGIS UNDERSTOOD THAT THE SOURCE HAD OBTAINED THE INFORMATION ABOUT THE ALLEGED PLANS FOR CREATING AN INTERNATIONAL INCIDENT INVOLVING KISSINGER THIRDHAND. THE WIFE OF A MAN WHO WAS

END PAGE TWO

SECRET

[redacted]

3

SECRET

PAGE THREE MM 105-22871 CONFIDENTIAL

CONNECTED WITH A MEMBER OF THIS GROUP HAD OVERHEARD HER HUSBAND TALKING ON THE TELEPHONE ABOUT KISSINGER'S VISIT TO VENEZUELA AND HAD REPORTED THIS INFORMATION TO THE SOURCE.

STURGIS ADVISED THAT NOW THAT KISSINGER'S VISIT TO VENEZUELA HAD BEEN CANCELLED, HE UNDERSTOOD THAT ALL PLANS "HAD BEEN ABORTED" AND THAT THERE WAS NO IMMEDIATE DANGER OR CONCERN. ALTHOUGH NO DEFINITIVE PLANS OF THE GROUP WERE KNOWN, STURGIS UNDERSTOOD THAT THE GROUP HAD ONLY DISCUSSED POSSIBLE PLANS FOR AN INCIDENT INVOLVING BOTH KISSINGER AND THE PRESIDENT OF VENEZUELA DURING SUCH A VISIT IN ORDER TO DISCREDIT UNITED STATES-VENEZUELA RELATIONS.

STURGIS POINTED OUT THAT THE CUBAN EXILES ARE ALWAYS TALKING, CONSPIRING AND PLANNING SOME SORT OF ANTI-CASTRO ACTIONS, BUT IT IS PRIMARILY IDLE AND HOPEFUL GOSSIP AND RUMORS THAT COME TO NOTHING.

STURGIS STATED THAT ALTHOUGH HE FELT THERE WAS NO IMMINENT DANGER IN THESE ALLEGED THREATS, HE HAD PROMPTLY REPORTED THIS INFORMATION TO AN ACQUAINTANCE OF HIS IN THE U.S. CUSTOMS AGENCY, MIAMI, FLORIDA. THIS U.S. CUSTOMS AGENT HAD ADVISED STURGIS THAT HE WOULD PROMPTLY REPORT THIS INFORMATION TO THE U.S. SECRET SERVICE, MIAMI, WHICH AGENCY HAD PROTECTIVE JURISDICTION FOR U.S. CABINET MEMBERS. ACCORDINGLY, STURGIS UNDERSTOOD THAT THIS

END PAGE THREE

CONFIDENTIAL

SECRET

PAGE FOUR MM 105-22871 [redacted]

MATTER WAS BEING APPROPRIATELY HANDLED BY THE U.S. GOVERNMENT.

SOURCES FAMILIAR WITH CUBAN GROUPS AND ACTIVITIES IN THE MIAMI, FLORIDA AREA HAVE FURNISHED NO INFO INOF INDICATING THE EXISTENCE OF ANY GROUP CALLING ITSELF THE LATIN AMERICAN ANTI-COMMUNIST LEAGUE.

ON APRIL 7, 1975, A CONFIDENTIAL SOURCE, WHO IS FAMILIAR WITH CUBAN COMMUNITY ACTIVITIES AND HAS FURNISHED RELIABLE INFORMATION IN THE PAST, REPORTED AS FOLLOWS:

ON MARCH 24, 1975, REVEREND MANUEL ESPINOSA DIAZ, MINISTER OF THE PENTECOSTAL CHURCH, ACCOMPANIED BY FOUR CUBAN EXILES, BOARDED THE BOAT "WAHININI II" AT KEY WEST, FLORIDA, WHICH BOAT WAS PILOTED BY ANOTHER CUBAN NAMED JOSE CARDENAS. THE GROUP CLANDESTINELY WENT TO THE NORTH COAST OF CUBA AND REVEREND ESPINOSA CARRIED A LIST OF OVER THIRTY THOUSAND CUBANS WHO HAD BEEN UNABLE TO COME TO THE UNITED STATES TO JOIN THEIR RELATIVES. REVEREND ESPINOSA HAD AN INTERVIEW WITH FIDEL CASTRO IN AN EFFORT TO ARRANGE THE LEGAL DEPARTURE OF THESE PEOPLE. (U)X

SUBSEQUENTLY, ON MARCH 31, 1975, IT WAS LEARNED IN MIAMI THAT THE "WAHININI II" HAD RETURNED TO MARATHON, FLORIDA, ESCORTED BY THE U.S. COAST GUARD. ON THE SHIP, IN ADDITION TO REVEREND ESPINOSA AND HIS CUBAN EXILE COMPANION, WERE TWO U.S. NEWSMEN

END PAGE FOUR

[redacted]

5

Chapter Twenty

Kaiser in Israel

In the early evening of January 7th, 1976, my mother and father got into an argument about Dad needing to go out of town for a few months. She said, "What am I to do with the kids all by myself? Scott needs to go to football practice and someone needs to pick up Elizabeth at her godparents. Why are you doing this now when we have lots of bills that need to get paid?" But Dad couldn't give her an answer.

Later that night, I heard some digging just outside of my bedroom window. I looked outside, and in the backyard I saw dad wrap his briefcase in a black plastic bag. He placed the bag into the hole he just dug under the avocado tree and covered it up. When my father came into the house, I asked, "Dad, why did you just bury your briefcase in our back yard?"

He was surprised at the question I had just asked, but even more surprised that I had seen him do what he did. He said, "Son, I buried it there to keep it safe, lets just keep this between ourselves Okay?"

I replied, "Okay, dad!"

The next morning we all got up as if it was another normal day. Elizabeth and I were getting ready for school, and Dad was walking out the door with Mom. She said, "Make sure your rides are coming

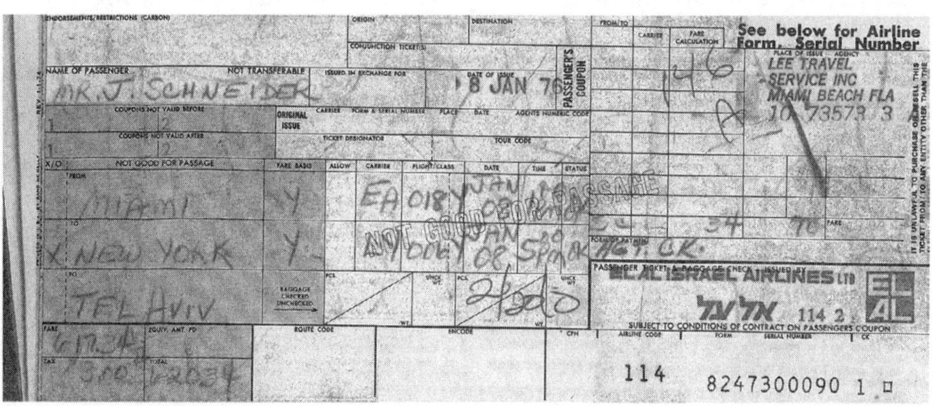

ENDORSEMENTS/RESTRICTIONS (CARBON)
ORIGIN
DESTINATION
CONJUNCTION TICKET(S)
See below for Airline Form, Serial Number
NAME OF PASSENGER NOT TRANSFERABLE
MR. J. SCHNEIDER
ISSUED IN EXCHANGE FOR
DATE OF ISSUE 8 JAN 76
PASSENGER'S COUPON
PLACE OF ISSUE AGENCY
LEE TRAVEL SERVICE INC MIAMI BEACH FLA
10 73573 3
COUPONS NOT VALID BEFORE 1 2
COUPONS NOT VALID AFTER 1 2
ORIGINAL ISSUE
TICKET DESIGNATOR
TOUR CODE
X/O NOT GOOD FOR PASSAGE
FROM MIAMI — Y — EA 018 Y JAN
TO X NEW YORK — Y
TO TEL AVIV
NOT GOOD FOR PASSAGE
BAGGAGE CHECKED UNCHECKED
FARE 617.34
TAX 3.00
TOTAL 620.34
FORM OF PAYMENT AGT. CK.
PASSENGER TICKET & BAGGAGE CHECK — ISSUED BY EL AL ISRAEL AIRLINES LTD
אל על 114 2
SUBJECT TO CONDITIONS OF CONTRACT ON PASSENGERS COUPON
AIRLINE CODE FORM SERIAL NUMBER CK
114 8247300090 1
IT IS UNLAWFUL TO PURCHASE OR RESELL THIS TICKET FROM / TO ANY ENTITY OTHER THAN THE

to pick you guys up for school, I'm taking your father to the airport, and I'll see you kids after I get out of work." My father was off on a El Al flight to Israel from Miami through New York.

A few months went by, and our family had received several letters from my father, letting everyone know that he was doing okay. He described how beautiful Israel was, wishing we could all see what he was seeing. He wrote, "It seems like a step back into time."

My little sister, Elizabeth and I just wanted our dad back home. Then my Mom received a letter that read: "I've been caught and I'm now in an Israeli prison, I'm hoping to see you all soon. Ed."

The FBI came over to the house, and they started to ask my mother questions: How did Dad manage to get to Israel? And how did he get a hold of a passport? They wanted to know if she ever saw him with a passport?

She said, "No! He told me that he had some unfinished business to take care of. I wasn't sure how he was getting to Israel. All I know is that he had a ticket to go, and he showed it to me. I thought that you guys might have given it to him. How else could he enter into another country?"

It turned out that ...

On January 9, 1976, Edwin Kaiser successfully entered Israel bearing a passport in the name of Jerome Schneider.

A CIA report on Kaiser was generated on July 8, 1976.

Edwin Benjamin Kaiser, Jr., aka Jerome Schneider,
Passport and visa matters - forged and altered passport.

Re: Bureau telephone calls July 7, 1976 and July 8, 1976 for illegally entering another country on a forged passport of Jerome Schneider. Kaiser altered a passport by removing Schneider's photograph and replacing it with his own.

The CIA was interested in my dad and a memo was issued on him, dated June 25, 1976. The memo was almost withheld/redacted in its entirety. The only legible text is, "This did not indicate sophisticated trade craft. The American Embassy in Tel Aviv has pouched Schneider's passport and forwarded it to the State Department. Schneider's passport was issued on August 10, 1971."

After spending two more months in the Israeli prison, the CIA placed him on a plane back to the United States. When my father arrived at JFK Airport in New York, he was arrested by two FBI agents. They handcuffed him as soon as he walked out of the tunnel from the airplane. My father was immediately transferred to the SDF (Southern District of Florida) and escorted back to Miami where they booked him into the Miami Dade County Jail. A few months later, he was released from the Miami Dade County Jail.

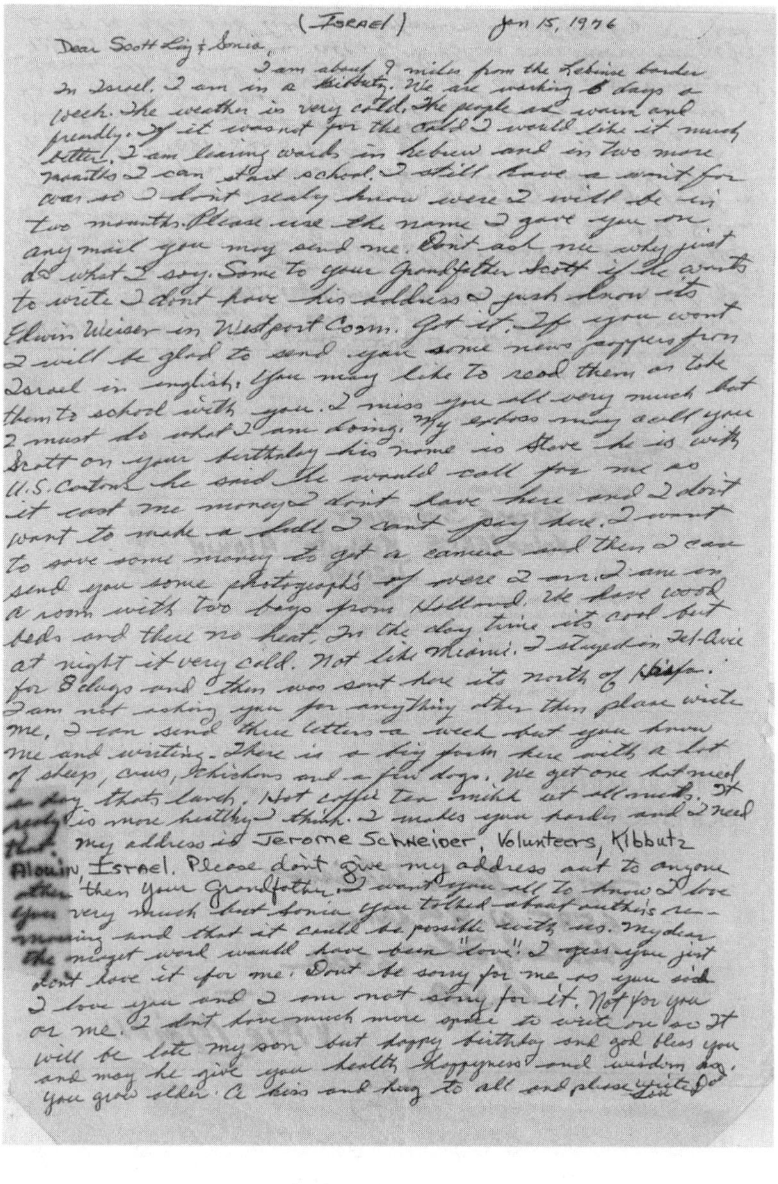
(ISRAEL) Jan 15, 1976
Dear Scott Liz + Sonia,
I am about 9 miles from the Lebanise border
In Israel, I am in a kibbutz. We are working 6 days a
week. The weather is very cold. The people are warm and
friendly. If it wasnt for the cold I would like it much
better. I am learning words in hebrew and in two more
months I can start school. I still have a wait for
war so I dont realy know were I will be in
two months. Please use the name I gave you on
any mail you may send me. Dont ask me why just
do what I say. Same to your Grandfather Scott if he wants
to write I dont have his address I just know its
Elwin Weiser in Westport Conn. Got it. Iff you want
I will be glad to send you some news pappers from
Israel in english. You may like to read them or take
them to school with you. I miss you all very much but
I must do what I am doing. My exboss may call you
Scott on your birthday his name is Steve he is with
U.S. Custom he said he would call for me so
it cost me money I dont have here and I dont
want to make a bill I cant pay here. I want
to save some money to get a camera and then I can
send you some photograph's of were I am. I am in
a room with two boys from Holland. We have wood
beds and there no heat. In the day time its cool but
at night it very cold. Not like Miami. I stayed in Tel-Aviv
for 8 days and then was sent here its north of Haifa.
I am not asking you for anything other then please write
me, I can send three letters a week but you know
me and writing. There is a big farm here with a lot
of sheeps, cows, chickens and a few dogs. We get one hot meal
a day thats lunch, Not coffe tea milk at all much. It
realy is more healthy I think. I makes you harder and I need
that. My address is Jerome Schneider, Volunteers, Kibbutz
Alouin, Israel. Please dont give my address out to anyone
other then your Grandfather. I want you all to know I love
you very much but Sonia you talked about authers re-
marring and that it could be possible with us. My dear
the magic word would have been "love"! I guess you just
dont have it for me. Dont be sorry for me as you said
I love you and I am not sorry for it. Not for you
or me. I dont have much more space to write on so It
will be late my son but happy birthday and god bless you
and may he give you health, happyness and wisdom as
you grow older. A kiss and hug to all and please write Dad
Love

[FPC] Finger Print Classification, apparently the FBI couldn't or wouldn't want to identify my father.

Dear Scott, Liz & Sonia,

I am about nine (9) miles from the Lebanon border in Israel. I am in a Kibbutz. We are working six days a week, the weather is very cold, the people are warm and friendly, if it wasn't for the cold I would like it much better.

I am learning words in Hebrew and in two more months I can start school?**** CIA School?**** I still have a want for war, so I don't know where I really be in two months. Please use the name I gave you on any mail you may send me. Don't ask me why just do what I say. Same to your grandfather Scott if he wants to write, I don't have his address I just know it's Edwin Weiser in Westport Conn. Got it! If you want I will be glad to send you some news papers from Israel in English you may like to read them or take them to school with you, I miss you all very much, but I must do what I am doing.

My ex-boss may call you Scott on your birthday his name is Steve he is with U.S. Customs he said he would call for me as it would cost me money I don't have here and I don't want to make a call I can't pay here, I want to save some money to get a camera and then I can send you some photographs, of where I am. I am in a room with two boys from Holland, we have wood beds and there's no heat. In the day time it's cold, but at night it's very cold not like Miami. I stayed in Tel Aviv for eight (8) days and then was sent here it's North of Africa. I am not asking you for anything other then please write me. I can send three letter's a week, but you know me and writing, there is a big farm here with a lot of sheep, cows, chickens and a few dogs. We get one hot meal everyday, that's lunch, hot coffee, tea, or milk at all meals, it's really more healthy I think. It makes you harder and I need that.

My address is Jerome Schneider, Volunteers, Kibbutz, Alouin, Israel. (The correct spelling would have been Alon, Israel), my father then goes on to say, "*Please don't give my address out to anyone*" other then your grandfather, I want you all to know I love you very much, but Sonia you talked about other's sin morning and that it could be possible with us. My dear the magic word would have been "love" I guess you just don't have it for me. Don't be sorry for me as you said I love you and I am not sorry for it. Not for you or me, I don't have much more space to write on so it will be late my son, but happy birthday and God Bless you, and may He give you health, happiness and wisdom as you grow older a kiss and hug to all, and please write. Love, Dad.

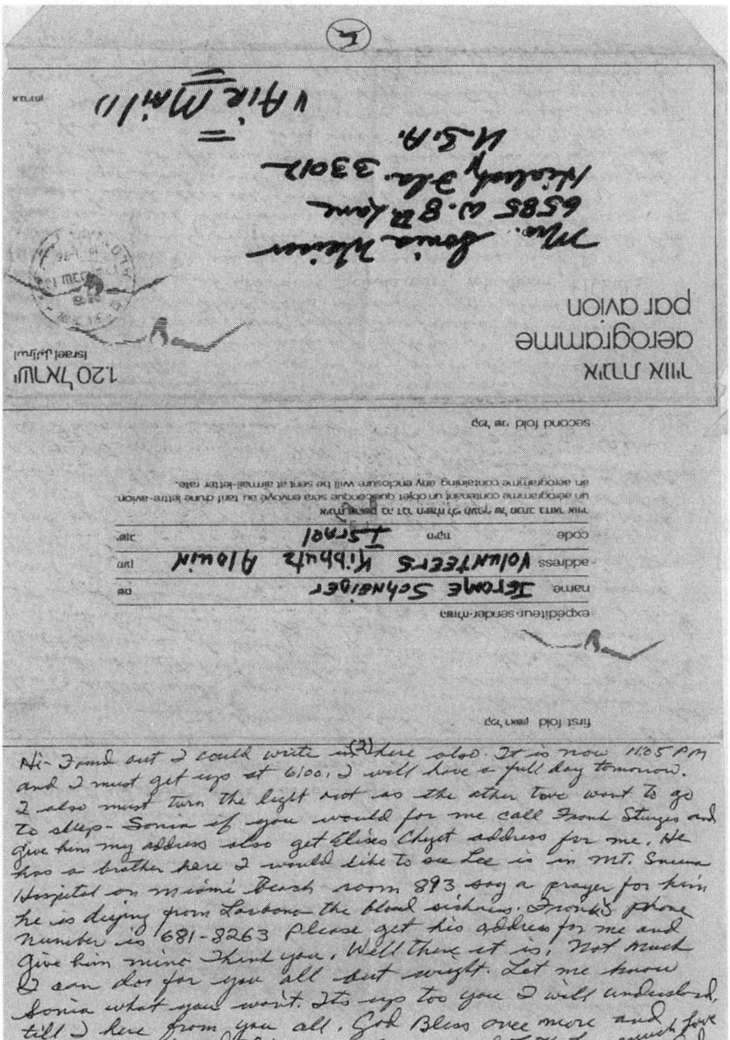
Mrs. Sonia Kaiser
6585 W. 8th Lane
Hialeah, Fla. 33012
U.S.A.
Via Air Mail

aerogramme
par avion
1.20 Israel

expediteur-sender
name Jerome Schneider
address Volunteers Kibbutz Alonim
code Israel

second fold

first fold

Hi- Found out I could write in (2) here also. It is now 11:05 PM and I must get up at 6:00. I will have a full day tomorrow. I also must turn the light out as the other two want to go to sleep- Sonia if you would for me call Frank Sturges and give him my address also get Eliss Chyet address for me. He has a brother here I would like to see Lee is in Mt. Sinai Hospital on Miami Beach room 893 say a prayer for him he is dying from Leukemia the blood sickness. Frank's phone number is 681-8263 please get his address for me and give him mine. Thank you, Well there it is, Not much I can do for you all but weight. Let me know Sonia what you want. It's up to you I will understand. till I here from you all. God Bless once more and Scott be good and take care Mom and Little Liz. much love Dad.

Hi- Found out I could write in (2) here also. It is now 11:05 PM and I must get up at 6:00. I will have a full day tomorrow. I also must turn the light out as the other love want to go to sleep - Sonia if you would for me call Frank Sturgis and give him my address, also get Elises Chyet for me. He has a brother here I would like to see Lee is in Mt. Sinai Hospital on Miami Beach room 893, say a prayer from him he is dying from Leukemia the blood sickness. Frank's phone number is 681-8263 please get his address for me and give him mine thank you. Well then it is not much I can do for you for you all but wait. Let me know Sonia what you want. It's up to you I will understand till I hear from you all. God Bless over more, Scott be good and - take care of mom and Little Liz. Much Love Dad.

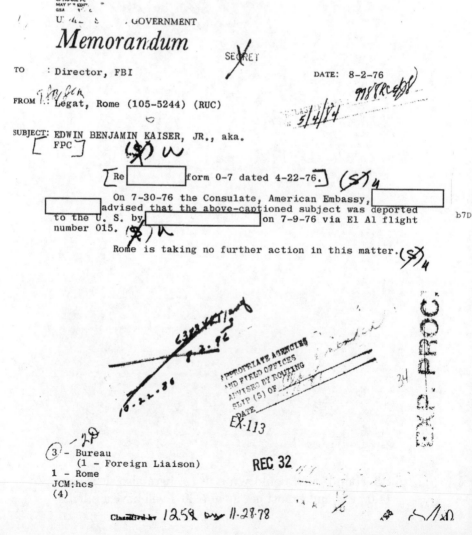

U. . . GOVERNMENT

Memorandum

SECRET

TO : Director, FBI DATE: 8-2-76

FROM : Legat, Rome (105-5244) (RUC)

SUBJECT: EDWIN BENJAMIN KAISER, JR., aka.
[FPC] (S) u

[Re [redacted] form 0-7 dated 4-22-76.] (S) u

On 7-30-76 the Consulate, American Embassy, [redacted] advised that the above-captioned subject was deported to the U. S. by [redacted] on 7-9-76 via El Al flight number 015. (S) u b7D

Rome is taking no further action in this matter. (S) u

APPROPRIATE AGENCIES
AND FIELD OFFICES
ADVISED BY ROUTING
SLIP (S) OF
DATE

EX-113

REC 32

EXP. PROC.

3 - Bureau
(1 - Foreign Liaison)
1 - Rome
JCM:hcs
(4)

Classified by 1259 Dg 11-28-78

What was known to my mother, was that my father was on a kibbutz. The kibbutz (Hebrew word for "communal settlement") is a unique rural community; a society dedicated to mutual aid and social justice; a socio-economic system based on the principle of joint ownership of property, equality and cooperation of production, consumption and education; the fulfillment of the idea "from each according to his ability, to each according to his needs"; a home for those who have chosen it.

My father was on a kibbutz for many months. We have several letters from him while he was there. We also have letters from my father's friends who remained in the Israeli prison, my father received these letters after he had been caught and returned to the United States.

An even larger anomaly is that, it seems, as though my father was making friends with Palestinians at the same time! This is evidenced by at least one letter from a young Palestinian Liberation fighter, who wrote to my father.

Was his time in Israel and overseas in general, a cover, or an exercise in infiltration of a group or groups? Below is an excerpt of a letter from that Palestinian Liberation Army resistance fighter.

In this letter (shown on next page), he is describing to my father the mindset of his people as well as the recounting of an incident in which he and his friends came upon a contingent of Israeli soldiers. This man is writing to my father in an attempt to have him understand the Palestinian plight. How did my father meet this man and in what context?

In an interview of Gerry Patrick Hemming, conducted by Alan J. Weberman, the following was revealed:

Frank Sturgis and Gerry Patrick Hemming knew what my father was doing in Israel. Hemming stated, "Ed Kaiser was doing a hit for a colonel in the Israeli Defense Force in Nablus, I flew the guy, he went with me around the Bahamas, he turned himself into the U.S. Marshals. We use their people and they use ours. Ed Kaiser was arrested as he was leaving". Hemming said, "Why was he arrested if the Israelis used him?"

Once he was captured and extradited, a report was generated by the CIA regarding my father This report dealt with identifying my father through known photographs and comparing them with the passport he used to enter Israel.

countries weapones to help us;
Let me tell you about whats happened
to me.(one of my Patroles);
or Before 3 years I was with my friends
we were armed when we were walking
across the fields we saw agroup from
the israelys army, we took our Places,
we went with them in fighting and
throughing the bombs at them which
exploed between them, we used our
machen guns, four 20 minutes and
we killed all of them who were 6. one
of us was died, we took his body in
our withdrawing and give him to his
famely and all the camp made to
him a celepration in burning him.
In same day all of his famely were put
in the prison and exploved his home and
stayed there for 9 monthes but his brother
still in prison. After that the Revolution
helped his famely.

To: Washington field office from Miami,
Matters: Forged and altered passport, three prints of each of the arrest photographs of Edwin Benjamin Kaiser, Jr. have been compared.

Our results of examination:
While some characteristics in common were noted between the photograph contained in the passport and the known photographs of Edwin Benjamin Kaiser, Jr. A definite conclusion could not be reached as to whether they are the same individual due to lack of specific individual identifying characteristics. Q1 and K1 are returned with a copy of this report to their respective contributors. [FBI-Photo Laboratory Investigation D-760716017 PN].

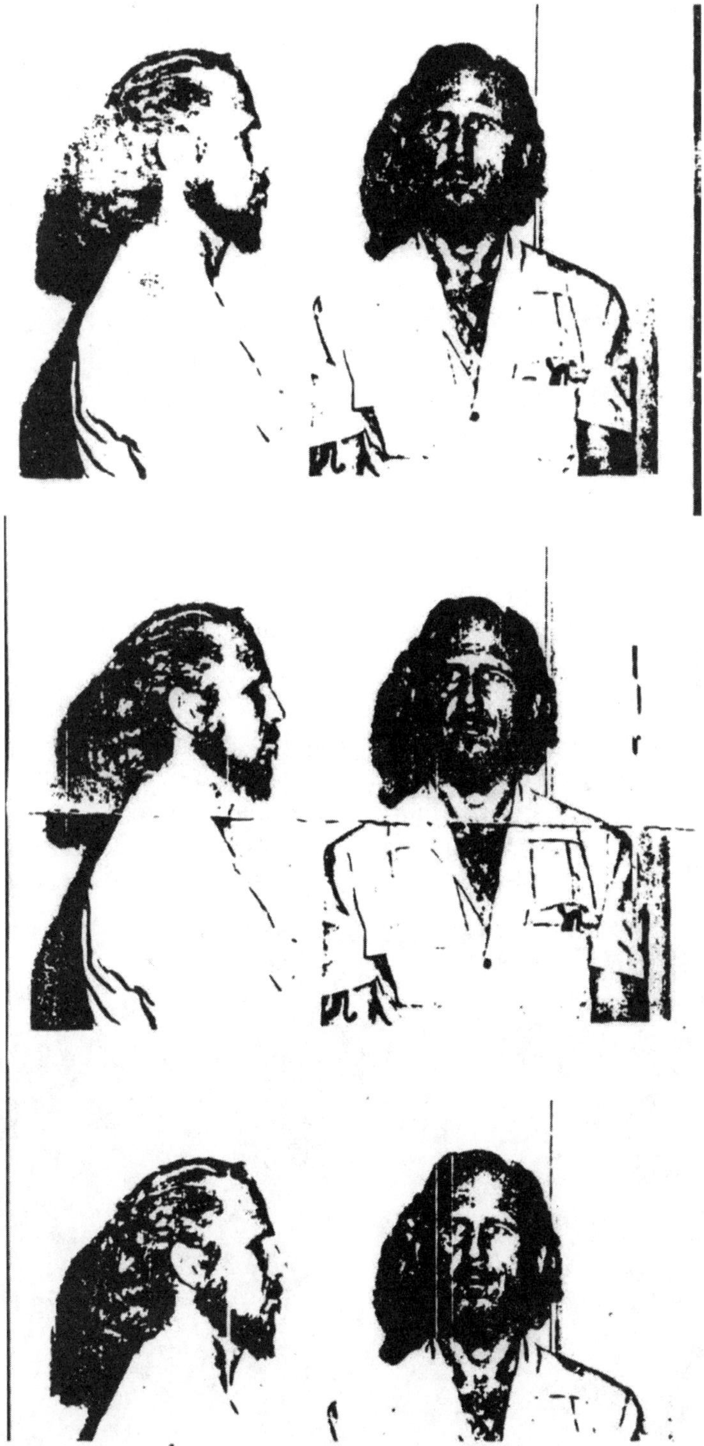

Even though my father was conducting actions that were ordered and sanctioned by someone at high levels, he was so far off the radar that our general government had no idea what he was doing. This did not help him when it came to the judiciary system.

Uncle Frank convinced my father that journalist Gaeton Fonzi could find a way to get out of his legal troubles. He spoke with Fonzi several times. Unknown to my father, his legal problems had already ended. The U.S. Attorney in Miami could not determine where my father had left, from the southern part of Florida or from some where else the U.S. (Despite the existence of the receipt of his plane ticket that I show on the previous page.) The District State Attorney dropped all the charges. A few days later two constables arrived at our home delivering a notice that all the charges were being dropped.

It should be noted that the judge that allowed my father to go free was Judge Palermo.

The following is a description of Judge Palermo from the *Legal Legends of Miami* web page:

> Judge Peter R. Palermo is a tireless problem-solver with a heart, and these qualities have served him well during his lifetime in the military, as a mayor to West Miami, and as a magistrate judge. In 1971, Judge Palermo was appointed among the first United States Magistrate Judg-

> es in the nation. Among his greatest achievements is his role in helping to establish and guide the growth of the new system.
>
> Today there are 587 United States Magistrate Judges in 89 District Courts throughout our country. As a United States Magistrate Judge, Palermo has testified before Congress on a number of legal issues from extradition to the Bail Reform Act of 1984. He has also had the honor of presiding over, and swearing in more than 600,000 new United States citizens at well over one hundred naturalization ceremonies throughout South Florida.
>
> http://www.historymiami.org/legallegends/past_events_09_nominees.html

It is interesting to me that Judge Palermo had presided over and sworn-in more than 600,000 new United States citizens throughout South Florida. What nationality do you suppose the majority of these new citizens held before they were sworn in, in south Florida?

Is it safe to say that he was a friend of the anti-Castro Cuban community, and may have helped my father get his charges dropped. My mother tells her knowledge of the events surrounding my father's trip to Israel in a FBI interview of Sonia Kaiser.

My mother was questioned at her place of business and she said: "He was in Israel and he was arrested for tapping wires, don't ask me whose wires, because I don't know. It's all on some arrest report that I have, he was not arrested entering Israel with a false passport, he had a false passport, that's true.

He was in Israel for quite awhile, I got letters from him. He sent letters to my children, his children. He was there on a kibbutz for a while. He was already living there. I had a lot of papers from him, and they were all stolen. All the papers that he gave me are now gone."

But all of the letters and papers were not gone. My mother had managed to keep the letters from my father in Israel. After all, they were written to the woman he still loved and children whom he loved more than anything else! Mom had kept them hidden from everyone.

Upon the charges being dropped, my mother couldn't believe what had just happened, she said, "Ed, not that I want you to get into any kind of trouble, but what the hell is going on here? How can they say that they don't know where you departed from? How could they not know? I'm the one that took you to the Miami International Airport, and you departed on the El Al Flight. I don't get it? What is it that there are covering up? What did you get yourself in to?"

But, my father didn't have an answer to give her.

That weekend my father dug up his briefcase that he had buried under the avocado tree and brought it into the house with him. Everything started to seem different, things weren't the same and our family started to fall apart. Mom and Dad were already divorced. Dad was dating other women and Mom had a new boyfriend. My sister and I were trying to figure out why everything was just one big fall out, and why our parents were no longer together. Just like in any other family having to deal with a divorce, what do you say to the kids?

I knew that Mom loved Dad and Dad loved Mom. Looking back I think it's because they just took life for granted. Not life, but maybe each other, and the love wasn't there like I remembered when I was a little boy. Although they were divorced they started living with each other again. I didn't care, we were just glad Dad was back.

Chapter Twenty-One

Dead Man's Cay

In the last months of my father's life, he was traveling quite extensively in and around the Bahamas. In particular and ironically, he spent a number of weeks or months on Dead Man's Cay. I have discovered legal pad pages detailing several day-to-day activities of his time on the island. He and one natives of the island were trying to form a co-op of some sort. They were canvassing the small island, talking to the residents, trying to raise an accord among the people in regards to the formation of this co-op.

These pages detailed his efforts on the island, right down to the penny but were still vague enough to not give away the motivations or end goal of his mission. It may have been a personal quest for my father. He was a man of great empathy and compassion. I believe that these qualities are what drove him to constantly search out oppressed people and fight for them, even at the sacrifice of his own family and his life.

Notes of my father's detailing his end of the week activities on Dead Man's Cay.

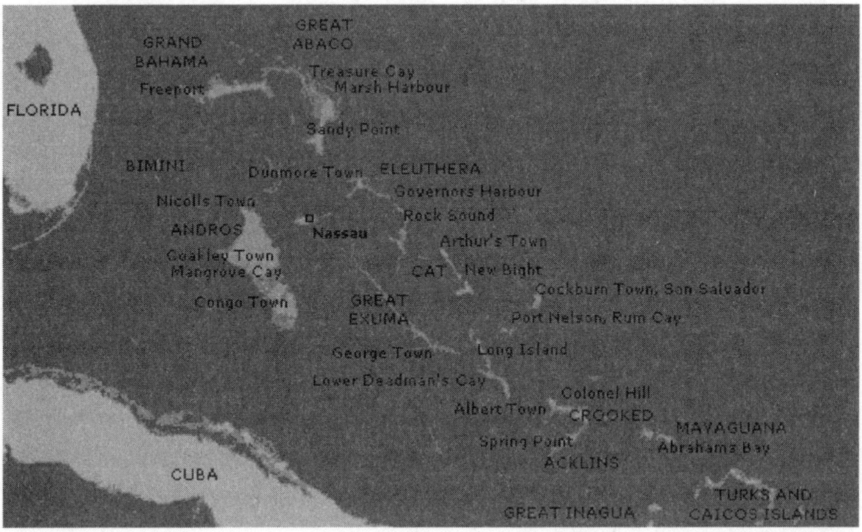

Went up North 68 miles to Howard Stoore talk to some people letting them know I was Comeing so the word would get around and more would come to meeting. then back Home Dinner at Mr + Mrs Salasz. Home to bed at 10:30 —

Sun Out early today went down to last settlement to make shore everone would be at the meeting but I am shore there will be the renny around that is also never after the meetings. My back is giving me more proplems now then yesterday I should stay in bed for a few days. Maby I will get some rest tomorrow. Maby not as Father Paul lissens to my plan on a co-op and he thinks it is a good Idia now that he knows the hole plan. Had dinner with him + Leas this evening. He said I could use his boat with motor to help and show the fisher men how to fish with the tosh. Had the last meeting to the South today and I hope Tuesday to pick up over a 100 more names for Nassau then. Things are going just fine step by step, and slowly even if I move fast. I have travelld over 900 miles by car since I have been here so you can see I am

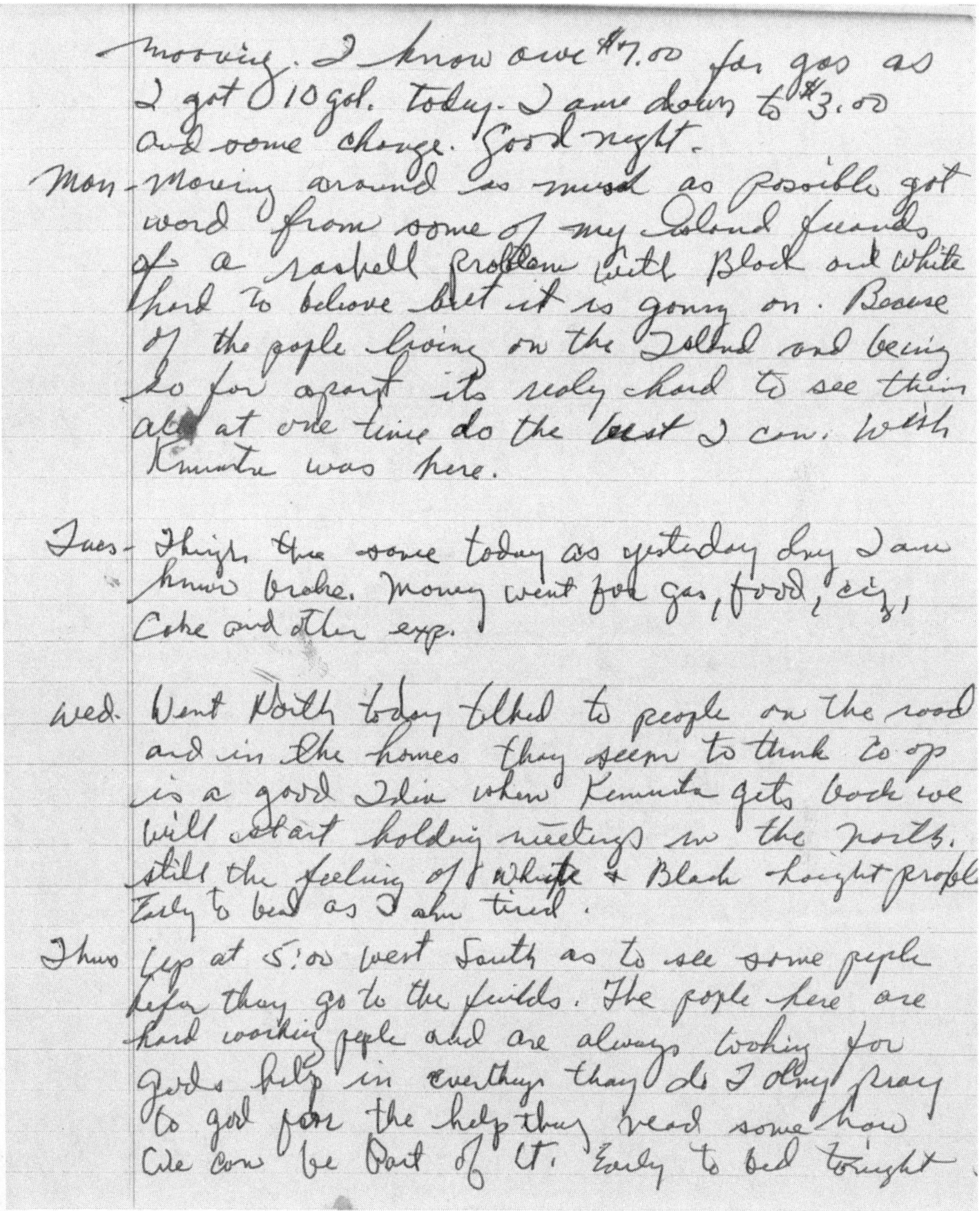

mooving. I know owe $7.00 for gas as I got 10 gal. today. I ame down to $3.00 and some change. Good night.

Mon - Moving around as much as possible got word from some of my Island freands of a rashell problem with Black and White hard to believe but it is going on. Becouse of the pople living on the Island and being so far apart its realy hard to see them all at one time do the best I can. Wish Kimmetu was here.

Tues - Things the same today as yesterday day I am know broke. Money went for gas, food, cig, Coke and other exp.

Wed. Went North today talked to people on the road and in the homes thay seem to think Co-op is a good Idia when Kimmeta gets back we will start holding meetings in the north. still the feeling of White & Black -haight people Early to bed as I am tired.

Thurs Up at 5:00 went South as to see some people befor thay go to the fields. The pople here are hard working pople and are always looking for Gods help in everthing thay do I alwys pray to god for the help thay need some how We can be Part of it. Early to bed tonight.

Last night I also had some problem (Small)
at the Kentucky Club. George Nores (Shorty)
Paul the greek's brother in law. Had some
Hard time explaining to me about "Don't help
these Niggers". As Paul the Greek's brother in law
put it. When Kimentan comes back we can
go and talk to the bastards in language they
may understand. I will take the white and
Kimentan can take the black that way there
can never be anything said and maybe they
can see that white and black can leave
togethe happy and along the way a mans
heart and his actions should be judge not
color. Going out the afternoon for Conch diving

Fri- Yesterday got 321 conch gave it to the Womans
club to sell dinners and raise money
to build a park they need shrubs concreet ect.
Things work out fine they raised over $200.00,
Was looking for the plane belt to no avail.
Worked with the people helping as much as possible
Looked at Father Pauls roof and will fix it when
the material comes in. Hopeing Monday or Tuesday.

Sat. Went North talked to the people meet some
other Americans who have been here for
3 months. They like the idea of a co-op
and I think they may be of some helps.
I find it hard to get people to gether as they
are so spread out. Some of the people in

Chapter Twenty-Two

My Father's Death

On February 7, 1977, just five days before my father's birthday, my sister and I had been planning a surprise birthday party for Dad. It was 6:30 a.m. I usually roused myself from bed closer to 7:00, and then leave the house about 7:15, because school didn't start until 7:45. But for some reason this day felt different.

My father entered my room and sat at the edge of my bed. It felt a little weird. He had never done that before. He would usually just get dressed and leave for work. My father asked me to go into the bathroom, and wash my face. I guess it was because he wanted me to be alert for what he had to say. I went back into the room and sat on the bed with my father. He said, "If anything were to happen to me, I want you to know, that your Uncle Frank isn't as nice as you think he is."

I just sat there on the bed listening to what he had to say. He said, "I want you to hear this tape." So he played it. I heard my dad and Frank talking on it. There was a section of the tape that really grabbed my attention. I heard Uncle Frank say, "I shot the president".

I asked my father, "What did he mean when he said, I shot the president?" My father replayed the tape and this time, I could clearly hear my father asking Frank if he knew what happened to President Kennedy.

Frank said, "I shot the president." I couldn't believe it. I was in shock. I didn't know how to react or what to say.

My father said to me, "And Frank wanted me to help him kill President Nixon too. Your uncle Frank said, 'Here, this is the gun I used to shoot Kennedy with.' Then Frank gives it to me. So I say to Frank, 'I don't believe you,' I say, 'Frank, I really don't know what to believe.' So Frank says to me, 'In case anything were to happen to me, I want you to have the gun.'"

I saw a frightened look on my father's face. He said, "And all this information I'm giving you, you mustn't tell anyone. I want you to keep this to yourself." He continued, "You don't need to be telling your mother, do you understand me?" Then he walked into the kitchen, grabbed some breakfast, kissed us goodbye and walked out the door. I didn't realize then, this would be the last time I ever saw him.

I continued to think about the tape my father had played that morning. I was thinking about it all day at school, and I wanted to tell someone. I wanted to tell my friends, but who would believe me? I was hoping time would just fly by. I couldn't wait to get out of school. I just wanted to go home. I was constantly looking at the clock, waiting for the bell to ring.

For some reason I began to feel sick to my stomach. When the sixth period bell rang, I was excited, hurried out of the classroom, and I started to walk home. I didn't get very far from school, when my mother's car approached. She stopped the car. My Aunt Dot was in the car. Both of them had glassy looking eyes, like they had been crying, but they weren't.

Mom said, "I have to go somewhere right now, and I'll meet you at home."

Something just didn't feel right. I started to wonder why my mother didn't give me a ride home, and where was she going? I started to think, "Why ... what was going on?"

I kicked a rock all the way home. When I got there, I looked around for dad. No one was at the house, I was alone. A few hours later my mother and Aunt Dot showed up. I was sitting on the sofa watching TV when my mother said, "I have something to tell you."

I sat on the sofa quietly as I watched tears coming from my mother's eyes. She said, "I can't."

My Aunt Dot said, "Your father is with your grandmother now." I didn't understand how my father could be with my grandmother if my grandmother was dead.

I said to my mother, "What is Aunt Dot talking about?"

My mother said, "Your father is in Heaven now".

That day, I remember was the worst day in my short thirteen years of life, it had started with a phone call to my mother at her work. My mother was crying uncontrollably as if she were gasping for her last breathe of air, she held me tight as she would cry, her tears hit my shirt like bullets as she said, "Your father is dead."

After I cried, I thought to myself what happen? My home is no more, my family is torn apart ... what is going to happen to us now? The security I once felt as a kid was now gone in a blink of an eye. The Christmas before my father was killed had I asked for a BB-gun and a bike. I got both, I always wondered, if I had asked for something less expensive at Christmas would my father still be around?

On the day of his death a hard knock on the door woke me up later that evening. The FBI was standing outside the front door talking to my mother. I looked up to the sky, as if I was waiting for something to happen, but nothing did. My mother had no family to lean on other then my Aunt Dot, who had accompanied my mother to the morgue to identify my father's body. But the "CIA" and the mortician would not allow my mother to say good-bye to her husband.

My mother had two children to support and raise on her own, without their father. I asked myself, "Why bother going to school or get good grades if my father is not around to see them?" Was I just being selfish, not wanting to please my mother? When I walked to school and saw the school buses parked at the front of the school I felt like throwing up.

A few days later, when I arrived home from school, I discovered that our house had been broken into. I had gone straight to my bedroom to play my guitar, when I immediately noticed glass on the floor and saw the screen ripped out of the window. That was proof to me that we had been burglarized.

I walked into my parent's bedroom, and the first thing I noticed is that the gun my father gave me was missing. The burglars had rummaged through my parent's closet and had taken everything, but the clothes and shoes. I called my mother at work and told her what had happen. She said, "Don't touch anything, I'll call the police, just stay there and I'll be right home."

When the cops knocked at the front door, I opened it, and noticed that the front door was unlocked. I let them in, and they asked if I had touched anything, I said no, so they started to dust for finger prints. They dusted my window sill where the burglars had most likely broken in.

The cop was able to lift a large palm print, but no finger prints. The cops repeatedly asked me if I knew what was missing. I didn't know how to answer them. I didn't know what to say about the rifle my father had given me for my birthday. All I heard, over and over in my head, was my father telling me *not to say anything to anyone.*

So, instead of mentioning the rifle, I said, "They took some jewelery" Then, because I noticed the front door had been unlocked when the cops arrived, it appeared to me that the robbers broke in through my bedroom window, and after robbing us just walked out the front door. They made it look as though someone was at home. I immediately caught on and went to my neighbors, asking questions. To my disappointment, no one had seen anything.

My mother said, "They didn't take the 8mm film that your father took at President Kennedy's funeral."

On February 7, 1977, Edwin Benjamin Kaiser, Jr. fell off some wooden planking while at work aboard a ship. The official report states that he died due to multiple injuries and blunt trauma to the head. He was 42 years old.

Sonia Kaiser said, "He carried a lot of papers and tapes in his attaché case. It was missing right after he died. I saw him with it in the morning, before he left the house for work. I know he had it. But the day he died I never saw it again ... after that, never."

In 1978 Gerry Hemming was asked about the death of Edwin Kaiser. Hemming said, "He fell on the job. The FBI didn't know what happened. The CIA didn't know what happened." Hemming said, "Sturgis didn't know. I saw Sturgis at the funeral that night. Nobody else was there. Hey, he could have just 'up and died? He had to get out from under this shit. All he needed was a phony death certificate. He was under investigation for a phony passport thing into Israel. He may have contracted to do a Middle East hit and gotten into trouble. He may be in Shangri-La!"

Mom had no doubt that her husband was murdered. "Someone pushed him into the manhole. I wasn't there, of course. But he told me that he was working on a ship that needed repairs, and there was an area on this ship that was dangerous. He said he had warned all his men that were working for him not to walk across the boards, because they were not safe for weight.

"Then they tell me that he walked across the boards and they broke and he fell in. I said, 'Why would he be so stupid if he's telling everybody not to walk across those boards, why would he be so stupid to do that?' They didn't know of course. Then I got a lot of strange visits from a lot of strange people and a lot of strange phone calls, like yours for instance, asking me questions."

These are photographs from the scene of my father's "accident." The position of his body seems a bit suspect to me. I am not an expert but a person who fell from a height of two stories, in my mind, would not likely land flat on his back with his arms resting on his stomach. At the very least, it looks as if he was moved. At the most, his death was faked, and he went into hiding somewhere.

About Edwin's death, Gerry Hemming said, "It wasn't a matter of pushing him into the manhole. I went to check on all that

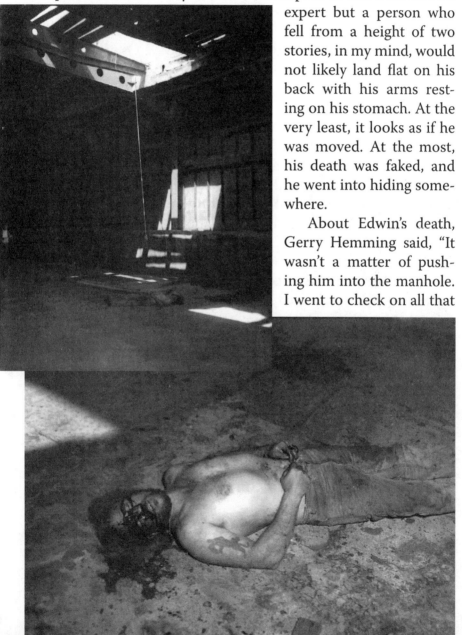

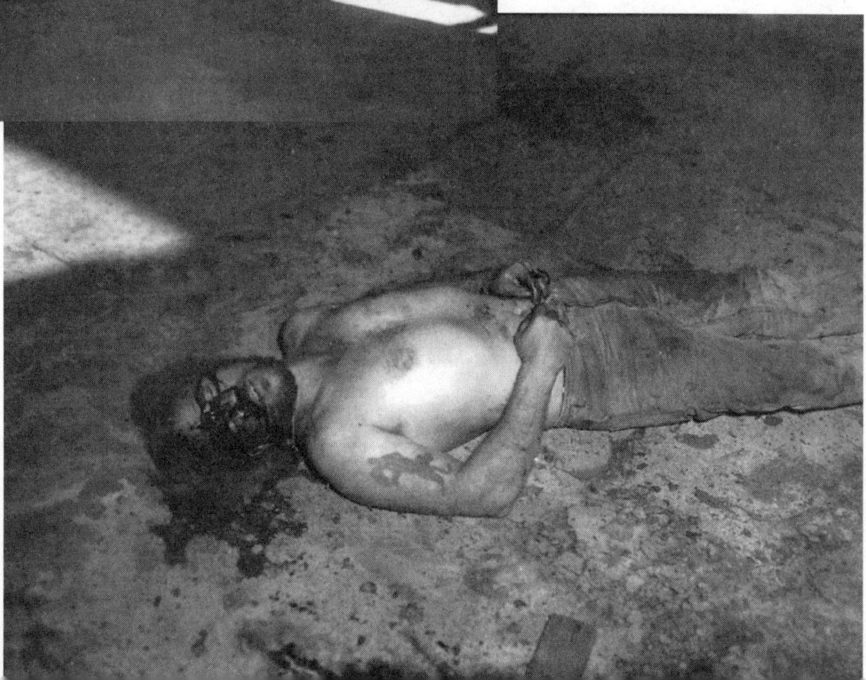

kind of bullshit. I went to the medical examiner's office. Dwyer was there. He ain't supposed to be dicking around in that territory, it ain't his case. Dwyer wants to know from me, did he fucking die? Was that him? What he stepped on, did it really collapse? He knew he wasn't supposed to step on it. It happened to another one of my other guy's about the same time, only he flew through the roof of the shithouse. Later, he overdosed on dope. People don't listen. Sturgis wasn't worried about being snitched out. Somebody knew that Kaiser was talking out of school. A criminal investigation was going on. They didn't want him testifying before a Federal Grand Jury. They took care of the situation. The guy had 'Oswald" stamped on his forehead.'"

I guess it is safe to say that the "in-crowd" knew why my father was murdered. If it was general knowledge that my father knew too much and was "taken out of school," then it would make sense that sinister forces behind the secrets may want to silence him.

After all, he was showing off pictures of the Watergate burglars, may have even been one of them. He had secretly training anti-Castro Cubans and had worked daily with some implicated in the JFK assassination. He also had little black books filled with names of important and infamous people.

If he did not know outright, it wouldn't be a stretch to believe that my father had developed a well informed, highly accurate theory as to who was involved in the assassination of JFK. Below is a discovery that I think details my father's theory on who ordered and carried out this brutal killing.

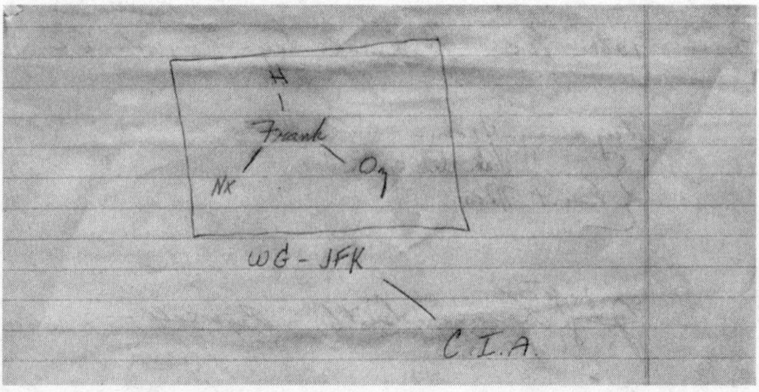

During the course of research, I came across this diagram on the back of a page in my father's legal pad. I almost missed it, but noticed it as I was removing the page from the scanner. One possible interpretation could be that, "Frank"=Sturgis, "H"=Hunt, "Nx"=-Nixon, "Oz"=Oswald and "WG"= Watergate.

My father used a yellow legal pad for a planner and daily journal. Most of these pages, plus numerous other items were stolen immediately upon my father's death. Luckily, they missed a few items. While removing one of the legal pad pages from a scanner, I noticed a diagram in pencil on the reverse. I was stunned. It didn't require a lot of speculation on my part to figure out what the crude diagram represented.

After my father's death, the FBI questioned my mother about his relationship with Frank Sturgis. She said, "Before Watergate Frank was at our house practically every day. But I never knew what they talked about, because they never talked in front of me. They would always be outside in the back yard. We used to go to Frank's house too."

At his funeral, I was sitting in the front pew waiting for them to bring my father's body out, but all I saw was a pedestal and this little box sitting on it. I wasn't sure what I was looking at, so I asked my mother, "Where's Dad's body?"

Mom said, "They cremated him."

I was thinking to myself, "Who are they?" Then I saw Uncle Frank. Gerry Patrick Hemming was also at the funeral that night. Nobody else was there, but the immediate family and my sister's godparents. Sturgis was standing in the back of the room, near the exit doors. I walked up to him and said, "Hey Uncle Frank, do you know what happen to my Dad?" He just looked down at me shrugged his shoulders and said, "I don't know."

A few days after my father's death, my mother consulted with three attorneys. They all refused to take the case. One of the attorneys said, "You can't sue the government." Approximately two weeks later, the CIA took the ship out into deep waters, blew it up and sunk it.

This is pure conjecture as to why they sunk the ship, I believe that the CIA was destroying evidence that could lead to the identity of my father's murderer. Given what my father told me, extensive research and the interviews available from A.J. Weberman, I believe whole-heartedly that Frank Sturgis played a large part in, if not single-handedly, killed my father.

I want to share one last story.

One afternoon, when I was thirteen, I was in the kitchen with my father. We were making sandwiches. I opened the refrigerator and accidentally hit my dad in the head with the door.

I heard a loud thud!

My dad was lying on the floor with blood coming out of his mouth, and he wasn't moving. I shook him and tried to wake him, but he wasn't responsive. I was terrified! I started to call out to my mother to come help me. Just then, my dad sprang up and started to laugh harder than I had ever heard him laugh. He told me to calm down. That it was only a joke.

"Its just jelly" he said.

I punched him as hard as I possibly could.

Appendix One

Bullet Points on the Life of Edwin Kaiser

- Ed Kaiser joined the United States Marines in 1952 and received a dishonorable discharge for assaulting his superior officer.

- Ed Kaiser then joined the French Foreign Legion in 1957 and lost his American citizenship for taking up arms for another country, his citizenship was revoked in 1959, and he was not allowed back into the United States. A letter from Mamie Eisenhower was received by my grandmother on April 10, 1959 indicating that she was doing all that she could do to get him back into the United States.

- Ed Kaiser landed in the United States in 1961 under a laissez-passer visa and was convicted of assault and theft of Government property, the sentences were later diminished..

- Ed Kaiser helped move his mother from Norwalk Conn. to Miami Beach Florida in November 1962. When he returned from Florida, he mentioned to his wife Sonia that he met several Cubans in Miami, among them were Frank Sturgis and Lee Oswald.

- Ed Kaiser moved to Miami in 1969, and over a period of time he was introduced to E. Howard Hunt, David Morales, Gerry Patrick Hemming, Mike McLaney, James E. Flannery, Gaeton Fonzi, Robert Dwyer, Frank Castro and many more.

- In 1969 Ed Kaiser helped to form an anti-Castro organization called Cubanos Unidos and used the *Miami Herald* newspaper as a way to communicate with everyone in the organization.

- Ed Kaiser's goal of the Cubanos Unidos was to form a Cuban government-in-exile in Haiti so that a new Cuban regime would take over after removing Fidel Castro. Ed Kaiser was the head of the military section of the Cubana Unidos. He also plotted the assassination of "Papa Doc" Duvalier.

• In 1971 Ed Kaiser wore a lieutenant's uniform impersonating an officer and used fraudulent military identification. He entered several military bases such as Homestead AFB, U.S. Coast Guard Base in Opa Locka, Miami and San Juan, Puerto Rico AFB. He was stealing weapons, grenades, guns, medical supplies and classified documents to supply his mercenary men in their training in the South Florida Everglades. He would also sell arms with Frank Sturgis in Nicaragua.

• In 1972 Frank Sturgis got Ed Kaiser involved with Watergate. Ed Kaiser collected information and secretly taped Frank Sturgis, as "they" were plotting to take out President Nixon and put Agnew in office at the Miami Beach Convention.

• Frank Sturgis unsuccessfully tried to recruit Ed Kaiser to help him kill innocent people and cause a riot between the VVAW and protesters at the 1972 Republican Convention.

• Ed Kaiser taped a conversation of Frank Sturgis confessing to the assassination of JFK.

• In 1973 Ed Kaiser testified before a Senate Select Committee on the Campaign Activities regarding the person or persons involved in financing the project called "Secret Eyes," concerning the demonstrations against the VVAW at the Republican Convention. Frank Sturgis refuted Ed Kaiser's testimony.

• In 1974-75 Ed Kaiser continued training his mercenary men for another invasion of Cuba.

• In 1976 Ed Kaiser successfully entered Israel under a false passport in the name of Jerome Schneider. A colonel in the Israeli Defense Force contracted Ed Kaiser to perform a hit in Israel, Ed Kaiser was caught wire tapping (Hemming said he knew this because he had flown him out of the country and around the Bahamas). The Israelis arrested Ed Kaiser, and the CIA brought him back into the United States. Ed Kaiser was later released in July 1976 on identical charges. The Florida State U.S. Attorney General could not determine whether Kaiser left from the southern parts of Florida or from somewhere else, so the U.S. Government dropped all charges.

• A CIA report on Kaiser was generated on June 25, 1976. This was withheld in its entirety. According to my father's friends in Miami my father was hired to assassinate the Prime Minister of Israel.Yitzhak Rabin, serving two terms in office, 1974–77 and 1992 until his assassination in 1995.

• The CIA reports on my father indicate he was caught for wire-tapping, my father was living there for three months until Frank Sturgis received word from my mother on the whereabouts of my father. Within a few days my father was arrested. Many believe that my father tried stopping the assassination of the Prime Minister of Israel by preventing the leftist wing groups from carrying out their plans. I believe that my father was set up.

• In 1977 Ed Kaiser was killed for holding onto too much information, it is my belief that Frank Sturgis killed Ed Kaiser, Hemming testified that Sturgis wasn't worried about being snitched out. Somebody knew that Kaiser was "talking out of school." They didn't want Ed Kaiser to testify before a Federal Grand Jury so Frank took care of the situation. Gerry Patrick Hemming said that Ed had "Oswald' stamped on his forehead."

• Sonia Kaiser was asked about her husband's relationship with Sturgis. She said, "Before Watergate, Frank was at our house constantly. Ever since my son was a baby, Scott would call Frank 'Uncle Frank.' Right up to the age of thirteen when his father was murdered on February 7, 1977. We would go over to Frank's house too."

Bullet Points, Son of Edwin Kaiser- Scott Kaiser

• Father: Ed Kaiser; mercenary, soldier of fortune, CIA contract agent, anti-Castro activist, weapons thief, illegal weapons seller, partner of Frank Sturgis.

• As a child Scott went to the Everglades many times and witnessed his dad and Sturgis testing and firing automatic weapons and detonating explosive devices for use in paramilitary operations.

• Witnessed his father wearing a fraudulent U.S. Military uniform with fake I.D. to gain entrance into Homestead Air Force Base Weapons Depot. Scott saw his father and Sturgis steal and load weapons into an El Camino.

• His father kept a closet with automatic weapons and grenades ready for immediate use.

• Scott lived in constant fear of unknown forces coming to his home and killing his dad and family. (No explanation was given for this).

• Their home was searched by the FBI, minutes after his father had fled with the weapons and explosives. His mother and children were left many times alone and frightened for their lives and the life of their father.

• Scott was constantly embroiled in devastating family arguments between his mother and father.

• One day when Scott was 13, his father told him about his work for the government and how his own life was in danger, He confessed to plotting an assassination attempt on Nixon with Sturgis. Ed Kaiser also confessed to Scott that Sturgis had admitted playing a part in a conspiracy to kill JFK.

• Ed Kaiser played a secretly recorded tape to Scott regarding conversations with Sturgis about killing JFK, and plotting to kill Nixon.

• Ed Kaiser constantly kept an attaché case cuffed to his hand.

• Kaiser revealed to Scott that no one could be trusted especially Sturgis.

• Kaiser was led to Israel for the purpose of having the CIA arrest him and retrieve the contents of the attaché case. In fact, Kaiser was arrested by the Israelites and brought back to the United States by the CIA where he served several months in prison without being charged. The contents of the attaché case were never recovered by U.S. Intelligence Agencies. Kaiser had buried it and Scott had witnessed this.

- After Kaiser's release, he was killed under extremely suspicious circumstances.
- Scott knew immediately that Sturgis had murdered his father over the contents of the case.
- The family lived in absolute terror for the next few years.
- Scott turned to a life of drug addiction at a young age.
- Scott enlisted in the Navy but was discharged after a fight.
- Scott used to play Russian roulette with a hand gun and was saved from suicide by his friends and a pastor.

Appendix

Documents

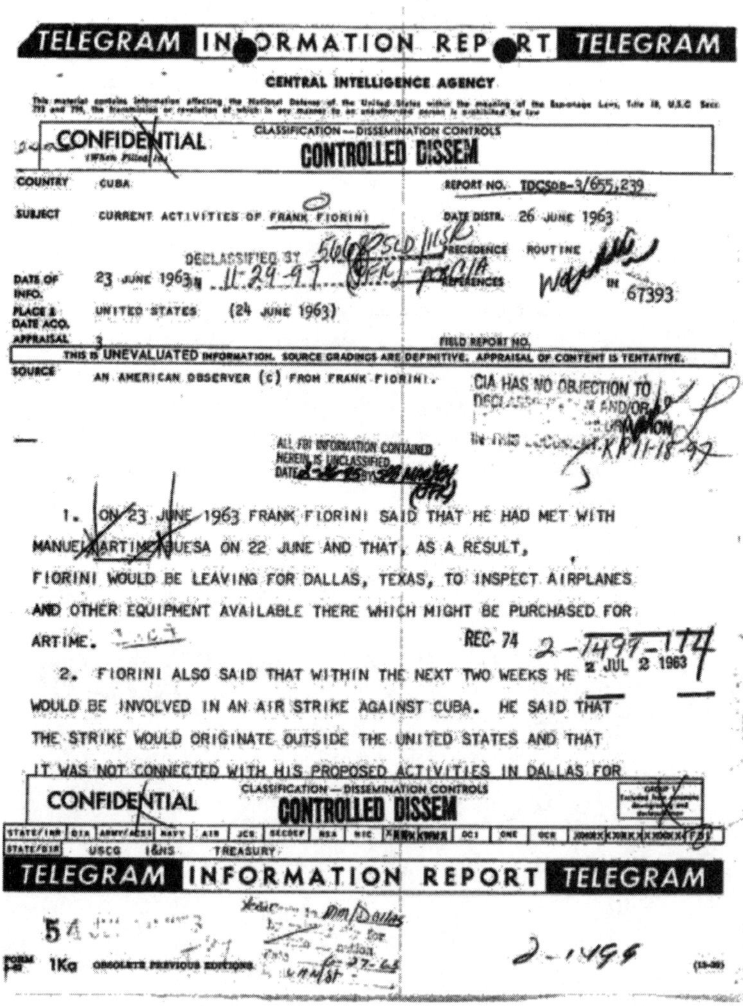

TELEGRAM INFORMATION REPORT TELEGRAM

CENTRAL INTELLIGENCE AGENCY

CONFIDENTIAL

CLASSIFICATION—DISSEMINATION CONTROLS

CONTROLLED DISSEM

COUNTRY CUBA

REPORT NO. TDCSDB-3/655,239

SUBJECT CURRENT ACTIVITIES OF FRANK FIORINI

DATE DISTR. 26 JUNE 1963

DECLASSIFIED BY ... 11-29-97

PRECEDENCE ROUTINE

DATE OF INFO. 23 JUNE 1963

REFERENCES IN 67393

PLACE & DATE ACQ. UNITED STATES (24 JUNE 1963)

APPRAISAL 3

FIELD REPORT NO.

THIS IS UNEVALUATED INFORMATION. SOURCE GRADINGS ARE DEFINITIVE. APPRAISAL OF CONTENT IS TENTATIVE.

SOURCE AN AMERICAN OBSERVER (C) FROM FRANK FIORINI.

CIA HAS NO OBJECTION TO DECLASSIFICATION AND/OR RELEASE OF CIA INFORMATION IN THIS DOCUMENT. 11-18-97

ALL FBI INFORMATION CONTAINED HEREIN IS UNCLASSIFIED

1. ON 23 JUNE 1963 FRANK FIORINI SAID THAT HE HAD MET WITH MANUEL ARTIME BUESA ON 22 JUNE AND THAT, AS A RESULT, FIORINI WOULD BE LEAVING FOR DALLAS, TEXAS, TO INSPECT AIRPLANES AND OTHER EQUIPMENT AVAILABLE THERE WHICH MIGHT BE PURCHASED FOR ARTIME.

REC- 74 2-1499-174

2 JUL 2 1963

2. FIORINI ALSO SAID THAT WITHIN THE NEXT TWO WEEKS HE WOULD BE INVOLVED IN AN AIR STRIKE AGAINST CUBA. HE SAID THAT THE STRIKE WOULD ORIGINATE OUTSIDE THE UNITED STATES AND THAT IT WAS NOT CONNECTED WITH HIS PROPOSED ACTIVITIES IN DALLAS FOR

CONFIDENTIAL

CLASSIFICATION—DISSEMINATION CONTROLS

CONTROLLED DISSEM

STATE/INR DIA ARMY/ACSI NAVY AIR JCS SECDEF NSA NIC OCI ONE OCR

STATE/DIR USCG I&NS TREASURY

TELEGRAM INFORMATION REPORT TELEGRAM

FORM 1-63 1Ka OBSOLETE PREVIOUS EDITIONS.

2-1499

CIA Telegram describing the activities of Frank Fiorini (Sturgis) and Manuel Artime (brigade 2056) in and around the Dallas, TX area in June of 1963. These activities involved inspection of planes and other equipment for purchase by Artime. This document also discusses Fiorini's plan for an airstrike (from outside US) on CUBA and the fact that it would not be connected to Fiorini's proposed activities in Dallas for...?

1 - V. Kolombatovic
1 - E. Smith
1 - R. W. Feuer

CODE TELETYPE NITEL

TO LEGAT, TEL AVIV (105-1392) MARCH 10, 1976

FROM DIRECTOR, FBI

EDWIN BENJAMIN KAISER, JR., AKA; [FPC]

RETELTELS MARCH 3 AND 4, 1976, CAPTIONED WITH CHARACTER IS - ME. CHARACTER HAS BEEN CHANGED TO [FPC]

BUREAU FILES DISCLOSE THAT EDWIN BENJAMIN KAISER, JR. WAS BORN FEBRUARY 12, 1935, AT NORWALK, CONNECTICUT. HE HAS AN EXTENSIVE PRIOR ARREST RECORD UNDER FBI NUMBER 243 334B WHICH INCLUDES ARRESTS FROM 1952 THROUGH 1975, ON NUMEROUS CRIMINAL CHARGES INCLUDING BURGLARY AND LARCENY, AGGRAVATED ASSAULT, ASSAULT WITH A DEADLY WEAPON, THEFT OF GOVERNMENT PROPERTY, POSSESSION OF DRUGS, BREACH OF PEACE, DRINKING IN PUBLIC, RESISTING ARREST WITH VIOLENT ASSAULT AND BATTERY ON POLICE OFFICER, PASSING WORTHLESS CHECKS, ETC. HIS ARRESTS TOOK PLACE THROUGHOUT THE UNITED STATES, FROM ALASKA TO FLORIDA. (U)

RECORDS OF THE IMMIGRATION AND NATURALIZATION SERVICE DISCLOSE THAT IN A SWORN STATEMENT KAISER STATED HE ENLISTED IN THE FRENCH FOREIGN LEGION AND SERVED IN THAT ORGANIZATION FROM AUGUST 31, 1957, TO DECEMBER 12, 1958. IN AN INTERVIEW

RWF:cap
(5)

SEE NOTE PAGE 4

FEDERAL BUREAU OF INVESTIGATION
COMMUNICATIONS SECTION

TELETYPE

CIA HAS NO OBJECTION TO DECLASSIFICATION AND/OR RELEASE OF CIA INFORMATION IN THIS DOCUMENT.

56 APR 22 1976

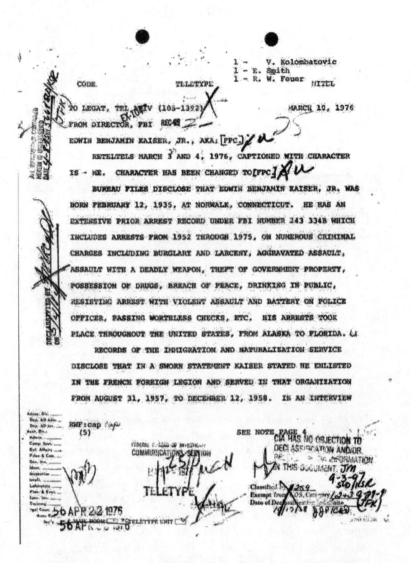

March 1976 Letter from The Director of the FBI to the Legal Attaché in Tel Aviv, Israel, concerning the identification of Edwin Benjamin Kaiser, Jr

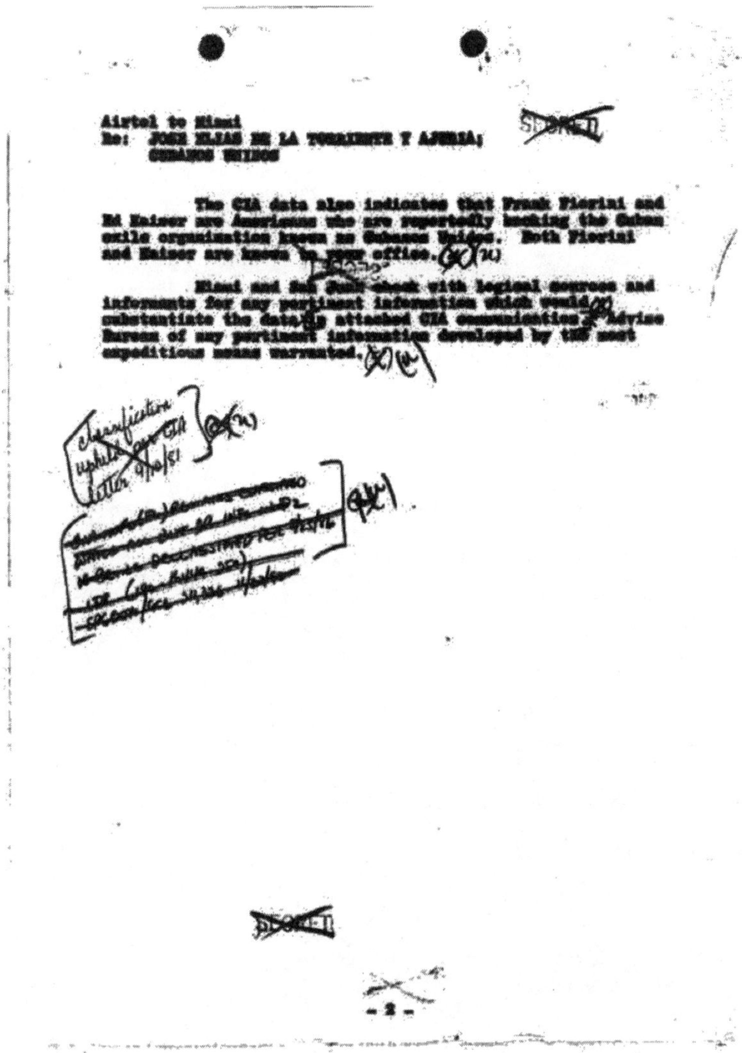

SECRET

Airtel to Miami
Re: JOSE ELIAS DE LA TORRIENTE Y ABRIA;
CUBANOS UNIDOS

The CIA data also indicates that Frank Fiorini and Ed Kaiser are Americans who are reportedly backing the Cuban exile organization known as Cubanos Unidos. Both Fiorini and Kaiser are known to your office. (X) (U)

Miami and San Juan check with logical sources and informants for any pertinent information which would substantiate the data in attached CIA communication. Advise Bureau of any pertinent information developed by the most expeditious means warranted. (X) (U)

classification upheld per CIA letter 9/10/81

SECRET

- 2 -

Airtel correspondence confirming that Edwin Kaiser and Frank Fiorini (Sturgis) were known to the CIA and were heading up the anti-Castro Cuban group called Cubanos Unidos.

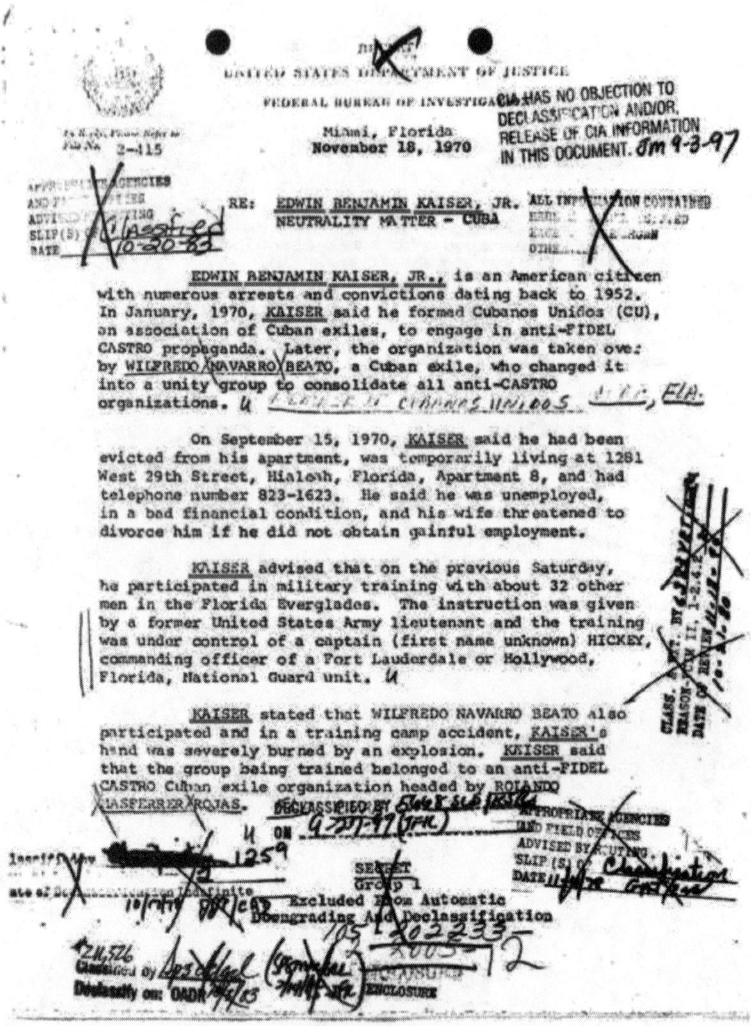
UNITED STATES DEPARTMENT OF JUSTICE

FEDERAL BUREAU OF INVESTIGATION

CIA HAS NO OBJECTION TO DECLASSIFICATION AND/OR RELEASE OF CIA INFORMATION IN THIS DOCUMENT. 9-3-97

In Reply, Please Refer to File No. 2-415

Miami, Florida
November 18, 1970

RE: EDWIN BENJAMIN KAISER, JR.
NEUTRALITY MATTER - CUBA

EDWIN BENJAMIN KAISER, JR., is an American citizen with numerous arrests and convictions dating back to 1952. In January, 1970, KAISER said he formed Cubanos Unidos (CU), an association of Cuban exiles, to engage in anti-FIDEL CASTRO propaganda. Later, the organization was taken over by WILFREDO NAVARRO BEATO, a Cuban exile, who changed it into a unity group to consolidate all anti-CASTRO organizations. U

On September 15, 1970, KAISER said he had been evicted from his apartment, was temporarily living at 1281 West 29th Street, Hialeah, Florida, Apartment 8, and had telephone number 823-1623. He said he was unemployed, in a bad financial condition, and his wife threatened to divorce him if he did not obtain gainful employment.

KAISER advised that on the previous Saturday, he participated in military training with about 32 other men in the Florida Everglades. The instruction was given by a former United States Army lieutenant and the training was under control of a captain (first name unknown) HICKEY, commanding officer of a Fort Lauderdale or Hollywood, Florida, National Guard unit. U

KAISER stated that WILFREDO NAVARRO BEATO also participated and in a training camp accident, KAISER's hand was severely burned by an explosion. KAISER said that the group being trained belonged to an anti-FIDEL CASTRO Cuban exile organization headed by ROLANDO MASFERRER ROJAS.

DECLASSIFIED BY ... ON 9-23-97 (JFK)

[redacted] 1259

SECRET
Group 1
Excluded From Automatic Downgrading And Declassification

105-202233-
2-2005-72

ENCLOSURE

Airtel correspondence confirming that Edwin Kaiser and Frank Fiorini (Sturgis) were known to the CIA and were heading up the anti-Castro Cuban group called Cubanos Unidos.

SECRET - NO FOREIGN DISSEMINATION

RE: CUBANOS UNIDOS
(UNITED CUBANS)

They advised that PILIN MENDOZA, a well-known figure in the Cuban Authentic Party in exile, is closely associated with CARLOS PRIO SOCARRAS, former President of Cuba and head of the Authentic Party. MENDOZA said that PRIO would make a $1,000 contribution to CU. CU refused the contribution for fear PRIO would attempt to take over the organization at some later time.

He also stated that JUANITA CASTRO, sister of FIDEL CASTRO RUZ, present Prime Minister of Cuba, told the CU that she has United States Government backing and offered to furnish money and arms to CU. CU refused the offer because JUANITA CASTRO reportedly is not to be trusted and has a bad reputation in the Cuban exile community.

On July 9, 1970, MM T-4, a Cuban exile closely associated with CU members, advised that WILFREDO NAVARRO frequently travels to Washington, D. C., seeking United States Government aid. NAVARRO also claims to have land outside the United States which can be used as a training camp site and from which an invasion of Cuba can be launched.

MM T-4 said that NAVARRO recently contacted Miami Radio Station WQBA and claimed that CU was operating a large scale training camp. NAVARRO invited newsmen to visit the camp in a CU airplane and photograph the installation. The newsmen accepted the invitation, but NAVARRO has not gone forward in making any further arrangements for the visit.

MM T-4 said that the newsmen feel there is no such training camp and NAVARRO was attempting to obtain free press publicity.

On July 29, 1970, MM T-5, another Government agency which conducts intelligence investigations, reported that CU was planning an armed expedition to Cuba and the following individuals are principals in the operation:

5.

SECRET - NO FOREIGN DISSEMINATION

US Department of Justice / FBI document from 1970 regarding Edwin Benjamin Kaiser and his participation in military training in the FL Everglades. During this training, Kaiser was injured in an explosion.

SECRET - NO FOREIGN DISSEMINATION

RE: CUBANOS UNIDOS
(UNITED CUBANS)

REVIEWED BY Army/JFK TASK FORCE
ON 7/8/98
☒ RELEASE IN FULL
☐ RELEASE IN PART
☐ TOTAL DENIAL

BOB RAMEY (phonetic), a commentator on Channel 4 TV, Miami, who will travel with WILFREDO NAVARRO.

WILFREDO NAVARRO, leader of CU.

JORGE NAVARRO, brother of WILFREDO and designated Naval Chief of CU.

(First Name Unknown) RODRIGUEZ ALONSO, designated Military Chief of CU.

GORDON DI BATTISTO, an Italian having Mafia connections.

EDWIN KAISER, reportedly with "U.S. French Legion".

MAURICIO FERRE, reportedly provides financial backing to WILFREDO NAVARRO.

PILIN MENDOZA, a friend of JOSE FERRE. (X)

[MM T-5] indicated that it was intended that mercenaries from Corsica would be used. (X)(u)

On July 29, 1970, EDWIN BENJAMIN KAISER, JR., 805 West 30th Street, Hialeah, Florida, advised that he knew no one named BOB RAMEY or (First Name Unknown) RODRIGUEZ ALONSO. KAISER said that he had previously been in the French Foreign Legion and knows former legionnaires who now live in all parts of the world. Many of these legionnaires would fight as mercenaries if contacted, but at the present time neither he nor CU has any plans to contact these people and does not have the funds to pay them or the military equipment to issue them. KAISER said that WILFREDO NAVARRO is a long-time friend of Miami City Commissioner, MAURICE FERRE, and the nature of their relationship is business interests.

KAISER advised he continues to be active in CU

6.

SECRET - NO FOREIGN DISSEMINATION

SECRET - NO FOREIGN DISSEMINATION

RE: CUBANOS UNIDOS
(UNITED CUBANS)

and may be considered one of the persons in charge of military operations for CU. He said he had recently been in contact with HERNANDO ENRIQUEZ in the Dominican Republic, who is in a position to order arms from Europe. If CU agrees to buy such equipment, delivery would be made outside the United States.

KAISER said that CU presently has a .50 caliber machine gun, a .30 caliber machine gun, some C-4 explosive, and a quantity of small arms. CU is considering a three-day infiltration and sabotage mission to Cuba in which about five men will participate. One of the tactics they plan to use is to kill a few Cuban Government soldiers and cut them up into small pieces to terrify other Cuban Government soldiers.

On July 30, 1970, KAISER advised he was then leaving for the Island of Martinique in the Caribbean where he would try to make arrangements to set up a military base for operations against Cuba.

On August 3, 1970, KAISER advised he had just returned from the Island of Martinique where he was arrested and questioned for 28 hours by French intelligence officials before he was released. The purpose of the visit was to obtain permission to set up a base for operations against Cuba. French authorities told him they would cooperate with him if and when he obtained such permission from the United States Government.

KAISER said his present military plans involve an operation which would leave the Florida keys by boat and attack the Cuban Naval Academy near Havana. About twelve persons would participate in the raid and after the mission, would return to the Florida keys. After about two days in the Florida keys, they would return to sea to meet a mother ship and then go to Haiti. KAISER said the military mission would leave the Florida area with arms and explosives aboard.

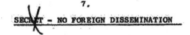

7.

SECRET - NO FOREIGN DISSEMINATION

For any of you interested in the Corsican connection to the JFK assassination, this document makes mention of an informant citing the intended use of mercenaries from Corsica in the anti-Castro activities of Cubanos Unidos.

[ELIAS CHAJET]

SAM J. ERVIN, JR., N.C., CHAIRMAN
HOWARD H. BAKER, JR., TENN., VICE CHAIRMAN
HERMAN E. TALMADGE, GA. EDWARD J. GURNEY, FLA.
DANIEL K. INOUYE, HAWAII LOWELL P. WEICKER, JR., CONN.
JOSEPH M. MONTOYA, N. MEX.

SAMUEL DASH
CHIEF COUNSEL AND STAFF DIRECTOR
FRED D. THOMPSON
MINORITY COUNSEL
RUFUS L. EDMISTEN
DEPUTY COUNSEL

United States Senate
SELECT COMMITTEE ON
PRESIDENTIAL CAMPAIGN ACTIVITIES
(PURSUANT TO S. RES. 60, 93D CONGRESS)
WASHINGTON, D.C. 20510

MEMORANDUM

TO: Fred D. Thompson
FROM: Howard Liebengood
DATE: June 12, 1974
SUBJECT: DIGEST OF INTERVIEW WITH ELIAS CHAJET
RE: STURGIS/ANDERSON

Elias Chajet, 48 years old, was interviewed by the writer at his Miami Beach, Florida home on July 11, 1973, in the presence of William M. Howell and Edwin B. Kaiser. Chajet was born in Havana, Cuba; has resided continuously in the United States since 1954; and has been a United States citizen since 1959.

Chajet has known Frank Sturgis well for two years, having first met Sturgis shortly after Chajet founded CHIPP (Citizens' Help for International Political Prisoners) in May of 1971. Sturgis was active in CHIPP, which Chajet described as a humanitarian venture designed to raise funds and petitions for Communist political prisoners throughout the world. Sturgis was a regular companion of Chajet, who would tell Chajet of his activities and how they would lead to funds to enable CHIPP to succeed and Sturgis to recapture Cuba. In early 1972, Sturgis spoke of a "big project" and mentioned that his boss was E. Howard Hunt, a "higher-up in the White House". Chajet recalls being introduced to Hunt, who was leaving Bernard Barker's office one day as Sturgis and Chajet were arriving. During this period of time, Sturgis was making frequent trips to Washington.

Chajet said that he took Sturgis to the airport on Friday, June 16, 1972, and that Sturgis indicated this trip was part of the "big project" that would give them enough money to liberate Cuba and fund CHIPP.

Chajet said he was aware that Sturgis had been very close to Jack Anderson. As Chajet understood it, Sturgis was born in the United States, went to Cuba to fight for Castro, and lost his citizenship. Sturgis regained his citizenship through assistance from Anderson and

This document describes Elias Chajet's and his anti-Castro group as a "humanitarian venture designed to raise funds and petitions for Communist political prisoners through-out the world". When in-fact Sturgis was planning on using that group as a front to recruit men, liberate Cuba and fund CHIPP.

Frank said, "this trip was part of the "big project" that would give them enough money". Is it no wonder Howard Hunt would try and extort president Richard Nixon for two million dollars?

2

Senator George Smathers. Chajet stated that Sturgis spoke of Anderson often and talked with him regularly on the telephone. Chajet remembers that Sturgis told him in July of 1971, when they were active together in CHIPP, that Anderson "owed him some favors." Chajet was of the impression that Sturgis was in contact with Anderson regarding the "big project" and was certain he would have confided in Anderson while in Washington, D.C.

Chajet noted that after the Watergate, both Sturgis and his wife were in contact with Anderson. Mrs. Sturgis told Chajet that Anderson had offered her funds and a place to live in Washington if she wanted to come up there. Chajet explicitly remembers Sturgis, while out on bond in the late summer of 1972, asking him (Chajet) for a ride to the DuPont Plaza Hotel to see Jack Anderson. Chajet drove Sturgis there and waited in the car for twenty minutes while Sturgis went inside. When Sturgis returned, he showed Chajet several $50 bills and told him the trip was successful, advising Chajet that he'd received the money from Anderson.

Shortly before Sturgis returned to jail after the trial, Chajet said that he detected a rift in the Anderson/Sturgis relationship. Sturgis told Chajet that he did not want to see Anderson any more. This surprised Chajet because of the closeness of their relationship before.

HL:go

This document shows how Frank Sturgis was able to regain his citizenship through Jack Anderson and Senator George Smathers. Anderson pays off Sturgis, but seems as though Anderson double crossed Sturgis and Frank told Chajet that he didn't want to see Anderson any more.

MEMORANDUM

TO: Fred Thompson

FROM: Howard Liebengood

DATE: July 12, 1973

SUBJECT: INTERVIEW WITH ELIAS CHAJET

I interviewed Elias Chajet, 48 years old, 803 82nd Street, Miami, Florida, at his home between 7:30 a.m. and 10:30 a.m. on July 11, 1973. Chajet was born in Cuba of Lithuanian parents and is Jewish. He is an extremely obese, nervous chain smoker who speaks softly with a Cuban-and-New York combined accent. He first came to the United States in 1946 but returned to Cuba for several profitable years as a jeweler. He finally returned to the U.S. to stay in 1954. He has been a U.S. citizen since 1959. He has a brother working with the Chilean Embassy (job title unknown). Chajet does not look well. His nerves are shot, he has high blood pressure, and a terrible cough. He takes 250 mg. of aldamont four times a day, and apresoline and hydroxiene (?) once daily for blood pressure. Despite his infirmities, he is very credible in his demeanor. He is a registered Democrat but actively supported Nixon (did canvass work in the Cuban Miami community).

Chajet has known Barker for ten years and Sturgis for two years. During the latter time, he has been Sturgis' closest friend in the Miami Cuban cult. He first met Sturgis shortly after Chajet founded CHIPP (Citizens' Help for International Political Prisoners) in May of 1971. Sturgis was introduced to Chajet by Kaiser. Both Kaiser and Sturgis were active in CHIPP.

Chajet states that he is a humanitarian, not a soldier (a fact corroborated by the other Cubans I talked with), and that he is dedicated to CHIPP, an organization designed to raise funds and petitions for Communist political prisoners around the world. (Kaiser advises that he and Sturgis are militants who, unknown

This document describes an interview with Howard Liebengood and Elias Chajet. It discusses Chajet's health, but nevertheless, come off very credible in his demeanor. Chajet has known Barnard Barker for ten years, but has been introduced to Frank Sturgis by Edwin Kaiser.

3

About the time of Hoover's funeral, Sturgis bragged about having the assistance of the CRP security coordinator, McCord, in the big project. Sturgis made at least four trips to Washington in the three months preceeding the Watergate arrests.

Chajet met Hunt downstairs in Barker's office one week after the Hai Phong Caravan. Sturgis and Chajet had walked into the building and seen Hunt and Barker in the downstairs area, whereupon Sturgis introduced Chajet to Hunt as the "big boss." Sturgis bragged a little while later that other big shots were coming to Miami from the White House. I questioned Chajet on names, and the names he could remember were McCord, E. Colson, and Mitchell.

Sturgis never worked hard at his employment. He changed jobs several times and was disinterested. He had serious financial needs, i.e., a 17-year old daughter with a drug problem and in the HIR drug program, as well as an aged mother who lived with him and his family. Nonetheless, in pre-Watergate 1972, Sturgis always had plenty of money. After Watergate, while Sturgis was home on bond, he also had lots of money. At one time he indicated that Carlos Prio (I believe a former president of Cuba) and an associate, Cristobal Mayo, were raising money for his defense. He also heard Barker and Sturgis talking about what a great fellow Artime was, and he (Chajet) assumed that Artime was also supplying them with funds. After Watergate Sturgis had no known contact with Martinez or Gonzalez but saw Barker regularly.

Chajet said that Sturgis had known Anderson for a long time and idealized Anderson. As Chajet understood it, Sturgis was born in the U.S. but went to Cuba to fight for Castro and, as a result, lost his citizenship. He had contact with Anderson during the revolution, and Anderson later assisted him, along with Senator Smathers, in regaining his citizenship. Sturgis spoke of Anderson often--nearly every day--and talked with him regularly on the telephone. Chajet remembers that Sturgis told him in July of 1971 when they were active in CHIPP that "Anderson owed him some favors." Sturgis has constantly spoken of Anderson as a source of assistance with CHIPP.

Chajet said that he knows that Sturgis discussed the big project with Anderson because he remembers Sturgis telling him months before Watergate that "Anderson had promised him full press

This document discusses Watergate, those involved in raising funds for the burglars defense and Jack Anderson knowing about Watergate prior to it happening so that Sturgis would rightfully receive his full press release.

4

cooperation with the big project." Chajet admitted to being puzzled at this and just thought Anderson was looking for information. Chajet is inclined to believe that Sturgis was in constant communication with Anderson until he left for the Watergate operation. Chajet indicated that on the Wednesday before Watergate, Sturgis asked Chajet to take him to the airport for a trip to Washington. Chajet took him to the airport on Saturday at 12:00 noon, he thinks. Before Sturgis got on the airplane, he was excited and told Chajet that as a result of this trip they would now have enough money to swing CHIPP and to liberate Cuba, indicating that he now had support from the "higher-ups" at the White House.

Chajet indicated that he has heard information he believes from the newspapers that Sturgis inadvertently ran into Anderson at the airport upon arriving in Washington on the day of the Watergate. He has also heard the story that Anderson appeared at Sturgis' bail-bonding hearing and believes that Sturgis told him that Anderson visited him in jail.

After the Watergate, both Frank and his wife were in contact with Anderson. Sturgis' wife had told Chajet that Anderson offered money to her while Sturgis was in jail the first time and offered to find her a place to live in Washington if she wanted to come up. Chajet knows that Anderson and Sturgis had for a long time talked about doing a semi-fictitious life story of Sturgis as a soldier of fortune, and understands from Sturgis that New York ghost writers visited him in Florida after the Watergate with regard to this book. He remembers that Sturgis got mad because all the writers wanted to talk about was Watergate. Chajet thinks that the writers were down there about one month before Sturgis came back to go to jail for the last time.

At the time of the Republican Convention in August of 1972, Sturgis asked Chajet to drive him to the Dupont Plaza so that he could see Jack Anderson. Chajet waited in the car, and Sturgis was inside about twenty minutes. This was at approximately 10:00 a.m. When Sturgis returned to the car, he had in his hand a fold of $50 bills, crisp and new, approximately one inch high. He felt them as he put them in his wallet and said to Chajet, "Well, my trip wasn't for nothing." Chajet estimates that there were at least 15 to 20 bills in his hand.

After the Watergate operation, Sturgis was always bragging and seemed proud of the fact that they were caught. Chajet got the

This document describes how CHIPP would soon have enough money to liberate Cuba. (Again, I believe this is where Hunt asks Nixon for money to keep his mouth shut). Chajet drives Frank Sturgis to the airport. Anderson pays off Sturgis.

"Chajet indicates that Sturgis was also a close friend of the chairman of the Young Democrats, a Greek". Could this be the same Paul the Greek my father says in one of his letter's to stay away from?

Chajet describes Sturgis as a man that would sell anything for money so long as it did not conflict with his desire to liberate Cuba. Sturgis believed that Anderson would never double cross him, and Sturgis must know this.

5

impression from Sturgis that Anderson had indicated this would provide better material for his book. Sturgis never mentioned anybody sabotaging the Watergate operation, but did state that the other guys were stupid for leaving the tape on the door. Macho (Barker) was stupid for using his notary seal. Sturgis was very optimistic about spending no more than two months in jail and was not concerned about Gernstein. Sturgis indicated that Anderson had said he would testify for him if necessary. Chajet remembers hearing Sturgis mention Anderson's name to Barker but doesn't remember the context or the time period involved.

Shortly before Sturgis returned to go to jail for the last time, Chajet detected a rift in the Anderson - Sturgis relationship. Sturgis had no longer discussed Anderson daily, and when Chajet brought his name up Sturgis said he "didn't want to see that bastard no more." Chajet assumed that the book had fallen through and that this was the problem. Chajet has not seen Sturgis since he left the last time, but he has talked to his wife once. Mrs. Sturgis only said that Frank "wanted this" and that she was behind him.

Chajet indicates that Sturgis was also a close friend of the chairman of the Young Democrats, a Greek (name unknown). Chajet and Sturgis visited the Young Democrats' office on West Flagler Street on several occasions after the Watergate break-in and before.

Chajet describes Sturgis as a "first-class mercenary" who would sell anything, including information, for money, as long as it did not conflict with his desire to liberate Cuba. He said that Sturgis was a big believer in Anderson and was convinced that Anderson would never double-cross the United States. He is certain that Sturgis kept Anderson informed on all aspects of the Watergate. Now Chajet feels that Anderson double-crossed him and that Sturgis must surely know this.

HL/go
July 12, 1973

SAM J. ERVIN, JR., N.C., CHAIRMAN
HOWARD H. BAKER, JR., TENN., VICE CHAIRMAN
HERMAN E. TALMADGE, GA. EDWARD J. GURNEY, FLA.
DANIEL K. INOUYE, HAWAII LOWELL P. WEICKER, JR., CONN.
JOSEPH M. MONTOYA, N. MEX.

SAMUEL DASH
CHIEF COUNSEL AND STAFF DIRECTOR
FRED D. THOMPSON
MINORITY COUNSEL
RUFUS L. EDMISTEN
DEPUTY COUNSEL

United States Senate
SELECT COMMITTEE ON
PRESIDENTIAL CAMPAIGN ACTIVITIES
(PURSUANT TO S. RES. 60, 93D CONGRESS)
WASHINGTON, D.C. 20510

July 13, 1973

MEMORANDUM

To: File

From: Howard Liebengood

Subject: EDWIN KAISER, JR. INTERVIEW

On July 10-11, 1973, I informally interviewed Edwin Kaiser at the Airport Inn in Miami, Florida in the presence of Bill Howell and Armando Certs. The following summarizes the highlights of that interview.

KAISER

Kaiser is a short, stocky, 38 year old native of Norwalk, Connecticut. He has had a stormy life history and is shabby in appearance. He was barefoot and dirty with a very serious burn on his foot. He will not discuss the circumstances of the injury but intimated that it arose from a recent revolutionary endeavor. He is one of the most militant people I have ever met. His stormy history started with an assault record when he was very young. He went into the Marine Corps but has a bad conduct discharge due to a fight. He then joined the French Foreign Legion where he saw combat in Africa in the late 1950's. He received a serious wound to his Achilles tendon while in the service of the Legion and was discharged as a result. He continues to receive to this day a disability pension from the French government. As a result of his foreign service, Kaiser lost his U.S. citizenship and returned to the U.S. in approximately 1960 on a foreign immigrant visa. He returned to Norwalk, Connecticut briefly, and then went to Alaska where he worked for two years in the Anchorage and Fairbanks area doing seismographic drilling and driving for an Alaskan bondsman with Mafia ties (named Duke Knuth). He returned to Norwalk in 1962, met his wife while visiting friends in Minnesota and married her(Sonia) in Watertown, South Dakota in September, 1962. They then returned to Norwalk for four to five years while Kaiser worked as a tree surgeon. They then moved to Alaska for two months and then to Hialeah, Florida four years ago. They have resided there ever since. His wife works for S & O Fixtures and Kaiser had a legimate car wash for a while but has no legal occupation. He has become embroiled in the revolutionary endeavors of the Miami Cubans and works toward the liberation of Cuba with them on a daily basis. He has two children, a boy nine years old and a girl five years old, to whom he is very devoted.

This document describes an interview Howard Liebengood had with my father in the presence of Bill Howell and Armando Certs. Mr. Liebengood says, "Kaiser is one of the most militant people I have ever met"as he goes on to describe my father.

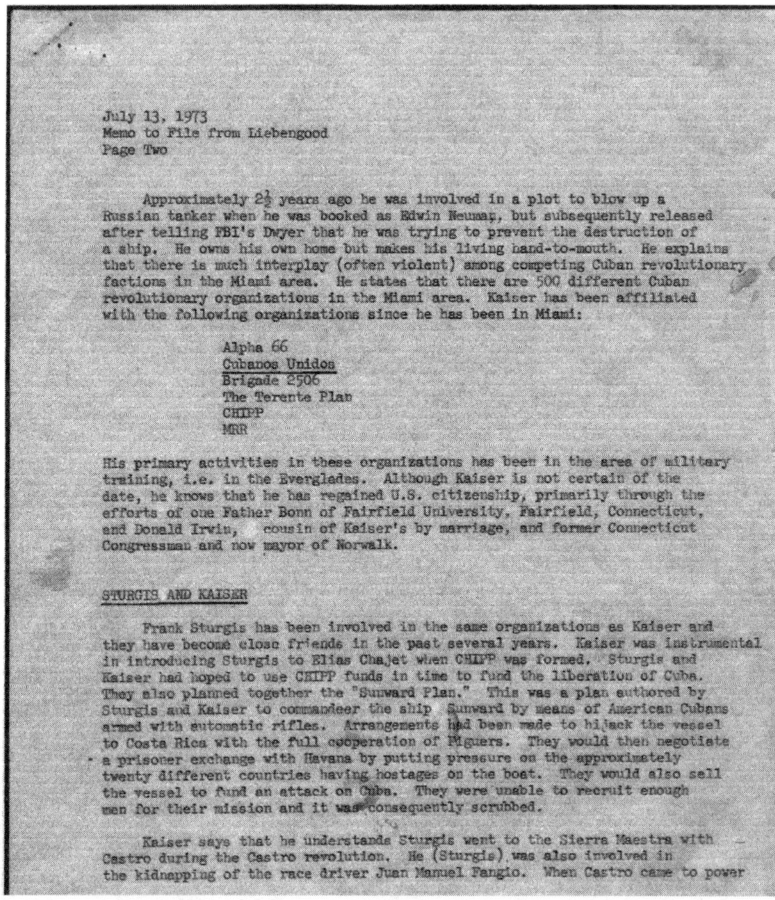
July 13, 1973
Memo to File from Liebengood
Page Two

Approximately 2½ years ago he was involved in a plot to blow up a Russian tanker when he was booked as Edwin Neuman, but subsequently released after telling FBI's Dwyer that he was trying to prevent the destruction of a ship. He owns his own home but makes his living hand-to-mouth. He explains that there is much interplay (often violent) among competing Cuban revolutionary factions in the Miami area. He states that there are 500 different Cuban revolutionary organizations in the Miami area. Kaiser has been affiliated with the following organizations since he has been in Miami:

Alpha 66
Cubanos Unidos
Brigade 2506
The Terente Plan
CHIPP
MRR

His primary activities in these organizations has been in the area of military training, i.e. in the Everglades. Although Kaiser is not certain of the date, he knows that he has regained U.S. citizenship, primarily through the efforts of one Father Bonn of Fairfield University, Fairfield, Connecticut, and Donald Irwin, cousin of Kaiser's by marriage, and former Connecticut Congressman and now mayor of Norwalk.

STURGIS AND KAISER

Frank Sturgis has been involved in the same organizations as Kaiser and they have become close friends in the past several years. Kaiser was instrumental in introducing Sturgis to Elias Chajet when CHIPP was formed. Sturgis and Kaiser had hoped to use CHIPP funds in time to fund the liberation of Cuba. They also planned together the "Sunward Plan." This was a plan authored by Sturgis and Kaiser to commandeer the ship Sunward by means of American Cubans armed with automatic rifles. Arrangements had been made to hijack the vessel to Costa Rica with the full cooperation of Figuers. They would then negotiate a prisoner exchange with Havana by putting pressure on the approximately twenty different countries having hostages on the boat. They would also sell the vessel to fund an attack on Cuba. They were unable to recruit enough men for their mission and it was consequently scrubbed.

Kaiser says that he understands Sturgis went to the Sierra Maestra with Castro during the Castro revolution. He (Sturgis) was also involved in the kidnapping of the race driver Juan Manuel Fangio. When Castro came to power

This document describes my father's involvement in a plot to blow up a Russian tanker. My father was booked as Edwin Neuman, another alias name you could add to the long list of alias' my father had. Apparently, my father was released from jail after telling FBI's Robert Dwyer that he was trying to prevent the destruction of a ship. My father explains there is much "interplay" (often violent) among competing Cuban revolutionary organizations. (Meaning a lot of killings were going on in Miami). My father states that there are more then 500 different groups. Kaiser has been affiliated with the following organizations since he has been in Miami: Alpha 66, Cubanos Unidos, Brigade 2506, The Torriente Plan, CHIPP, MRR

My father's primary activities in these organizations has been in the areas of military training. It appears that my father was able to regain his American citizenship that he loved so much through Father Bonn, who is found in my father's little black book and Donald Irwin, a cousin of my father's by marriage. Mr. Irwin was the former Connecticut Congressman and mayor of Norwalk.

The anti-Castro CHIPP although was headed by Elias Chajet would soon be secretly taken by Sturgis and Kaiser and used as a group to liberate Cuba. One of their plans used by this group would be an operation called "Sunward Plan". It was to hijack the vessel heading to Costa Rica and negotiate a prisoner exchange with Havana by putting pressure on twenty different countries they would also sell the vessel to fund an attack on Cuba. However, Kaiser and Sturgis were unable to recruit enough men for their mission.

Sturgis was also involved in the kidnapping of the race driver Juan Manuel Fangio when Castro came to power.

July 13, 1973
Memo to File from Liebengood
Page Three

Sturgis was made a Commandante (Major) in the Castro airforce. Approximately 1960, Sturgis flew a bomber to Florida to seek exile upon realizing Castro was a communist. He has been extremely active in anti-Castro counter-revolutionary measures since then.

Kaiser saw Sturgis often during the past year and was aware that he had contacts in Washington, D.C., particularly a brother in the Pentagon(name and position unknown) and columnist Jack Anderson, of whom Sturgis often spoke.

Kaiser recalls that in approximately March, April, or May, 1972 he was at Sturgis' home working on a military chain of command for the liberation of Cuba (Kaiser has this in Sturgis' handwriting and will furnish if necessary) when Sturgis received a call from Anderson. Sturgis returned from the telephone and sat on the couch and asked Kaiser if he wanted to make "big money." Kaiser asked what it was. Sturgis replied that it was an operation requiring that he start a riot against the Vietnam Veterans Against the War at the Republican convention in Miami. Kaiser asked if it were politically motivated and Sturgis said it was and Kaiser said he wanted nothing to do with it. Sturgis said that others in the anti-communist Brigade were involved and that Jack Anderson was backing it. Kaiser was not interested and nothing more was said about it. It was nonetheless this remark that caused Kaiser to later suspicion that Anderson had double-crossed Sturgis, noting that suspicion is a way of life in the Miami Cuban community where double agents abound.

It should be noted that Kaiser has a terrible memory for dates. He does not read the newspaper or follow current events other than those pertinent to the Miami Cuban military movements. Kaiser now feels that if he can prove that Sturgis was duped by Anderson he could save face for the Cuban movement and expose a source of long standing grief to both the U.S. and Cuban movement.

ARMANDO CERTS

Certs attended the interview with Kaiser and is the source of information pertaining to Carlos Armenias' knowledge of the McGovern related drug dealings. Unlike Kaiser and Howell, Armenias is a handsome, heavyset, well kept Cuban. He is friendly but cautious and committed to exposing those who have tricked Sturgis and discredited the Cuban movement. He is active in MRR which is Artime's organization (Movement for Recovery of the Revolution) which supposedly had some CIA backing from time to time. Certs was the youngest navel officer in the history of Cuba prior to his defection and by comparison very credible in appearance. Unlike Kaiser he does not tend to puff either his bravery or his accomplishments. Certs, Armenias, and Kaiser have made a tape which Howell has given me on which I'm told tells the Armenias story. Hence, I spend little time discussing the matter with Certs directly as his knowledge is second hand.

HSL:brc

This document describes that Kaiser knew Sturgis fought with Fidel Castro, and could furnish in Sturgis' handwriting a military list chain of command for the liberation of Cuba.

My father and Sturgis discuss the riots at the VVAW convention where president Richard Nixon was to speak. My father asked Sturgis if it were "politically motivated" and Sturgis said "it was". My father said. "He didn't want nothing to do with it" knowing that Nixon would be assassinated. This would have ended up in provocation with my father standing in the middle of it. This is what my father meant when he asked Sturgis if it were to be "politically motivated". President John F. Kennedy's assassination was also "politically motivated" and perhaps the reason it was called the "Big Event".

Armando Certs attended the interview with Edwin Kaiser and was the source of information pertaining to Carlos Armenias' knowledge of the McGovern related drug dealings. Armando is active in Manuel Artime's group, MRR.

Certs, Armenias and Kaiser have made a tape which Howell has given me on which I'm told tells Armenias story.

30 April 1963

SUBJECT: Ricardo CABRERA Amoedo, aka "Cayo"

1. On 18 October 1962 an untested source submitted information on Ricardo CABRERA Amoedo, aka "Cayo." He had secured this from a Cuban who was believed to have at one time been connected with G-2, who has been the subsource of information received by this office previously, and who has known CABRERA since at least 1957.

2. The information on CABRERA is as follows:

a. He was born in Habana, is about 35 years old, is married and the father of a minor daughter.

b. He was appointed to the National Police in 1952 by the BATISTA regime and remained in the Police until 1955 when his immediate superior, Major REY Castro (fnu), assigned him to duty in the Miami area to surveil the revolutionaries in asylum in the United States during the fight against the BATISTA regime. In Miami he became friendly with such Cuban asylees as Mario MASSIP, Mario AGUERREBERE, Carlos PRIO Socarras, and Antonio de VARONA.

[redacted] c. In 1957 CABRERA made contact with the late Policarpo SOLER and moved to the Dominican Republic, where SOLER was. At that time CABRERA became a TRUJILLO agent. He returned to Miami, made contact with some Cuban exiles, and suggested that they work under orders from SOLER and TRUJILLO. At that time CABRERA's friendship with PRIO grew and they began to move to the Dominican Republic Cubans who opposed the BATISTA regime. CABRERA was the contact with Caridad, SOLER's wife, who went back and forth between the Dominican Republic and Miami to persecute anti-TRUJILLO individuals in the Miami area.

d. After the fall of the BATISTA regime in January 1959, CABRERA went to Habana where he was appointed Port Inspector of the General Directorate of Customs. There he made contact with "Pepin" NARANJO, then Governor of Habana, through whom he was appointed Chief of Police of the Provincial Government. NARANJO made the following statement in the presence of the subsource and others: "Stay in your job as Port Inspector, and when I am appointed Minister of the Interior I will appoint you to the Secret Police because I need you to go to Miami to work under my direct orders." As soon

Page 2

as NARANJO was appointed Minister of the Interior, he appointed CABRERA Inspector of the Secret Police under the Interior Ministry. CABRERA was then immediately placed on detached service at NARANJO's orders and in late 1959 was sent to Miami by NARANJO so that he could submit reports on the anti-CASTRO elements in Miami. At that time CABRERA was paid through the Cuban Consulate then in Miami.

e. When the Secret Police was dissolved, CABRERA was recalled, and when he arrived in Habana he was informed by NARANJO that, as the corps to which he belonged was no longer in existence, he should present his resignation by mail, so that he could show this in Miami to counterrevolutionaries so they would have more trust in him. NARANJO also told CABRERA that he would recommend him to Ramiro VALDES, G-2 Chief, so that CABRERA could continue working since he knew how to work and how to watch the anti-CASTRO-ites in Florida.

f. In 1960, as an active G-2 member, CABRERA returned to Miami and continued working as an informer under VALDES' orders. During 1960 CABRERA made three trips to Cuba and had interviews with VALDES, Fidel CASTRO, NARANJO, and with Juan ORTA, who was then Secretary to Fidel CASTRO. During one of these visits ORTA told CABRERA the following: "One of your close friends in Miami has just submitted a report to the Prime Minister, assuring him that a group of you and LLANES Pelletier (fnu), a Rebel Army captain and aide to Fidel, are making contacts and having interviews with different revolutionary elements in Miami, such as Jorge SOTUS and "Nino" DIAZ, to "have a conversation and reconsider the Communist problems" (that were already arising in Cuba). CABRERA's last trip to Cuba was in the company of LLANES, who was arrested two or three days after his arrival in Cuba.

g. About late 1960 CABRERA sold some arms to Rolando MASFERRER, saying he was involved in a "fat deal" and was selling these arms under orders from Fidel CASTRO. Very shortly after this, CABRERA, returned to Cuba via Q Airlines from Key West and landed at Columbia Military Airport; CABRERA boasted that he was picked up at the airport by an Army jeep and taken directly to talk with Fidel.

h. In Miami CABRERA worked for G-2, together with PIMENTAL (fnu) and Pepe NOVA, who were the chiefs of the G-2 agents in Miami. CABRERA is still a man who would sell his mother and his best friend for a dollar. CABRERA became an American citizen and used to brag about being a member of the CIA.

3. The untested source was sufficiently closely connected with CABRERA at one time to have personal knowledge of some of the information reported in Para. 2 above. Apparently, they have now been at odds since about the end of 1960, but the possibility that some degree of personal animosity and denunciation may be involved in the above should not be overlooked.

4. Any additional information received by this office concerning this matter will be forwarded promptly.

MM 52-5383
2.

not donating money to KAISER's revolutionary activities. The police came. He was arrested and he gave the police a fictitious name and was booked into the Dade County Jail. A day later he was released and was never tried on any charges.

KAISER is in possession of a large quantity of index cards containing names, addresses and descriptions of persons involved in illegal drugs activity. KAISER said he stole these cards from U.S. Customs Office when they moved to another location about a year ago. He has gone out and contacted a number of these people. One such person contacted is an unidentified Negro male who sells KAISER stolen watches, rings and other jewelry which KAISER resells to employees at Maule Industry and other factories in the area and the Opa Locka area.

Appendix Three

Interview with Rudy Junco

Scott Kaiser: What kind of exciting stories could you tell me about my father?

Rudy Junco: There's quite a few stories, I remember your dad teaching me how to use weapons: hand guns and rifles. Your father was an expert on M-1 and M-15's and all that. He was an expert at shooting, man, I mean with or without scope.

SK: That's amazing.

RJ: I mean he was good, sharp like you have no idea.

SK: He was a sharp shooter huh?

RJ: Yeah, in hand combat he was bad, I mean bad-ass. He could kill anyone with his bare hands, easily and fast. He was trained for that. I don't know if you know that. He was trained by the government, man.

SK: Oh, trained, yeah, yeah.

RJ: He was well trained, and remember, he spoke a few languages.

SK: Yeah, laughing ... yeah.

RJ: He was a real asset for the government, he was definitely.

SK: Yeah, not long ago you and I were talking about, ah, Frank Sturgis and Howard Hunt and ah, ah...

RJ: David Morales and all those guy's were all involved, ah, they, they all knew your father.

SK: They all knew my dad?

RJ: Yes, I remember one day your father asked me to give him a ride, and I knew it, he didn't say anything after he did. He got what he wanted. He went to the CIA Headquarters here in Miami, and he took some envelope, big photographs and documents, and I remember.

SK: Really wow!

RJ: Something related with Kennedy's assassination, you know. I remember those days, they were very delicate, I never, I never talked to anyone of those document or pictures since your father's passed away.

SK: Really, so you never said ...

RJ: Yes, I have, I always believed he was killed, man, I don't think it was ....

SK: What were the pictures about? What were they?

RJ: I believe it was in Dallas Texas. Because I remember seeing one, they were black and white, you know.

SK: What was black and white?

RJ: I remember seeing their face, I remember there was a motel, I can't recall the name of the motel, they were standing outside, I can't recall the name of the motel that was a long time ago, shit, it was about 40 something years ago.

SK: But what was black and white the motel or the photos?

RJ: The pictures, the pictures, the pictures!

SK: – Ah, the pictures were black and white

RJ: You don't have the faintest idea what was there because you're talking about forty something years ago.

SK: Shit! You know you're the first person to ever give me this news, because I've been trying, I mean, I've been raking my head for five years now trying to figure out where my father got these photographs. From, how he got them and what were they about, because I talked to so many people in Miami about these photographs, and ah, none of them said that it was ah about Watergate. And I assumed that those pictures were about Watergate because my father. I found out through Eugenio Martinez that my father was the sixth burglar in Watergate that nobody knew about.

RJ: Ah, your father was an expert breaking into anywhere.

SK: Laughing, yeah, I know every time I say my dad was a thief everybody laughs cause they know it's the truth. (Laughing).

RJ: Yeah, yeah, yeah, I tell you those were the days. I remember your father taking me to a restaurant, a very expensive restaurant and buying bottles of wine of $1,700.00. Shit, I would never spend that money on stupid bottle of wine.

SK: Damn! Were in the hell did he get the money from, cause he sure didn't bring it home.

RJ: Well you know that they get their money from the government you know that, we all know that.

SK: You know, I also read some reports about him going to Puerto Rico AFB and Homestead AFB. I remember him taking me out to Homestead AFB, when I was a kid and, ah, we had some good times, but I never knew he was into all this stuff. I didn't know anything about this until five years ago. And, I found out because my mother was in California visiting her sister, and, ah, I was looking for some pictures to hang up on the wall. And since my mother moved in with me, she hadn't completely unpack, and so I was going through her chest, you know, I opened up her hope chest to look for some picture to put up on the wall to kind of make her feel more at home, when she arrived back. And I found a large envelope of FOIA documents given to her by a researcher by the name of AJ Weberman, who gave her all this, I mean there had to be three or four inches of paper work and he gave her a book. I forgot what it was called, but anyways it was a book written by AJ Weberman and Michael Canfield. And, I asked my mother when she got back, how come you never told me anything about these? And, ah, she started crying, she said she didn't want me to ever find out what my father was into.

RJ: Your father was into a lot of things with the government, you know, your father was like every time I saw the movie, oh shit um, Identity, how do you call that shit?

SK: Bourne Identity?

RJ: Bourne Identity, I think your father was like that, because I remember your father having so many ID's.

SK: (Laughing) Wow!

RJ: And passports.

SK: Laughing, yeah, yeah, he had a fake passport going to Israel.

RJ: They were not fake, bullshit, he could go to any airport they were not fake, bullshit.

SK: Yeah, he just had a bunch of different ID's, oh wow, this is incredible. This is like really incredible news. Ah, you know this information you're giving me, you don't mind me using it for, ah, in my book. You don't mind me, uh, uh, displaying this information you're giving me, making it known to the public do you?

RJ: (A pause), of course not, go ahead and do it, just remember that he use to carry different thing, and he was so easy in talking different languages that's why may be the government, or who ever the agency was give him all this documents, because, ah, he could fake any nationally man.

SK: That explains why he was in Israel.

RJ: He could talk like a Colombian, he could talk like an Argentinean, whatever. He could change his accent right on the spot.

SK: Wow, that's amazing.

RJ: And, really, he could turn upside down anything if he wanted to.

SK: Makes me feel like I was living with a real 007. I didn't know anything about my father.

RJ: You bet your butt, he was, (Laughing). A real one, not a fake one.

SK: You know I really appreciate your story, and telling me about the photographs, and telling me what had happen. Because without you, without you, I would not have had this story, because I wouldn't know really how my father got a hold of these photographs, other then a lot of hearsay from other people telling me that they were stolen out of the CIA's office in Medley. Did the CIA have an office in Medley? In the Opalocka area?

RJ: Right I use to remember he would get together with a guy, a big guy from the CIA, it was like an Italian guy. A big guy you know what I mean?

SK: Oh yeah. That's the life!

My father's body had been identified by Rudy Junco of Rudy's Meat Market in Hialeah, Florida. It was in the basement of the meat market where I would attend secret Cubanos Unidos meetings with my father.

Appendix Four

Interview with Tosh Plumlee

Tosh Plumlee: Do you know him? Do you know him before he died? Now you know he died.

Scott Kaiser: What's his name?

TP: Huh?

SK: What was your buddy's name?

TP – Sergio, the Dark Horse Bar. I took a picture of him, and then, ah, he had a replica of his monkey that he use to put on his head. He would talk like the monkey, and he had what I called this "sick monkey."

Now that was back in the 70s when the House Select Committee was starting. And, me and Greg was trying find him, everybody was trying to find him. His parents lived in Havana. He use to be with the M26-7. He was in support of Castro in 57-58, so this goes back a lot of lineage.

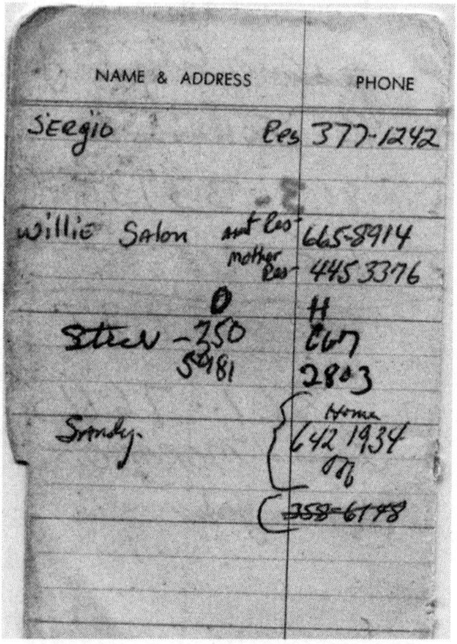

Is the Sergio in my father's address book, the same person, whom Plumlee mentioned?

Sergio was working with a special unit that was out of the Pentagon. He was military Cuban. He was not in the Bay of Pigs. He was a trainer at Latula on Operation Tide, if that means anything to you. Christian and Gonzalez were two pilots that crashed their plane in the Nicaraguan jungles, and they did not find that plane, but they knew it was there. But they did not retrieve the bodies until sometime in the 80s or 90s. Ah, you can look that up through, ah, I think Gordon Winslow and his site as that, or the Mary Ferrell, somebody!

But anyways, Christian and Gonzalez, that was an aircraft known as 933, it came out of Miranda Air Park Salvage yard, it was retro fitted for an LB Smith Aircraft and it was flown in the Bay of Pigs. I myself as Buck Pearson not Parson, we trained those pilots down there from Latula on an operation, known as the Operation Tide.

I don't know if you know any of this or not, but anyways you can check this out, it's available. In fact it's available on the CIA website. Those documents are now released. Actually, those documents have been released since 1996, till about 1998, when they recovered the remains. I don't know if you know this or not, but your dad used to carry around a St. Christoper medal.

SK: Yes he did. He use to carry around a St. Christoper medal, and he use to carry around a St. Barbara medal. A big, big medal on his chest, yes. That's correct.

TP: Okay, alright, now he gave me that medal at Marathon Key in Florida to give to this 826 that Christopher was taking down over to Latula over at Nicaraguan, um at the training base. They crashed. They went down there. They flew, they came back. They flew not with Gonzalez, but with Strumburger, who is a good friend of mine. But I don't want to get into all that. But ah, so anyway, they crashed and all that. They overshot, went into the jungle and crashed into the mountains. And the bodies were left there, and the CIA knew they were there. They did not expose them to compromise, so they went by code and procedures. That wasn't even discussed until 1998. And, they went in there and found them, now the reason why I'm telling you this story is because your dad give me those medals at that Jack Pars restaurant at old Marathon Key. Who got them down there, and the airport was right across the road from the Marathon or Jack Pars you know, and ah. So, Christopher and Gonzalez was taking that 826 out of Marathon going into Nicaraguan. I handed them the St. Christopher's medal, and they put it on the yoke of the airplane. And in 1996 when they found their remains stuck up in the trees in the jungles of Nicaraguan, your dad's medal was still on the yoke of that airplane.

SK: Wow! Wow, now that's incredible.

TP: Now that's a story for yeah, I wanted to tell you that story. Regardless of what you read about me, it's these little details, like

I told you. You're the son of a good friend of mine. To give me a medal to give to Christopher and Gonzalez, two Cubans pilots that used to fly for Regina Cargo, and another one was a little airline that worked for LB Smith Corporation. Hell I don't know if you're familiar with these names or not.

SK: No.

TP: We use to all meet there at that Sloppy Joe's there on Biscayne Boulevard right next to the McAllister Hotel. That's where your dad hung out at and ate in meetings, did you know that?

SK: No, I knew he would take off every single day and leave with Wilfredo Navarro or Frank Sturgis or somebody, but he was all over Miami Beach.

TP: Okay, your dad, your dad, your dad and John Martino, Frank Sturgis, your dad, ah golly.

SK: He use to work for William Pawley.

TP: Say again.

SK: William Pawley in Miami Beach, they called him Bill Pawley

TP: Bill Pawley is on Operation Tilt as they call it. I went in there to help remove missile technicians out of Cuba. Your dad is one of the guys, who gave me a map, ah road map so that we could get in pass the mountain range, we didn't have an aeronautical map at that time so your dad gives us an ESSO, I think it was an old road map, laughing.

SK: Wow! That's incredible.

TP: So we could get in and out of Cuba. (Shared laughter).

SK: Yeah, he visited, he's visited the islands quite a bit and the surrounding islands around Cuba, but I don't know if he's been into Cuba. It's hard to tell. I've never gotten a full story about my dad. I didn't know anybody I could talk to. I talked to Tony Calatayud, who also worked with my dad, but Tony couldn't, he gave me some information, but not a whole lot, not as much as your giving me.

TP: Most of those guys yeah, see I was a pilot. I was a real "operative." But, I, I knew all these guys. I was a personal pilot for John Roselli you know.

SK: Did my dad know Roselli?

TP: Yeah, he knew him as Colonel Rawlston at JM/Wave, and remember I told you about the Rodney Plaza? Your dad use to hang out there at the Rodney Plaza, and all those guys. Masferrer and all the weapons, Masferrer, had at the house do you remember that?

SK: No, but I know my dad had a bunch of shit in the closet. He had ammunition, grenades, bazookas.

TP: Yeah, I'll tell you what, now I don't know if you heard of this one guy. He and I before he died. Um. I don't talk about dead people, but uh, Gerry Patrick Hemming, I don't know if you know him or knew of him.

SK: He stayed at our house for like a week, and my mother made my father kick him out, because Gerry Hemming, not only did he stay at our house, but he didn't want to go to work. And according to my mom, he ordered some *Solider of Fortune* magazines and had them delivered to the house. That pissed off my mother, and then she told my dad that he needed to kick Jerry out of the house, because he didn't want to do anything.

TP: Well, that's the problem I had he tried to do a number on me, number one he's a convicted felon, number two, drug convictions as well as weapons convictions. A wanna-be solider of fortune, he worked with a lot of the rich Cubans to con them into supporting their "CIA operations" on this Interpen. That's all bullshit. And when I come out with research, he attacked me on an open forum saying he knows all these Cubans and nobody knows me. I'm a hot check writer and he's got a file on me fifteen inches thick, you know, all kinds of shit. And finally I just ignored him.

So, I come out, and he made a statement onetime that he had a meeting in the White House with the president and blah blah blah. So I came out and I happen to know something about the White House and the East Room was Jackie Kennedy's bedroom at that time. So, ah convicted felon is not going to get into the White House especially on a drug conviction. But, anyway I don't want to talk about him.

SK: Do you know if Oswald was in Miami in 1962? Between November 1962 and January of 1963.

TP: Was I in Miami?

SK: Do you know if Oswald was in Miami at that time.

TP: Yeah, that's the whole reason why I testified at the House Select committee. I went into a closed door session with them. I'll tell you two things about Lee. Lee was ONI intelligence, and he worked out of Grand Prairie TX. It's the old naval station there at Grand Prairie. He also worked out of Botmans Lake. Botmans Lake is at the end of the runway at Love field. Those are the places that Lee worked out of, alright.

Now, sometime later, I didn't know Lee. I didn't know anything about him, other then I met him one time before at a training base in North Carolina. He went to Hawaii and that's the only time I had contract with him. I just knew him as a another person at that time.

Now, the Dallas Cubans, who was Fernandez, Jose – the people that would run the base down at New Orleans, we use to run guns through the National Guard Armory. The Dallas Cubans had an apartment right behind Texas Street, where Oswald later rented a room. I took pictures of all that before anyone knew about that safe house, also I carved my initials in the draining board of that safe house back in the Spring of '62. And Jim Marrs and I, all of them went in there and took pictures of it. Later with Oliver Stone, I took them on a guided tour, and I told them. I said there's an apartment house where the Cubans lived, and I said that's where Oswald rented a room. They said, you're full of shit. We checked that area out, and there is no apartment house. I said, I'll take you over there.

And, then there's only one way to get to that apartment house you gotta go down the block come up turn around and go down the alley. The entrance way to that apartment house was directly behind the deal. I took a series of pictures. Put them on the damned Internet trying to help researchers, only to have those pictures stole and then and while someone else was taking them, they said they discovered the deal to put a feather in their hat for research. Can you believe that shit? That's what I get for trying to help out the researchers. I just wanted to open this up to you out of the respect for your father.

SK: This is all interesting, and I love to hear your stories, especially when it comes to my father. Because he was killed when I was only thirteen, and I believe it was Frank Sturgis and Richard Poyle who ended up killing my father. What do you know about my father and Roselli?

TP: I don't know that much other then your father, Roselli and Sam Giancana all that Miami bunch that went from that lobby out to, hell, Frank Sinatra use to come down there, they use to all paw-paw around there with everyone. I don't know if I ever told you stories about that they use to have meetings there at the Fontainebleau. When the Fontainebleau opened up, your father went to the opening of the Fontainebleau when it first opened up. Did he ever talk to you about that?

SK: No, but I use to go to the Fontainebleau with him, when I was a kid and we use to drive around in his red Jeep.

TP: Yeah, well he was there all the time, that was the meeting place, your dad, John Martino, Frank Sturgis would attend. I was reluctant to give you a call, but out of respect for your father I thought we should talk.

We ended our conversation discussing the photo of Barry Seal's Operation 40 photo.

Appendix Five

Letters from Israel

"Dear Ami and Ronnie

I hope you took that trip to Tiberias and had fun. I appreciate the fact that you and your mother were willing to go to court with me as character witnesses. I have happy news. I will be leaving prison and travelling to Miami USA on July 8th. I would like to be there on July 4th, for as you know they are celebrating the Bicentennial, but since I cannot be there I hope to celebrate my release.

I would very much like to see you and your family before I leave for Miami. I would thank you to bring me some photos, which I know you have, as a souvenir, and also a photo of your Sea of Galilee if you have one, as I have no photos of you or of Israel, and I would like to show them to Michael. If Michael's father or mother want me to bring him something, let them bring it to me here and I will bring it to him.

Ami, I would appreciate it if you can do me one more favor, and bring me three gifts from Tel-Aviv for my wife and children, inexpensive ones, and I will send you a refund once I have reached Miami

As you may or may not remember, Elizabeth is 7 and Scott is 13. If you come to visit me sometime next week with the family, I would be happy to say goodbye and thank you for your kindness and help, which has encouraged me in difficult moments.

I really don't know what to say, but I am happy to leave. I thought I would remain here forever. I shall not forget all you have done for me, and hope to someday return to you the kindness that is your due. I also hope, of course, to see you again.

With this I end for now and I am your friend,

Edwin Kaiser

"deposited Belongings of the detainee Kaiser, Edwin, made out on 01-mar-1976, 1400 hours at Kishon detention house, by 12342 Ispector Nissim Azrad in the presence of Master Sergeant Davidson and Sergeant 1st class Ben-Zvi , detainee escorts. following is a list of the property:

3 big suitcases
1 small bag
2 trousers
1 grey (military?) coat
1 grey sweater
7 colored shirts
26 underpants
5 t-shirts
6 pairs of socks
1 raincoat
3 pairs of trousers
2 longjohns
1 bathrobe
7 pairs of shoes
5 belts
3 framed photos (or pictures) - various photos
1 wooden jewel-box
1 medallion colored gold with a statue of Miriam [probably the virgin Mary - Ran]
1 silver bracelet with 7 green stones

[signatures of the officers]
the deposit was made in the presence of the detainee

[Edwin Kaiser's signature]"

Translated from Hebrew by Ran Daniels.

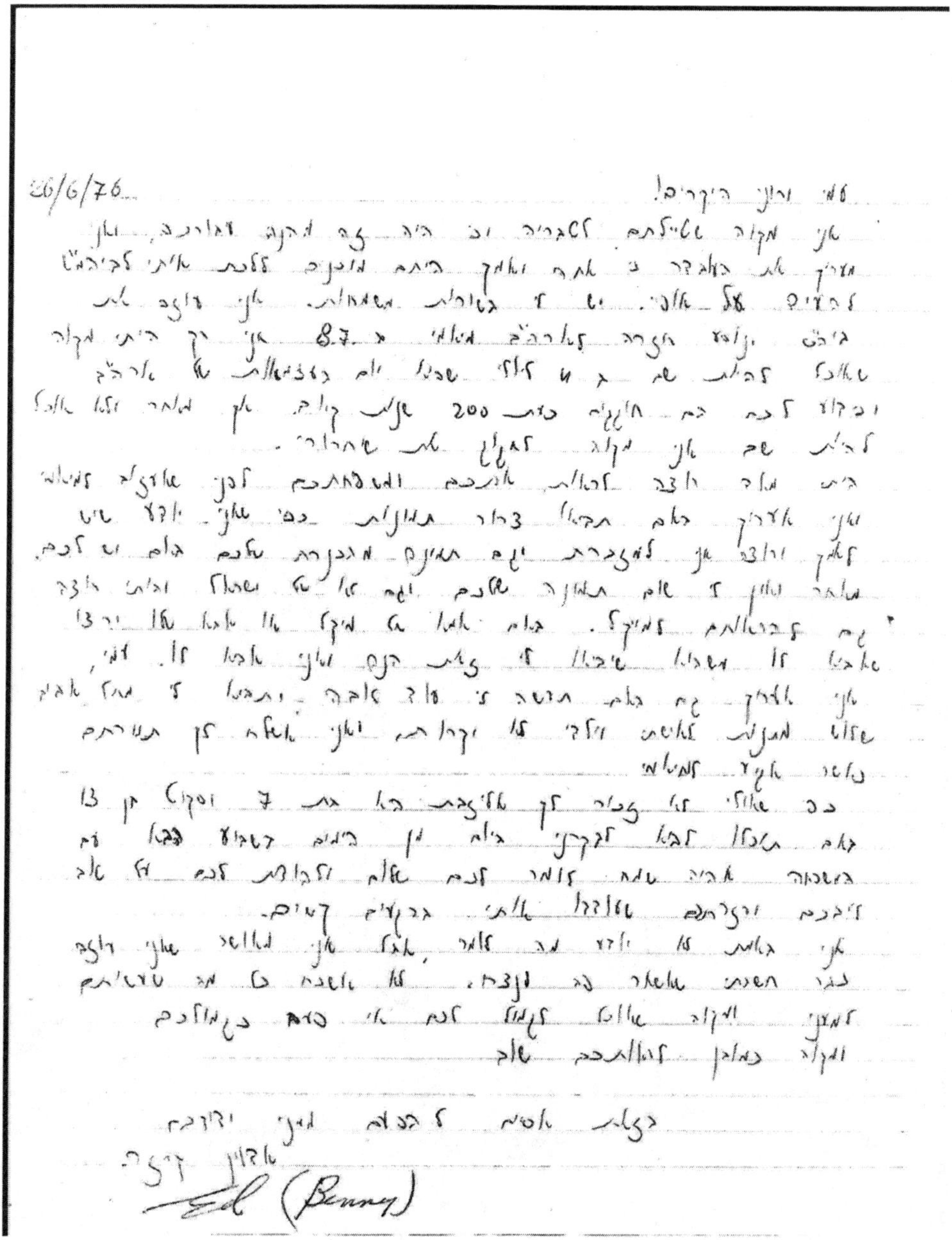
26/6/76
אמי ורוני היקרים!
Ed (Benny)

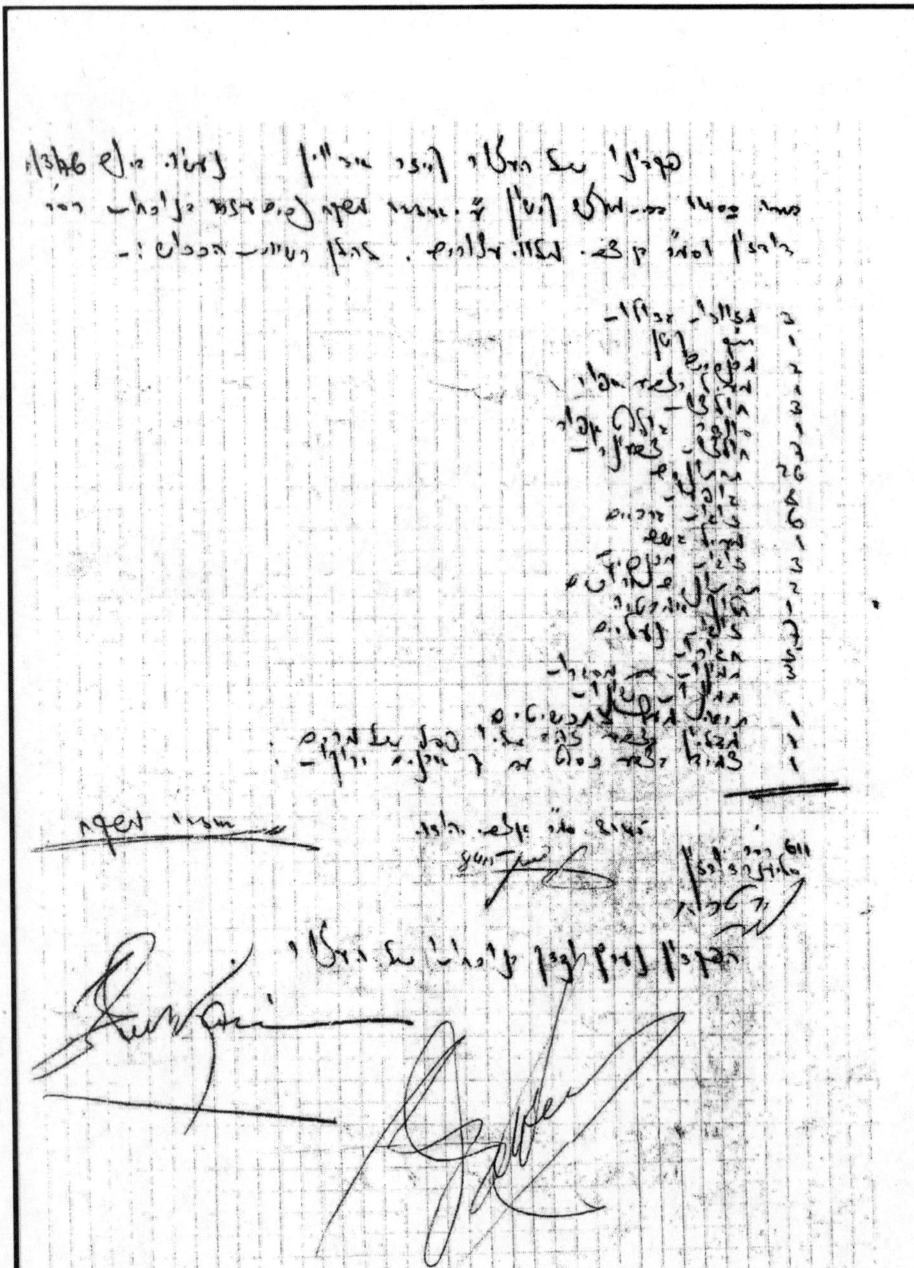

Index